THE KING OF THE BEGGARS

The Court of Miracles

LUIZ CARLOS CARNEIRO

By the Spirit

Louis E. Amedée Achard

Translated to English by:
Maryna Mendoza Lozano
Lima, Peru, June 2024

Original title in Portuguese:
"O Rei dos Mendigos"
© Luiz Carlos Carneiro, 1994

World Spiritist Institute
Houston, Texas, USA
E–mail: contact@worldspiritistinstitute.org

Contents

DEDICATIONS..4

INTRODUCTION...5

FIRST PART..7

    Chapter I The Birth..8

    Chapter II The Departure...17

    Chapter III The "Witcher"...46

SECOND PART..77

    Chapter I The Unexpected 78

    Chapter II Friends Jean and Jeanpaul..99

    Chapter III Leonardo da Vinci 184

    Chapter IV The Death of Planchet...217

THIRD PART..225

    Chapter I War, Always..226

    Chapter II On a single Horse 242

    Chapter III The Apparition 260

    Chapter IV The Ambush 275

    Chapter V The Black Figure...295

DEDICATIONS

To the couple Octavio Augusto and Mrs. Marylice, with thanks to God for having them as friends.

To Rodolfo and Mrs. Lucía.

To Antonio and Mrs. Gilda

God bless you.

Mes amis.

Avec amour.

The story that I'm writing now, thanks to the incarnate author, I do it naturally since I am not dead.

The events within this work, by bringing back characters from *Love is Eternal*, for me is a tribute to Luiz Carlos Carneiro, since this book of ours is fiction within history, and a story that took place in the same period of the real one.

We are one. A single spirit, and we can encourage anyone who has an uterus, breasts, ovaries; that is, a woman... and we are men with testicles and sperm to fertilize. But the spirit has no sex. Simply changes its wrapping. Thus, I, Louis Engine Amedée Achard, have found the one that allows rewrite our books. The events are, as I said, a tribute to this friend.

I hope you understand.

Peace.

Amedee Achard

Salvador, Bahia, October 17, 1993

INTRODUCTION

"Blood ties do not necessarily establish links between spirits. The body comes from the body, but the spirit does not come from the spirit, because the spirit of the reincarnated existed before the formation of the body.

It is not the father who creates the spirit of his son. The father does nothing more than provide the physical envelope, but he must help the child in his intellectual and moral development, to make him evolve.

Spirits that incarnate in the same family, especially as close relatives, are, most of the time, spirits that sympathize with each other, united by previous relationships that are revealed by their reciprocal affections during their earthly life. But it may happen that these spirits are completely strangers to each other, separated by equally previous antipathies, which are also expressed by their antagonism on Earth, to serve as a test for them. True family ties are not those formed by consanguinity. They are those that are born from the affinity and communion of thoughts, which unite the spirits before, during and after their incarnation. For this reason, two beings born from different parents can be more brothers in spirit than if they were brothers by blood. They can attract each other, seek each other, become friends, while two blood brothers can repel each other, as we see every day.

"This is a moral problem that only Spiritism could solve, through the plurality of existences."[1]

---

[1] *The Gospel according to Spiritism*. Topic 8, chapter XIV – Allan Kardec.

FIRST PART

Chapter I
The Birth

− Sacré bleu!² Is this a girl being born right now, when I was longing for a boy?

− Calm down, Planchet! Are others, at this very time, not giving birth? Are you not the king of beggars? You can do everything.

− Voilá,³ ragbag, I'll kill you, viperine tongue! Can't you see I'm worried?

− With what? You're getting old.

The frustrated father jumped from the already half-collapsed wall, grabbed his interlocutor by the rags, pulled him with a firm hand and shouted:

− Bochet, one day I will finish you. You bastard! Getting older, damn, that I can do everything? That? No sons...

− Let go of me, Planchet! Is it my fault you only know how to make girls? Look up your other women... who knows, maybe one of them has given birth to a child? Come on, let me go.

Planchet removed the blindfold from his left eye that covered one good eye, held it up, and then put it in the bag on his shoulder. He was wearing tattered and smelly clothes. His long hair

---

² Damn blue.

³ It's here.

flowed in the wind that blew underground in Paris. Short, a little fat and already gray. But he possessed the necessary attributes to assume the position of King of the Beggars: cunning, courage and leadership. Strong as a bull. Everyone obeyed him. They went up from the sewers to the squares, begging, accepting any invitation to kill, to steal in exchange for money that was taken to the Court of Miracles, very close to the Cathedral, or rather under it.

– Francisco is the king up there. And you, Planchet, the king down here. How much have we already accumulated?

– You are not missing anything, animal.

– Well, what about your son who hasn't appeared until now?

– Listen, discuss. This one who was born, and only few know it, will be a boy.

– Huh? – Bochet was startled –. But she's a girl.

– I have you in my hands.

– And the midwives?

– No worries. They are my mother and my grandmother. This girl will be a man. I can't live just by having daughters. Mendiant![4]

– How are you going to do it, man?

– Spread the news that I have a son.

– But...

– I'll take care of the rest.

– Keep in mind that they will want to see it.

– They won't see anything. He is a man, my son, do you understand?

---

[4] Beggar.

– Of course, of course. Like you said, you have me in your hands. One word from you and I die.

– I like you as a friend. Go out and tell everyone about Jean's birth, the first and only one. I will raise her like a man.

– And when they find out?

– I won't be here anymore. He will be my successor, the King of the Beggars of the Court of Miracles. Good?

– Oui

– Now go. I trust you.

✳ ✳ ✳

– He has born, my friends, Jean has born, the first and only! – Bochet shouted, sinking into the mud of the sewers.

– Which first Jean is this that was born? The one I know is already old, up there. It's the parish priest.

– I don't know… what do you mean, Bochet?

It was the underworld of Paris, with its sewers, its galleries full of beggars and the unemployed who crowded there. The immense community was feared even by the king's armies. The most scandalous plans were hatched there. There were people for every task.

– What's wrong with you, Bochet? Who is this Jean that was born?

– The king's son.

– King's son? What king?

– Planchet, the king of the beggars.

– Planchet? – A woman shouted –. Well, I have two daughters with him.

– I have three.

– There is no way – argued another –. Planchet only takes the form of a woman.

– Jean, Planchet's first son, was born!

The crowd fell silent.

– Bochet, are you serious? – A man exploded, standing up and removing a piece of bloody dog meat from his leg.

– More serious than your leg, which has nothing.

– So he managed to make a man?

– Well, if he was born...

– It must have been the last drop – Laughter broke out.

– Silence, stray dogs. I announce the birth of Jean, the only one, king of the beggars. Planchet already has a successor.

–And who gave birth to him? – A woman shouted –. He only gave me daughters!

– This time he got it right – shouted another, repairing an artificial wound on his thigh.

– We want to see.

– You cannot yet – warned Bochet.

– I have to see it to believe it.

– Shut your disgusting mouths, you disgusting sewer rats! – Bochet's voice roared, brandishing the cane he carried.

– You saw?

– I saw it. He's a man, Jean.

– And the party?

– Don't worry, there will be.

Paris, at the time of our story, lived in two worlds: one, that of pomp, not so much, but of those who worked, sellers, soldiers, blacksmiths, upholsterers and the rich; the other was bustling, with its particular inhabitants – the outlaws, the beggars, the unemployed – underground, the sewers, whose enormous galleries looked like squares, through which rainwater or the Seine River flowed freely, when it was full. However, they had a king! They had an army! They fought against the musketeers and these were afraid to look for them. The labyrinths of the sewers made them appear wherever they wanted. Get rid of them? How? All of Paris would collapse. The power of these beggars was respectable. They even received rich lords in audience with the king, who offered to pay them in gold for shady services.

– Paulette also gave birth and no one talks about it.

– Is she Planchet's daughter?

– Don't know! He just kept dragging his wings towards her.

– It can't be yours. It's a girl?

– Yes… then, yes.

– It doesn't matter. What matters is that Jean was born and is the successor.

Actually, yes, it mattered. Paulette, although always harassed by Planchet, never accepted him. She gave herself to a nobleman and became pregnant. On the same day, at the same time that Planchet's daughter was born, Paulette's son came into the world. It was not a matter of curiosity to know her sex, since the king was the father, she was consequently a girl. And all the fuss was about a lie, regarding the sex of the child. Thus, the boy, given the fame of her father, was considered a girl and the other, a girl, was considered a boy.

Paulette tried to hide what happened and, at the first opportunity, requested a meeting with the nobleman who was her father. The old church of Our Lady of Paris was the chosen location. The nobleman Jean of Luzardo, son of the Duke of Luzardo, was fascinated by the child he had taken in his arms and admired his resemblance to him.

– What are we going to do, Paulette?

– Up to you.

– You can't stay in that den with this child. She's blonde like her father!

–And where would I go?

– I'm going to provide. Be here early tomorrow.

– Where are you going to take us?

– For a property I have in the countryside. You won't lack anything.

– And your wife?

– My wife is sick, I don't think she will live long. She will understand.

– I'm sorry, Jean.

– Me too. She is a good woman.

They talked a lot about her being a witch. The young man smiled.

– That's true, but that's over. The cardinal himself absolved her. Just for doing good to so many, welcoming the poor and the crippled.

– And talk to the dead.

– Oh! This peculiarity is part of his illness.

– I love you very much, Jean.

– I know, Paulette. You also don't ignore that my feeling is the same. I'll take care of both. Go, come back tomorrow.

– One of Planchet's wives also had a son.

– Planchet, the king?

– Yes. And it's a boy.

– Now! So old Planchet has a successor? Excellent! How happy you must be.

– And everyone thinks that my son is theirs.

– But...

– You know better. I just let them think that way. Imagining that it was a girl, they didn't even want to look at my daughter.

– I understand. From what they say he only has daughters.

– I had nothing with him. Do you believe me?

– Paulette! I never doubted you. And as for Planchet's bravado, who knows, half of his daughters aren't even his?

– Could be.

– Planchet is a good man. He would be a great ambassador. He has easy words, he is brave, magnanimous and, perhaps honest, in his own way.

– I'm leaving, Jean, but what will we name our son?

– Do you have any preference?

She covered the child, lowered his head, and then thought:

– Your name is Jean, mine, Paulette... our son will be called Jeanpaul.

– Jeanpaul? – The nobleman laughed.

– Jean and Paulette.

– So be it, my love, so it will be. It is the combination of two names that we love. Tomorrow then?

– Yes, early.

– I love you Jean.

He uncovered the child's face, kissed him on the forehead and declared:

– By God, Paulette, I love this boy so much.

– Is yours, honey. I'm leaving.

※ ※ ※

There were three days of celebration in the city's underworld and in the Court of Miracles, under the royal jurisdiction of Planchet. This neighborhood of Paris, feared by the entire population, including the king's soldiers, was the place where criminals, thieves and murderers gathered at night to share the day's profits. It was also where they exchanged the "wounds" with which they deceived the population, when they begged. Of course, no one with common sense would dare go there, not even in the sunlight, unless, of course, businessmen or politicians looking for someone to carry out revenge on, or any illicit work, which was not uncommon.

France, for its part, was not going through good times. The alliance signed by Francis I with Suleiman, the so-called heretic, shocked the entire Western people. Christians allied with atheists, heretics? Impossible! But Francis I,[5] despite enjoying the good life, riding horses, having parties, hunting, had a terrible sense of state affairs. The so-called Treaty of Capitulations, signed between him and Suleiman[6], became a scandal throughout the West. Would a Christian king ally himself with a barbarian? And there was so much talk at the Court that, more to satisfy himself, as he had given one of his great parties, where the Council was meeting, between bottles of wine, he said:

– I can not deny it. My greatest wish is for the Turk to become stronger.

---

[5] King of France from 1515 to 1547.

[6] Soliman, the Magnificent, Turkish sultan from 1520 to 1566 ally of Francis I against Charles V

– But, Your Highness, he is a heretic!

-Does matters? Does it bother you that we are Christians? I want them well strengthened, ready and prepared for war. Of course, I personally ignore it. He is an infidel, as you say, and we are Christians. However, gentlemen, only he, as you know, can weaken the power of Charles V – he took a sip of the drink in his hand –, who will have to open the coffers, consequently, he will incur great expenses and become weaker. . You see, gentlemen – he continued, getting up and placing the glass on a sideboard – when the interests of the country demand it, our faith does little to disturb it – and he went to dance, calmly, in the beautiful hall.

And that's how it always was. Affairs of state, not infrequently, were discussed or resolved in a hunting camp, on horseback rides or in evenings in their different palaces. As far as the city is concerned, the magician Leonardo da Vinci[7] was in charge of providing it with his wonderful inventions. To achieve this, he spared no effort.

---

[7] Artist of the School of Florence, 1452 – 1519, painter of *La Gioconda*, sculptor, architect, engineer, musician and anatomist.

Chapter II
The Departure

The next day, Paulette returned to the Cathedral and did not have to wait long. Jean arrived in his carriage. He jumped out quickly and, approaching her, took the child in his arms and asked:

– Leave your belongings behind.

– Why, Jean?

– Please, you won't need rags, dear.

– Jean, in these packages I bring everything I have and the child's belongings.

– Come on, *mon amour*, we're in a hurry. And I own everything and for you, in my house. Please don't argue.

Paulette, although she lived in those holes, beneath Paris, had what was hers and, naturally, she did not want to part with what she had achieved with so much sacrifice. Therefore, with reluctance and with a pitiful expression, he tossed the bundle aside. Her clothing, far from being that of a lady, was; However, it was "the latest fashion" in the Court of Miracles and was kept as clean and orderly as possible.

– So, shall we go? – Jean insisted.

– Yes, let's continue.

He made her enter first, then handed her the child, going up in turns, when he ordered the coachman to go on. The coach set off, the horses trotting and the wheels hitting the uneven cobblestones of the streets of Paris.

– Where are we going?

– I already told you, dear.

– I know, Jean. I ask you where your country house is located.

– Alenzón.[8]

– I've never heard of it.

– Great, this way you will open a new scenario. It is near Mont-Saint-Michel. The sea air will be good for Jeanpaul.

-What will happen to me?

– It's not far from Paris, love.

– How far?

– Definitely about ten days.

– Inside this contraption?

– Calm down, Paulette. The best awaits us there.

–And you, will you stay with us?

– No, just for a while. I have my business in Paris.

– And your wife?

– My wife? Well, you're going to stay with her!

– Jean, what do you mean?

– You'll see when we arrive.

– My God!

– We will not stay inside this contraption, how you classify our vehicle. There are towns and police stations along the route. Don't worry.

---

[8] City in France with 35 thousand inhabitants.

– And the thieves?

– From time to time there are. We will avoid traveling at night.

– I don't understand. Will your wife stay with me?

– I already told you about the matter. Take it easy. There's no need to worry, she knows everything.

✶ ✶ ✶

Damn it! – Planchet roared at one of his henchmen, busy freeing him.

He pulled out a large piece of bloody horse meat from his chest, before taking the parts from both legs, one on the knee and the other on the thigh of the other member.

– What do you want, Planchet?

– Don't you see, son of the filth at the bottom of the Seine, that these "wounds" are of no use?

– How not? – And the interrogated man looked at the face of the king of beggars, leaning over him –. I have about ten pistoles in my *bag*.[9]

– A couple of *louises*.[10]

– Hoodlum!

– How, Planchet? What happens now?

– What happens now? I want you to really look like a beggar, a beggar, to honor my name.

– What did I do wrong?

– The horse, animal!

---

[9] Old French coin worth 10 francs.

[10] Old French gold coin worth 20 francs.

– Am I the animal or the horse? – And he continued with the task of removing the bloody rags.

– Both of you are animals. With so many horse, donkey and even breast fillets? With a wound like that you would already be dead! There are more two in the legs. You're exaggerating, man! Get an eye put out, a cut on one leg, but don't use all my horse. Do you know what you are going to do?

– That?

– Eat those steaks and donate everything you received. You are a walking sore, an undead, dung!

– Give you everything?

– And, now, the meat will serve the community just like the horse.

– But, Planchet.

– Now I have a son. I will raise taxes. Come on, Bochet, collect all this. And do the right thing, animal. After all, I'm honest, indeed.

– Are you really going to take everything from me?

– Who is the king here? – Bochet asked, holding the saddlebag that the man had in his hands, opening it and taking out the coins.

– Leave him one – Planchet recommended.

– One? I also have a family.

– I know. You are a successful beggar. You have a good house, a wife who always waits for you at dusk, you have bread, barley for your two horses, in short, you lack nothing.

– And do you need everything I won?

– And the horse?

– Horse? What horse?

– The one whose flesh you used to make the wounds?

– Was it yours, by chance? The animal was dead, in the middle of the street.

– I am lord of life and death, here, make no mistake. Go, change your clothes and come home tired, I see it. I'm tired, woman. I worked a lot...

– And without money.

– You will only pay what is stipulated for tomorrow, today the treasure is for my successor's dowry. Go, don't be late. Do you want to lose your job?

* * *

Young Jean's country house looked more like a palace. Located on a gentle hill, completely covered with grass, it stood out for its large Greek columns, which surrounded the entire residence, supporting the building, especially on the porch, flowers of different colors bloomed around it, mixing with the apple trees and vines...

– This is our house, Paulette.

– What a cute thing! – She praised enthralled, sticking her head out of the carriage screen.

– Yes, it's very pretty, but a little sad, with my wife's illness – Paulette looked at him a little moved and asked:

– Why did you bring me here? I don't want to be an obstacle between you and your wife.

– It's a long story, which you will soon learn. But wait, we're getting there.

In fact. At the sound of the carriage, some helpful servants appeared.

– Sire! – Said one, by way of greeting.

– How are you Pierre? And the Lady?

–Oh! Lord, a little better, but the crises...

– I see – the young man observed, lowering his head. – What can be done?

– Come Lord. We will take care of everything. Is this the young woman you told us about?

– Yes, I'm Paulette.

– And your son?

– Yes, Pierre.

–Mon *Dieu* ! How cute it is! Ma'am, will you let me carry it?

– Take my son? – Paulette reacted, hugging the little boy to her chest. Pierre smiled.

– No, do not worry. Do you see this one? – pointed to Jean – I carried him since he was a newborn. I just want to take you and him to your rooms.

– Okay, sir – Paulette agreed, embarrassed – handing the little one over to the care of the elderly Pierre, who received him affectionately in his arms –. She looked at Jean who was smiling.

– And you?

– Go, love, I'll see you soon.

– Are you going to see your wife?

– I will, I will, yes. I'll call you right away and, Pierre, ask the maids to prepare a bath for her. The dust from the road adhered too much to our bodies.

– It will be done.

– And my dogs?

– They missed you, especially...

– "Diana" – Jean interrupted.

– Yes sir. Sometimes she howls like a wolf, longingly.

– Oh!

– Should I let her go?

– No, not now. I'm going to see the lady. And, Pierre, see that they have anything they need.

– Sire...

– Yeah.

– Mrs. Suzanne asked me to bring the child to her as soon as I arrived. What I do?

– What she asked for, my friend. Is that why you went ahead?

– Sorry, it was.

– Answer her and tell her that I will be with her right away.

– You suffer, sir, I know.

Jean put his hand on the servant's shoulder and with eyes full of tears, he confirmed.

– You know, she is the one who doesn't love me.

– Sire...

– Pierre, I changed my mind.

– How?

– I'm going to see Diana. Go, take the child and do as I asked you. Do you have the key to the kennel?

– Yes, please take it out of my pocket.

Jean took the keys. Paulette followed the maids who soon arrived and entered the mansion. Pierre followed them. Jean walked away, thoughtfully playing with the key on a chain.

✶ ✶ ✶

Now where? Which place? What dimension? Interested? In a place, brothers, to which we invariably go, after our work, bound to the shackles of the flesh. Where have I gone and where you will go, but beware, the path may be as easy as rocky and difficult to access, and there are several places to which we will go, "according to our own works." Well, as a journalist, let me explain to you about the two characters Jean and Jeanpaul, two among many who really existed. Well, these two creatures were summoned, let's say, to the Reincarnation Department, where they hurried to arrive.

– Well – the Director began – it is time for you to return to the body of flesh, to have another chance.

– When do we go? – Asked the male spirit.

– Immediately.

– I will undoubtedly be a man.

– How come you don't know? I'm tired of being a woman.

– The spirit is always the same.

– It doesn't matter what body you have – the girl said – and as long as you don't separate from it.

– Very good, daughter of mine. Your parents have already been chosen. It is close to the moment of birth.

– Will we be born together?

– In the same day.

– And will I be a man?

The Director gave an enigmatic smile and responded:

– In a way, yes.

– How, in a way?

– You will know. Isn't it important for you to be with those who have kept you company in so many reincarnations?

– Definitely.

– It's just that. You can go to the corresponding section.

– Just one more question.

– Yeah?

– What is the reason for this tremendous dream that has overwhelmed us? And dreams that, according to what she tells me, are very similar to mine?

– Without sleep, without dreams, you have been in your mother's womb for a long time. But those maternal caresses seem like dreams to them.

They love you, they are happy to receive you and, therefore, they pamper you and give you confidence.

– It's here?

– That's right. Now go and learn your lesson this time. God protect you always.

Thus, they were born, Jeanpaul, son of a nobleman and a beggar, and Jean, the name that the foolish Planchet, who had no son, gave to the girl who came into the world. There was the "in a way yes" from the Director.

Planchet complied and enforced what he wanted. He never let his pseudo son, like so many others his age, show his sex. From the moment he was born he prohibited visitors and always left the child in clothing that completely concealed any sign of his true sex. He himself followed all the boy's movements. The only ones who knew the truth were him, his mother, the boudoir midwives and Bochet. The girl grew up as a man. Bochet was alone at home. And she learned to enjoy living as a man. She had more freedom. Her legs were also hidden with thin leather pads, almost up to the groin. Planchet was very careful in dealing with the daughter he wanted as a son. He had just forgotten one thing: that everything that is born has to die. And he began to feel the proximity of such an event. Jean had grown as strong as a bull. Of course, she knew her status as a woman, but to please her father, she obeyed him sweetly. And nobody suspected it. She brandished the sword like any swordsman of the time. With her thin leather pants, blouse with loose sleeves that reach to her forearm, with the vest underneath, which hid her youthful breasts, everything made her look masculine. One day he called his daughter, sitting in her favorite armchair, stolen from a furniture seller, and said:

– Jean, I can no longer accompany you through the streets, I am increasingly weak and ill. It's age, son.

– Well, father, why should you do that? I provide everything.

– I know, I know, you are strong, you are manly, even if you are a girl.

– Father...

– Wait. Let me talk. Your mother is also old and can no longer take care of you like she used to. Bochet, you've seen it, he speaks even to himself.

– It doesn't matter, dad. I will take care of you, my mother and Uncle Bochet.

– Daughter...

– Daughter?

– We are alone, Jean.

– So...

– I think I made the biggest mistake in the world when I hid your sex. It was a big mistake and my pride was hurt for having only brought daughters into the world!

– Dad, I am a woman, at least for you.

– Yes honey, just for me, you said it right. However, the day will come when you will need to have contact with a man. It's natural, it's part of life.

– Don't worry, father – and he kissed the hand of the devastated Planchet.

– I'm going to gather everyone and tell them the truth.

– No, please, dad.

– I don't want to leave you this legacy of lies that I, madly, created. I will free you from this immense burden.

-No, I do not want to! – She screamed -. If you die, father, I will be the King of the Beggars.

– No daughter, you deserve much more than this. France is growing, do you see how many artists and men of letters Francis brought us? I have a friend who will educate you.

– Dad, don't do this. The entire community of the Court respects you; underground too. Telling what happened now will only hurt you. Let me do this myself, someday.

– And they will execrate my memory.

– No, no, because I will know how to do it; not convene the Council.

Planchet made a vague gesture with his hands and replied:

– Well; However, can you look for the friend I told you about?

– To educate me?

– Yeah.

– And who is it?

– Doctor Girardán.

– The wizard?

– He is not a wizard, Jean. He is a very good man and treats our illnesses and injuries without asking anything.

– Okay, I'll look for him.

– Excellent. Tell him that you are my son and that I sent you to study with him – and looking seriously at the girl's youthful and worried face -. Don't let me down, Jean.

– I won't, dad, I promise.

* * *

Jeanpaul grew up surrounded by the love of his parents. Let's go back a few years, to the moment they arrived at the Luzardos residence. While Jean went to the kennel, the footman, following orders, took the child to the room where Dona Suzanne's bed was. He knocked discreetly on the huge, artistic door. It opened and a maid appeared:

–Oh! Pierre! – And fixing his eyes on the child's:

– How beautiful! Give it to me, I'll take it to the lady.

–And tell him that Mr. Jean will arrive soon.

– Wait, Pierre. You will know if Mrs. Suzanne wants something – she took the baby and then returned –. Mrs. Suzanne asks the child's mother to come to her.

– I will give her the message, Ana – and he left.

Paulette was taken to a large room, where she took a bath and dressed in clothes she had never owned. Two maids helped her. Looking at herself in the huge mirror, while she was combing her hair, admiring the change, she heard one of the maids say:

– You are very beautiful, lady.

– Lady? I?

She had never been treated like this. Brunette, light brown hair, large eyes in an oval face, full and sensual lips, a set that finished off a slender body, measuring 1.70m. In fact, she was very beautiful. There was a knock at the door. One of the maids went to answer the call and then returned.

– A message for you.

– Whose?

– Lady Suzanne. She wants you to go to her rooms.

– Me? – And Paulette put her hand on her chest – Alone? – The maid smiled.

– Yes. Lady Suzanne doesn't bite.

– But...

– She was waiting for you.

– And Jean?

– Certainly, he will be there soon.

– *Mon Dieu*![11]

– Come on, lady. I direct it. She's pretty. This will please Ms. Suzanne. My name is Bella. Do not be afraid.

– And my son?

– He is with her.

– God!

– She loves children. She has never been able to have one.

– And does she wants mine? – She asked worried.

– No, no. Don't worry. The lady knows everything about you.

– Everything? – Paulette was startled.

– Come on, lady, let's go. She herself will tell you everything.

– God, I'm just a lover of her husband and she treats me so well? – thought –. In any case, I'll take my dagger.

Who knows!

Pretending something, she returned to the dresser and picked up the long, thin dagger that she always carried in the waistband of her skirt and put it in the same place. After all, Paulette was a beggar from the Court of Miracles and had spent her

---

[11] My God!

entire life defending herself. She had not killed, but she would defend herself without fear.

She followed the servant to the luxurious rooms of the lady of that house. Fearful, but with her mind focused on the dagger she was carrying and accustomed to the many vicissitudes and dangers she went through daily, she entered the room.

The smell of medicine filled her nostrils. On the enormous bed, supported by pillows, was Lady Suzanne. In her arms, the child. Paulette stopped by the bed. The woman waved her hand ordering the maids to leave. The newcomer, with her eyes fixed on that woman in the bed. Alone, what harm could she do to her, so fragile?

– Madam – he stammered – I am Paulette, the mother of this child.

– I know, dear – said the patient –. Come sit here on the bed, next to me. You see? Your son is already there. Let's talk – Paulette was reluctant.

– Come, don't be afraid. What I have is not contagious, sit down. Give me your hand.

Still reluctant, the young woman extended her hand and let herself be led to the bed, sitting in the indicated place. The patient affectionately placed the sleeping child next to her and, turning to the young woman, confessed:

– I so wanted to have one like this...

– And why not? You are so young, Mrs. Suzanne.

– Oh! Honey – and tears fell from her eyes.

– You're crying?

– Don't worry, this will pass. It's just that I can't have children. I seem young to you, I really am; However, I am disabled, I cannot move, my lower limbs do not obey.

– Paralyzed, madam?

– Yes, Yes.

– Oh! God!

– Do you know that it's not that bad?

– How not? Living immobilized, unable to go out, run, ride, how is it not so bad?

– God knows what he's doing, ma'am.

– Lying here, I gave myself to meditation, with a thousand possibilities of establishing conditions to better support the people who need me. However, I won't stay in this bed for long.

– Oh! I know, you will walk again.

Suzanne smiled, patted Paulette on the back and reflected:

– In a way, yes.

– Madam, you are Jean's wife. Why are you allowing me to stay here? I assume you know everything.

– Yes, I know and I am happy about it.

– I don't understand.

– I know. I called you here to inform you of everything.

– You speak, madam, as if you already knew me.

– And I do, darling.

– Me, a beggar from the sewers of Paris? From the Courtyard of Miracles? As?

Suzanne smiled again, but this time, looking away from the sleeping baby. Then, looking at her, he declared:

– Many years ago, Paulette, I did you great harm.

– Me, madam? I'm only 23 years old. As far as I can remember, no one has ever hurt me. Only life.

– That is what you think. You are simple. And the Creator of all loves the simple. So much so that He makes them forget the mistreat they received in another life – Paulette, in her total naivety, did not understand anything that Lady Suzanne told her.

– I have never been mistreated, ma'am, and, you said, another life? I had no choice, as I never went underground much, except to church.

– Where you met my husband.

– Yes it was. But I didn't know he was a married man. And I wanted to rob him. But after...

– Everything was already planned, Paulette. You don't need to blush so much.

– But madam, Jean is your husband, do you receive me with my son, who is his, and do not order me to be arrested or killed? And you treat me with such benevolence, madam!

– Wait. I'll tell you everything. Here comes Jean. In the evening I will explain everything to you.

The owner of the house entered, approached the bed and kissed his wife on the cheek.

–How have you been, Suzanne?

– Good, dear, good. And even better now that I've met Paulette.

From Jean's expression, it was clear that he did not approve of his wife's actions. He felt guilty. The lover and the spouse together? The scene hurt his pride.

– Have you seen your beloved, Jean? – He asked smiling, his eyes shining.

– Huh? As? – He reacted by taking himself seriously.

– Don't worry, I'm talking about Diana.

– Oh! – He smiled – Yes, yes, she is very beautiful.

– And she misses you.

– It's true. And now I have to find her a husband. She's in heat.

– The viscount, our neighbor.

– I know. He has a dog of her breed. I'll talk to him about it.

Paulette, embarrassed, listened to this conversation, feeling out of place.

Realizing this, Suzanne took his hand and said:

– He's crazy about the dog.

-Diana?

– Yes. Did you know her?

– No ma'am. It's a woman's name, right?

– Yes, and from a goddess too. Diana, the huntress. It will like you. From time to time she comes here. She is a Goddess who helps us: she jumps on the bed, licks my face, then rests her big head on my chest and it takes a lot of work to get it out. It grows in everyone. Sometimes I think we don't have her, she has us. Only Pierre can make her obey. Do you like dogs?

– Very much, madam. I've had a few.

– Excellent. She will love to meet you. Well, Paulette, in the evening, as I told you, after dinner, we will talk again. I'm going to tell you something that will make you understand our unusual situation. Take your son.

At this point everything should be ready in the room was assigned to you. And Mary, one of our maids, will be at your service from now on. Now go, dear. I wait for you at night...

Paulette received the child from the lady, looked at Jean and left, being escorted out of the room by the maid who was waiting for her.

– Only with his wife – Jean took her hands and, with a melancholic air, said:

– Suzanne, what is all this about? I do not like this.

– Do not worry dear. Do you know the reasons and you still haven't gotten used to it? Must be like this.

– It is a delicate situation. A wife who throws her husband into the arms of another.

– You promised to help me. I was frank with you.

– But, only because of dreams?

– Not just dreams.

– Communication with the dead? What if all of this is simply due to your health?

– Hallucinations? No, no, Jean. Be sure about this.

– And you are going to tell her everything.

– Yes, it is necessary, dear. Because only then I will be free.

– But I love you, Suzanne.

– I know. However, you don't belong to me.

– We lived very well until this damn accident. When we got married it was to live together forever. It is a deeply embarrassing situation.

– After all, don't you like her?

– Of course I like her, but...

– Take it easy. Soon she will be your wife. She is already the mother of your son.

– What if everything you think is nothing more than a chimera?

– No, honey, it's not. Your son is proof that this is not an illusion.

– And why don't remember it? Don't you say I was "there" too?

– Yes, you were, and without realizing it, you were the bone of contention.

– Just look! A life before this! Sometimes you act like Dr. Girardán in skirts.

– He is a good man, a very good friend of mine. And he knows everything about us.

– A witcher is what he is – Susana smiled.

– No, he is not.

–From what I have heard at Court, Margaret, the king's sister, does not have a very good opinion of him.

– Dear – and he squeezed his hands more – there is a secret. Not Dr. Girardán's, but hers. Please, darling, don't get involved in this matter. Be as you are and always have been. Go now, dear, dust yourself off and leave me in peace with my servants. You wouldn't want to see your wife being carried, put in a bathtub, washed, dried, dressed and put to bed.

– Suzanne, do you underestimate me?

– I asked you to do all this. You refused and now what do I do? I don't care what's happening, my love.

– I, your husband, have the obligation to do everything.

– Go, we will meet in the evening. Go away please.

And the he left.

At nightfall they met again. Jean, at his wife's request, took Paulette to the bedroom. Suzanne reclined against some comfortable cushions. She was wearing a diaphanous robe with wide sleeves. She had loose hair falling over her shoulders and her cheeks were rosy thanks to the cosmetics her maids applied to her.

She was already beautiful and the makeup enhanced her beauty even more.

– You look beautiful, ma'am – said Paulette, by way of greeting. Suzanne smiled slightly.

– Take a seat – she invited, pointing to two armchairs, which she had ordered to be placed next to the bed.

The maids served them tea and toast. They ate in silence. In the end, Suzanne began in a calm voice:

– Well, let's start our conversation. I warn you that what you will hear is the purest truth. Especially for you, Paulette, since Jean is aware of the issue.

– Are you okay, darling?

–Oh! Yes, fine, don't bother. Just listen, *mon chéri. Je t'aime.*[12] – Jean simply lowered his head. A sign that the wife could continue – "Fine" – She resumed, clearing her throat to clear her vocal cords. It all started I don't know if it was millennia ago. It was a Nordic town. Big ships, men in elephant seal and otter skins. It was extremely cold, that's why they dressed like that. The houses built with thick tree trunks, tied together by strong ropes, had no floor or divisions. The furniture consisted of cots, made of wood whose ends ended in an X, lined with leather strips, where the skins of furry animals served as mattresses. There, on that stage, was me – and she hit her chest –. Me, do you understand? I, who adored Sven, one of the greatest navigators and great hunter. However, Sven didn't have eyes for me. He only wanted you – and she pointed to Paulette – Only you!

– Me, madam? – And the girl, with an air of intense perplexity, put both hands on her chest –. How? I never left the Courtyard of Miracles – she reacted tearfully–. You must be

---

[12] Dear. I love you.

mistaken, ma'am. It wasn't me and I don't even know who that Sven is.

– Oh! But you will know. Be calm, just listen to what I tell you, and fear nothing. I don't wish you any harm – Back then, your name was Mira. Blonde, slender, dressed in those bearskin clothes that left your thighs exposed, you were his favorite – and she pointed to her husband –. He was Sven. I tried in every way to seduce him so he would to stay with me. After all, I was the daughter of the man who had the most ships, Father Holff. The richest. All the guys asked me, except Sven. He was poor, just one of the crew of my father's ship. Marrying me would make him rich, he would have his fleet, but he only wanted you.

– Madam – Paulette intervened, as if she were experiencing the drama – It wasn't my fault.

– Don't talk, just listen. All this happened in a life before this one, girl. I took advantage of my status as the daughter of the clan leader to achieve my purposes. You were my friend, without suspecting that I loved Sven. You thought I wanted to help you and that my position would make it easier for your fiancé to get a better position. However, I just wanted to separate you from him – she sobbed loudly, taking a handkerchief from behind the pillows and putting it to his mouth.

– Do you feel bad, dear? – Jean asked, leaning over her.

– No, don't worry – and talked to the maid –, light another lamp. It's dark – and she continued –. I came up with a plan to get rid of you. Sometimes we fished in winter, when the cold was intense, covering the entire lake with a layer of ice. I knew the region where the ice was thickest and could support the weight of a person. You, Sven, along with other men, cut wood to feed our fires on those freezing nights. Then I took you to the place where the layer of ice was as thin as possible and made you fall into that icy water, whose very thin layer fell on your feet. I saw you clinging to the edge, looking at me terrified, thinking I was going to help you. However, I turned my back on you and returned to the village, entered the house and spoke there.

The fishermen, a few hours later, found Mira lying on the edge of the ice, with her legs still submerged in the icy water. They took her to the town, where they gave her massages, hot broth, in short, they tried everything, in vain, since her lower limbs did not react. When I was asked to tell what had happened, I only said that we had broken up and when I came back, I thought she had come back.

You didn't frame me. Rushed to the city, with Sven pushing the horses beyond the limit, nothing could be done and both legs were amputated. And she was thilled by the fact. How would Sven love you now? For what? Oh! Now he would be mine. I was wrong!

Look, your suffering seemed to have encouraged the love he dedicated to you much more. He still married you! I wished you died. However, the problems arising from the operation did what I had not been able to do. Six months later, your funeral took place. I rejoiced. And I tried to win over my Sven. I spoiled him so much that he ended up marrying me. What happiness for me to have him as a husband! However, to him I was just his wife and his thoughts were focused on you. How many times have I heard him pronounce your name, even alone, in the deepest reverie?

– Lady Suzanne, how can you be sure of this? – Paulette asked with tears in her eyes.

– It's true, – Suzanne Jean intervened. – Let's forget all that. Make sure you sleep.

– No, *mes amis*,[13] I haven't finished yet. Patience. We had a little son who filled our house with joy, but for a short time. At three years old, for no apparent reason, he fell ill and all our efforts to

---

[13] No, my friends.

cure him were useless. He died. In desperation, I rebelled against the gods, blaming them for my misfortune. Of course, it would be revenge for what I had done to you. I wasted away and, one day, unable to bear the pain and remorse any longer, I drank a beverage that took my life. How I suffered on the other side of existence! I was in dark places, until they rescued me and took me to a hospital, where they cured my ailments. It was there that Sven and Mira came to visit me. She was complete, her legs were not missing, the very ones that I, in my foolishness, had caused her to lose. She smiled at me, treating me like a sister. I threw myself at her feet, sincerely sorry, asking for forgiveness and promising to return to my physical body and do everything possible to reunite them again. In this way I would redeem the debt I had contracted with both of them, giving them back the happiness I had stolen from them.

And we came back. Dr. Girardán helped me find you. We married. And when I reached the age Mira was when she lost her legs, there was an accident that left me paraplegic. The mount lost control, causing me to fall and fracture my spine. I suffered a lot, but I was happy, because I myself had asked for that way to redeem myself. I had to suffer all the misfortune I had put Mira through. I am happy and grateful to God for giving me this opportunity.

When dear Doctor Girardán gave me the news that you were incarnate and in that horrible place, I urged Jean to look for you. I knew that in a certain way the memory would reach your minds, in an atmosphere of mutual sympathy and you would unite.

– My God, what a story! – Paulette exclaimed.

– Dr. Girardán has the means to demonstrate the veracity of the facts that I told you. I ask you to look for it one day.

– My dear – said Jean – everything is fine . We will look for the good doctor. You tried too hard. You should rest.

– I'll do that. Dear ones, pay attention to Divine Providence. They found each other, they have a little son, whom I adore, like the one I lost so long ago. And rest assured, God is not vengeful, He never has been. To correct our errors, we are the ones who request the way to pay. He doesn't intervene. Didn't he give us discernment between good and evil? The rest depends on us. We feel so ashamed before His Image that we ask for approval. Didn't his Son suffer? Why not us? And how he suffered! "Father, take this cup from me " – He even said, because he was human, but soon he understood again. And he died on the ignominious cross, thinking about saving us – She took both of them by the hand and continued –. Nothing, my loves, is unfair under heaven. Think about this, Paulette! Take good care of your child. He will soon meet a young woman. They also have to walk together to learn. Look for Dr. Girardán – She looked at his husband, who was bathed in tears, and told him – Jean, we were happy, right?

– Of course, darling, of course.

– I love you for never complaining. This was already a sign of the truth that I told you. Can you forgive me?

–Oh! Suzanne...

– Do not Cry. Remember that oak tree at the end of our property?

– I know where our initials are, made by me.

– I want my body to be buried among its roots.

–Suzanne...

–Madam... –Paulette accompanied, but, at a signal from the patient, they both fell silent.

"The body in not hat matters" she continued calmly, "it can be buried here, there or anywhere else. However, we are happy about it, because it brings back good memories and a longing that unites us to the place where so many loved ones were left. Then we stop being interested, since, studying in the school of life, we learn so much that one day we will be so far away. In another 'abode' of the Creator, those worldly feelings, coming from the earth's crust, fade away. However, we will continue to remember those who were close to us and perhaps guide them. Praise God!

– Sleep, dear – Jean advised, adjusting the pillows.

– Go, darling, educate your son. Find Dr. Girardán. And you, Paulette, look, make him happy. Goodbye.

– Goodbye? – Jean's voice sounded dismayed.

– See you tomorrow, darling – raising her hand, she caressed his face.

– Remember the oak tree. Leave me with my maids. Go, you have a lot to talk about, I know.

Jean kissed her on the forehead. Paulette, in the hands.

– Kiss your son for me.

– If you want, I'll bring it to you so you can do it.

– No, my dear. The little one sleeps and I'm going to sleep too.

They left. In the enormous room, Jean, with his right hand on his forehead, reflected:

– Why did she say goodbye with the phrase "See you tomorrow"? I didn't understand.

– Jean, the one who understands the least here, is me, an idiot – Paulette responded –. I had never heard or seen anything like it. I'm a beggar, you know?

– What, Paulette?

– How many bloody noses, lips and wounds do I have in my bag?

– Now, Paulette...

– You didn't let me bring the bag, but my work tools are there.

– What is that for? – Jean roared, holding her by the shoulders –. You are here, at peace and safe. Stop remembering the past, bury your nose, lips, ears, wounds, I don't know what else. Do you understand?

– You're hurting me – she shouted.

– I'm sorry – he apologized, letting her go –. But think about it, notice the difference from where I saw rats with this one.

– I realized... I realized right away. How am I going to get used to it from one day to the next? I miss my people, my friends, even stealing. What leisure can I have in the midst of such a transformation? I heard, especially this story about your wife. How do you want me to react?– Paulette –and Jean hugged her –I'm sorry. Let's walk a little, I think we have a lot to talk about – he took the young woman by the arm and they left the house, towards the well-kept garden.

– Do you know me as Mira?

– I'm not so sure.

– You're not very sure, how?

– Paulette, my raising was a bit, shall we say, radical. The saints, the Pope, the Catholic school, but, of course, we had the right to dream, not fleeting dreams, like everyone else, but something that, no matter how much it rejects us, leaves us some mark and, there, well far from my thoughts, I remember someone.

– Someone?

– Yes, let's sit on that bench. Someone who could have been you. I confess that Suzanne's whole story reminds me of... however, I can't pinpoint who. If you remembered something, who knows, together we could put this "puzzle" together?

– You know, Jean...

– Yeah?

– When you approached me, showing yourself so charitable and also affectionate, I wanted to steal you.

– I remember. Then you had an "animal-eaten" nose, on the left side – She smiled.

– Yes, that's how it was. You know, it's our weapon to move passersby.

– Yes I know. In the Court of Miracles there are miracles every day.

– It's true. But it was in the Cathedral of Notre Dame of Paris, on the stairs, and I couldn't steal anything from you, although my hand held your purse full of coins. Why? I saw in your eyes so much sweetness and a transmission of affection, of love, that prevented me from completing what I always did. Come to think of it, Jean, I believe what Lady Suzanne said. In fact, there is something that unites us, that attracts us. But, mon chéri, I didn't want it to be like that. Being a nobleman's lover is one thing. But being "the other", with the wife's permission, this moves me a lot. She's beautiful, poor thing, and she doesn't deserve this. But, Jean, she's the one who wants that whole story, so sincere. Oh! Jean, help me – and she hugged the man who had her in his arms, making her rest her head on his chest, stroking her hair.

– You're right. We have to look for Doctor Girardán. He seems to be the key to this whole mystery.

– Jean...

– Tell me, mon amour.

– We shouldn't touch each other, you know, I have real respect for your wife. I feel like I cheated on her and she doesn't deserve this. Do me this favor?

– Paulette, Paulette, do you know that I also think the same?

– I know, I'm sure.

– Well, you can also be sure that now I know that I love you even more – and he kissed the young woman's forehead.

Lady Suzanne gave her soul to the Creator two weeks later. She left smiling for her husband and for Paulette, without the slightest suffering. It seemed – and it was – that she was happy to leave this "valley of tears", in search for better places. Jean fulfilled her last wish: he placed her in the shade of the majestic oak and planted a cross that he made with the wood of the gigantic tree. And, after a heartfelt and painful prayer, accompanied only by the servants of the house, they returned to it.

– Poor thing – said Paulette, with her face flushed and wet with tears – Jean hugged her.

– No poor thing, dear.

– I say this because I know how much she suffered and I, my dear, am not worth that much.

– Paulette... – and he squeezed her tightly.

– Sir – Pierre approached, extending a glass to his boss –. Here. It's a hot brandy. You need it – Jean received the glass, looked at the old butler and said:

– Thank you Pierre. Take one too. Like me, I know you need it.

"God bless you, sir," he stammered.

– She is happy, Pierre.

– It's true and she always wanted it, sir, and you told me that you didn't want it!

– Pierre...

– Sorry *m'sieur*.

– *Oui*, I said that, but I don't think that way anymore.

-I know. She trusted me with many things. What do I do now? – And he wiped away the tears that fell copiously on his wrinkled face.

– You're my friend. You will always be with us, you and everyone.

– She instructed us, yesterday, in the bathroom – Mary intervened – that there was no solution to continuity. That the lady would now be Mrs. Paulette and that we would serve her as she wanted and so it will be done, lady – and she leaned down, taking Paulette's hand and kissing it. The girl, surprised by this sudden proof of submission, withdrew her hand, took the servant by the shoulders and, crying, they both embraced each other.

– Everything will be, dear, as if she were here – she said – nothing will change. Including the rooms in which she lived, which, I insist, remain as they are. As if she were there. It will be a sanctuary, where we will go to pray. I don't want anything that was hers taken away. And I want it happy, with flowers, everything organized.

– That's how it will be, madam.

✳ ✳ ✳

This is what happened. But we said that young Jean was handed over, to be educated, to the very good Dr. Girardán. So...

Chapter III
The "Witcher"

Jean, the daughter of Planchet, the king of the beggars, presented herself to Dr. Girardán. Saint Germain Street, on the outskirts of the city, was poor, with simple houses and uneven stone pavement. Illuminated at night by a few lamps that barely illuminated the place. Workers lived there, local people who worked in their workshops, blacksmith shops, etc. On this street, in a red brick house, with a door and a window, on whose wall a sign indicated – Dr. Girardán...

– Doctor – "our" Jean knocked on the door, with the large iron ring attached to the door. It wasn't long before it opened enough to allow a round head, completely devoid of hair.

– What do you want? – A booming voice resounded, scaring the young woman.

– Sorry, I come from Planchet, I'm looking for Dr. Girardán.

– Planchet?

– Yes, the King of the Beggars.

– Oh! Yes, Yes. He is waiting for you, young man. Come in.

Jean responded, a little suspiciously. She waited for the chubby man to handle the padlocks and chains securing the door and followed him, walking down a long hallway that led from the room to an open door.

– Mr. Doctor! – The man called, listening to the response from inside:

– Yes, Lenoir, what do you want?

– The visit you were waiting for.

The doctor left the room he was in. He was wearing an apron tied around his waist, naturally dirty with chemicals. Jean looked at that tall, thin figure, whose facial bones protruded from it, a detail softened by the bright eyes, expressing immense kindness.

– Oh! Young man, you are the son of friend Planchet, without a doubt.

– Yes sir.

– Hmm! Lenoir, bring us something to drink.

– Yes, doctor – and the man walked away –. The doctor began to examine the "child" with his eyes, who, distrustful and distant, did not look at him. Girardán smiled. His thick black hair, swept back, was held back with a leather ring. He put his hand on the visitor's shoulder.

– How are you miss?

– Huh? – And Jean took a step back – sir, I am a man.

– Oh! A man with almost developed breasts and about to have his first period! Very good... if you haven't already.

– Mister...

– Calm down, miss. Your secret will also be mine.

She, a little embarrassed, asked:

– Did my father tell you everything?

– Come, come, young friend, let's go to the living room, where we will talk better. However, you know, your father didn't tell me anything. He just asked me to be your preceptor.

–And how did you find out? – The doctor smiled.

—My friends, whom you don't see, told me everything. Therefore, have confidence in me, I will not betray you.

Arriving at the simple room, with simple furniture: a table, some chairs and a large cabinet against the wall, he made the girl sit down. The burly but friendly Lenoir returned with glasses and a vase on a tray which he placed on the table.

– Thank you, Lenoir.

– If you need it, call me doctor.

– *Oui* – and turning to Jean, while he filled one of the glasses with the reddish liquid.

– Raspberry juice. Do you like it?

– Yes sir.

Once served, he continued:

– I see that you have a beautiful sword at your waist.

– Yes, my uncle Bochet gave it to me.

– And I know you know how to use it because of the slots in the case, you've already taken it out a few times.

– It's true. I needed to defend myself.

– But you didn't kill anyone.

– No, sir, not yet.

– Not yet? And do you intend to do it?

She put her hat on her back, tied around her neck with a leather strap, revealing her head adorned with long black hair, trimmed just below the nape of the neck, as worn by young people of the time. Her large bright brown eyes were crowned by thin eyebrows and large eyelashes. Well above well-defined lips and chin, a funny little nose, a little upturned, which denotes rebellion and bravery. She wore a white blouse with loose sleeves that reached to her wrists and a black leather vest tied with braided cords between shiny metal eyelets. Black pants made of very soft leather, attached to her legs, inside boots that reached almost to her knees and then folded outwards. A wide belt held the sword, simple but very beautiful.

–When you fight, doctor, the only thing you think about is surviving. If this requires killing the opponent, let it be him, not me.

The doctor smiled slightly.

– I understand. To defend life, or that of third parties, this is allowed.

– *C'est ainsi.*[14]

– *Votre père*[15] asks me to be your preceptor.

– *Oui, mon précepteur, se vous accepter.*[16]

– *Oh! Avec plaisir, mademoiselle.*[17]

– Mademoiselle?

– *Pardon...*[18] boy.

– That's better.

Dr. Girardán had intimate fun contemplating that beautiful young woman transformed into a boy.

– You can read?

– Not much, I didn't have time to study.

– You write?

– In the same way as what I read.

– Didn't you have time? Why? What are you doing?

---

[14] That's how it is.

[15] Your father.

[16] Yes, my preceptor, if you accept.

[17] With pleasure, miss.

[18] Sorry.

– I help my parents and the community of the Court of Miracles.

– Yes, yes – the doctor crossed his fingers – and what does that help consist of?

– Well, sometimes I steal or cover for my friends when there is danger.

– I know, I know. And you also use those horrible wounds?

– No, that is for professionals and I don't like it.

– And what do you like the most?

– Well – and she crossed his arms – climb the vines to a balcony, or a window, enter a room and take the jewelry.

– Jean – the doctor warned in a serious tone –. I can't help you with these things. They are tasks that do not require study. What will we do?

– I told *mon père* , but he insisted, you know, he is old, sick.

– And he wants something better for you.

– Yes.

– And you, don't you want it?

– I wouldn't object but, thinking about it, knowing how to do it even helps. I can read the edicts of the kingdom, some secret documents...

– Which inform you where coins are being transferred...

– Yeah.

– Jean...

– Yes?

– How long has it been since you took off this vest?

– She looked at the doctor seriously.

– Why?

– I'm a doctor, girl, and I see that, since you wear it so tight, the veins in your neck are swollen and that's bad.

– So...

– So?

– If you want to continue in your life of deceit and lies, you have to take care of it. Come here – he stood up, extending his arm to her.

– Come with me to my office.

– For what?

– You will see.

She followed him, although reluctantly, to the room transformed into an office. There, among shelves with glass, instruments and books, in a corner there was a skeleton and a low, narrow bed.

– Take off all your clothes and lie down.

– Are you crazy?

– Well, a man cannot be ashamed of another – he mocked.

– But you know that is not the case.

– Come on girl, do you want help?

She took a step back and pulled the blade a few inches from its sheath.

– Hey, if you don't accept it – he said, pointing with his arms – so be it. You can go back to your den. I cannot help you.

– What does this have to do with having to take off my clothes?

– You want to know?

– Of course – and she was still in a defensive position.

– You stink.

– Me?

– I can hardly stand being in your presence without covering my nose with my hand.

– Do I smell bad?

– Like a skunk.

– How long has it been since you changed your clothes?

– Well, I change my vest and blouse.

– Month to month or more? And the pants?

– None of your business.

– But that's what matters.

– I thought, doctor, that you knew everything.

– Your father has just asked me to be your preceptor. He didn't add anything else. I will keep your secret, I assured you. I just want to help you to be more comfortable and without risk of infection. Do you agree to obey me?

She sheathed her sword and, looking the doctor in the eyes, responded.

– I have never been naked in front of any man.

– Perfectly, but I'm a doctor, Jean, and I just want to help you. I know your body like the back of my hand.

– My body? – She shouted with her eyes wide open.

– *Ma cherie*,[19] I read the body; that is, the female body, its organs, not yours precisely. Are you going to get naked or not?

– Completely naked?

– Completely.

– *Mon Dieu*.[20]

---

[19] My dear.

[20] My God.

– Choose. Will you accept and survive to continue deceiving, but in better conditions, or decline and you will not deceive anyone else, because you will die? How is it going to be?

She hesitated, walked a little, thought and finally decided:

– You are a doctor and an old man like my father, but even so, I'll keep my dagger in my hand... I accept.

She pulled the dagger out of her vest, unhooked her sword belt, and let it fall to the ground.

– Wait.

– What?

The doctor went to the door and called the servant Lenoir, to whom he said something. Then he continued.

– What did you say to your lackey? – She asked, seriously.

– Be calm. I only asked him to bring what I need.

– What if he finds out everything?

– He already knows. Lenoir is a good man, he is a seer, like me. He is aware of everything about you.

– But...

– Take it easy. Here, inside this house, only he and I live. As you may have already noticed, the house is large, we have several rooms. It's narrow, I know, but long. I have time for an appointment. Unless it's an emergency. Here you will wear women's clothing, so that your body can recover from the oppression it suffered.

– What if someone arrives?

– No one will see you. I just want you to stay in proper clothes for ten days. From time to time you will wear your men's clothing. You will learn how to do it.

– I don't know...

– Your father trusts me.

– I will be his successor.

– There will be no successor.

Lenoir arrived with a huge wooden tub in his hands. He entered, without saying anything, placed it next to the bed, returned and soon he was back with two small barrels – small for him – in his arms. He placed them on the floor, removed the lids, and poured their contents into the tub. It was hot water in one, as steam filled the room. He turned to the doctor and asked:

– Is that all, doctor?

– That's all, Lenoir, that's all. She and I will do the rest.

The servant left the office and closed the door behind him.

– Okay, come on, take off all your clothes.

She was no longer reluctant. She started to get rid of her clothes again. The doctor went to a shelf, picked up an amphora, poured part of its contents into the tub of hot water, then went to a small oven, which he lit, activating the embers with some pieces of iron.

– Ready?

He turned to the girl, completely naked. Without any emotion, he asked:

– Lie down on the bed.

She obeyed. Then the examination began, with expert hands. Using soft cloths soaked in potions, he cleaned the girl's entire body.

Then he massaged it all over.

– Look Jean, you are already a woman and all the blood from your menstrual cycle was stuck to you, which with the sweat and dirt could cause a serious infection, especially due to the lack of bathrooms. Your breasts almost atrophied from the excessive pressure, forcing your veins to swell. No, you wouldn't succeed your father like that. But come on, let's go to the bathtub now. And with large tongs he threw some pieces of red-hot iron into the liquid.

– Check the temperature. Get in, take this sponge and rub your private parts vigorously.

– It's hot there.

– But it is bearable. Get in.

So, she did, following the doctor's instructions. Within moments, the water was dark.

– Do you see, lady of the Court of Miracles, the filth that you brought from there, stuck to your body? Rub more. He waited a few minutes and addressed her again:

– Now get out.

She obeyed. He removed the lid of the tub, causing the water to flow down a previously arranged gutter and no doubt carrying the dirty liquid into the sewers. Then he refilled the tub, put a few more pieces of red-hot iron inside, and let her in. He poured the contents of a flask into the water and said:

– Wet your head and rub your hair.

She accepted everything meekly. There was perfume in the air now.

– Stay there for a few moments – She rubbed her hair, with a pleasant sensation all over her body, free of dirt.

– Get up – he continued, with a huge towel in his hands –. Dry yourself. I will provide you with clothes.

– And mine?

– They will be boiled, now you cannot wear them, including the boots. They smelled bad, honey.

– I never felt it.

– And of course! You lived with the bad smell, but whoever approached you... – and the doctor pinched his nose –. I will send Lenoir to find you suitable clothes, especially the underwear, where have you ever seen a young woman walking around in only leather pants?

– And what will I do in the meantime?

– We will start classes. Keep this towel around your body for two days and only remove it to return to the bathroom. And you will anoint your body with potions that I will give you. You already know how to do it. I will no longer embarrass you with my presence. By the way, how do you feel?

– Lighter, was I really that filthy?

– The certificate was the color of water. Now, girl, you are going to have some hot tea and then you are going to go to your room, where you are going to get some sleep. The essences I put in the water will make you sleepy.

– I never slept during the day.

– But now it is necessary.

He leads her to a simply furnished room: a ready-made bed, a dresser, and a small closet.

– Lie down and relax... When you wake up you will have your clothes. Don't worry about anything – and he shouted – Lenoir, the tea.

✳ ✳ ✳

Jeanpaul, son of Paulette and Jean, now of the same age as Planchet's daughter, had become a gentleman. Taught by teachers from Paris, in addition to mastering several languages, he was also an excellent swordsman, since, at that time, every knight had to know how to handle a sword. Carrying it simply as an ornament, it could even be something made of gold, with diamonds embedded in the handle. However, a noble's education would not be complete without this important detail. After all, at that time it was a passport to travel the streets of Paris and be equipped with a sword. Anyone who knew how to manipulate it would make criminals flee. On the contrary, he ended up knocked down, naked and with the stolen weapon when he was not murdered.

Jeanpaul had been carefully educated. Jean, his father, made him attend Mr. Fontein's academy, where classes were taught in the arts of defense and attack with swords and pistols. This institute was the most famous, if not the only, of its kind. When he got there, Jeanpaul already knew everything, he just needed to improve his skills, achieved thanks to the teachings of great teachers. At the same time he learned languages, science and mathematics. He was an interested scholar and was held in high regard by his teachers.

Tall, slender, blond, with dark, boisterous eyes, he was extremely given to adventures. He enjoyed hunting on the extensive estates of his father and his adoring grandfather, the Duke of Luzardo. The latter, already in his seventies, always spent several days at his only son's farm, just to be with his grandson. And systematically, when he was in Paris, he went to pick him up in his carriage. Jeanpaul idolized him.

– Tomorrow we will go to Alençon – his grandfather warned him, when he picked him up at the Academy.

– Tomorrow, grandfather?

– Yes, and very early. Because? Don't you want to go?

– No, it's not that.

– Well, your father entrusted you to me, here in Paris. You finished the course with honors, you deserve a vacation and your grandfather also wants to see those corners again; hunting, horseback riding and, don't you want to go?

– Grandpa, it's not like that. Precisely tomorrow morning I have to carry out an order from my father. I need to go to Saint Germain Street.

– Saint Germain Street? – The old duke asked surprised.

– Yes, grandfather.

– Have you ever heard of this street, Jeanpaul?

– It's not a pretty street, I know.

– But then, what did your father tell you to do there?

– Visit Dr. Girardán.

– *Sacre!*[21] But that is reckless! There is an ongoing case against him, my grandson. He can be burned at the stake at the king's request.

–Then I have to hurry, otherwise I won't find him again.

– Jeanpaul, that man is a witcher.

– No, grandfather, he is not. He is a charitable doctor, he cares for everyone. Grandma Suzanne loved him.[22]

– Oh! Son, Suzanne was a good girl, but she was also Dr. Girardán, in skirts.

– Grandpa... I will go alone, on horseback, to that street early tomorrow.

– I will provide you with an escort.

– There's no need. I know how to defend myself.

– *Sacre!* – Grandfather roared. – You are stubborn like your father.

– Then don't insist.

---

[21] Damn.

[22] This is how his grandfather treated Lady Suzanne, his father's first wife.

–And when will we go to Alençon?

– Tomorrow in the afternoon.

– Very well. I will arrange everything, you will see the Spanish muskets I bought. They are beauties. We will eat wild boar for a month.

– Apparently, you want to end the entire race.

–And I still bring something for the king.

Upon arriving at the Duke's palace, Jeanpaul changed his clothes, putting on a short-sleeved blouse, over it a purple vest, black shorts tucked into half boots with folded leather and a belt with a beautiful sword; He put a bright blue cloak over his shoulders, tossed it aside, put on his feather hat, and left.

– *Mon Dieu* ! – Grandpa exclaimed when he saw him put on the very fine leather gloves.

– Are you going to the whitcher's house or to meet a lady?

– Well, grandfather, after all, am I the grandson of the Duke of Luzardo or not? – The old man smiled satisfied and patted him on the shoulder.

– Be careful with the sword. Just draw it...

– ... to defend our honor or that of others – Jeanpaul completed – I already know this by heart.

– Very good. But wouldn't you go tomorrow morning?

– True; but I thought better about it and concluded that, since the trip would be exhausting, it would be better to leave early

The duke did not hide his joy.

–Oh! – He exclaimed, rubbing his hands –. Excellent! You thought very well. So, while you're visiting, I'll have everything ready so we can travel early tomorrow morning.– Make sure you don't forget anything, Grandpa.

– Who are you calling old, brat? Do it without subterfuge – he said, pointing his finger at his grandson, who smiled.

– No, no, don't even think about it – and he went to the door, which he opened quickly shouting – See you later, old man – and closed it behind him.

"You miscreant, come back here, brat," he heard his grandfather shout.

He went to the stable, chose a beautiful animal that he had harnessed, mounted it and started at a slow trot through the streets of Paris, heading towards the Rue Saint Germain.

✳ ✳ ✳

At that precise moment, Dr. Girardán was speaking to Jean:

– Well, with these clothes, dear, you look more like a little man. Isn't that right, Lenoir?

– Yes, doctor, yes. Only one thing is missing.

– Missing something? But what?

– Now, doctor, let him wipe a piece of paper or a cloth over his mouth… she has lipstick.

– *Saint Dieu* – exclaimed the doctor, running towards the girl with the suspended apron –. Clean those lips, Jean – he put his hand on his forehead – Ah! These are the things that will never make you a man.

– But it was so little...

– And where did you get this from?

– I stole it on one of my outings.

– *Mon Dieu* ! Is the feminine instinct predominant and I'm complicit, my God?

– It won't happen again, I promise, uncle.

– Uncle? – The doctor shouted. – What a great thing. To be your uncle I would have to be your mother's or your father's brother, I am neither of those things.

– Yes uncle.

– *Mon Père* !

– Finally, how am I?

– Now you are a little man – Lenoir agreed, with his big voice –. I already said it – shouted the doctor, who, deep down, was proud of his work – and without blushing –. Come on, go to the bottom and come back.

Jean was wearing, to better conceal her bust, a very loose shirt, and underneath a bra that, although it hugged her breasts well, nevertheless left space for them, without disturbing them; long trousers of very thick and soft wool, finished with high boots that reached almost to his knees; her black hair, cut to her shoulders and hidden by her feather hat, gave him a gentlemanly air.

– No! – The doctor shouted.

– No? What did I do wrong?

– Put your foot down, honey, heel first and keep those hips still, don't move them.

– But how?

– Don't know! I just know that this is not how a man walks and stops moving your arms.

– But I always moved like that and they never suspected it.

– Perhaps they were surprised and raised doubts that, out of consideration for their father, they never expressed. *Dieu* !

– Go, *petit* , go, walk, hit the ground with your heels, puff out your chest. No, no so much! Take your hand off your waist, hold the hilt of your sword! – Oh! Planchet! In science she learned quickly, she even speaks English. She is willing, if necessary, to interview any noble, but manners... how difficult... and in the warrior arts she knows everything. She wields the sword like any man. However, don't you know how to walk like one? Did I fail? – He thought.

– How am I?

– Lenoir, how is she?

– A woman dressed as a man.

– What? – She shouted, unsheathing her sword and advancing towards the huge man, who was smiling.

– Repeat that! – She shouted and Lenoir repeated.

– On guard! – and pointed the sword in his direction.

– How? Me without a weapon?

– Giddy Up! – she exclaimed, returning the sword to its sheath and throwing herself into the arms of the big man who carried her like a baby, caressing her black hair.

– I'm a fool, right?

– Yeah.

– So brute – and he started laughing.

– Come on, let's have a snack. By all the gods of Olympus – said Dr. Girardán – this work of mine surpasses the worst operation I have ever done – and told Lenoir –, put it down, elephant. This girl makes us look like moms.

– Can leave? – She asked.

– Of course – the doctor agreed –. Isn't that what we dress you for? Grab your snack and go.

– But make sure you don't go around kissing or courting any man – Lenoir added.

– Tiny! – she shouted, holding the hilt of his sword –. I'm a man.

– Oh my God! – Dr. Girardán whispered. And raising his voice – Go now, but don't fall in love with a woman, please.

– I will – He shouted –. I don't even know what I'm doing here, between two decrepit old men – and she headed towards the door, while both of them laughed. Then someone knocked on the door. She stopped.

– Who could it be, uncle? – Asked -. Take it easy. Wait here.

– You stay too, doctor. "I'll answer," said Lenoir, adjusting his clothes and dagger before heading towards the door.

– Who is it? – He asked, before opening.

– Jeanpaul, son of Jean de Luzardo, grandson of the Duke of Luzardo.

– Wait – Lenoir went to Dr. Girardán and repeated what he heard.

Oh! – He cheered, his face lit up, and Jean – Come, receive this visit.

– I?

– Definitely. You have good manners, you are polite, you listened to me. You are not a girl.

– Go... – and he slapped the girl's buttocks. She was, a little suspicious, and, with Lenoir unbolting the door and standing behind it, opened it. And they faced each other, Paulette's son with Planchet's daughter. They remained for a few seconds, eye to eye, and in their little heads the lightning, the spark of the past, like a fleeting light, made them smile at each other, as if they were acquaintances; However, the motive of the moment soon destroyed the first impression.

– Hello! – Jeanpaul expressed.

– Yes? – She answered.

–Gentleman, I would like to interview Dr. Girardán – and he took off his hat. Jean noticed that the sun's rays were gilding the boy's blonde hair. He cleared his throat.

– Who are you? – she asked, a little embarrassed.

– Jeanpaul... – Are you his son?

– No, no, grandson. Come in, please – and she stepped aside to give way to the young man, who, holding his beautiful hat, entered.

– Come on, I'll take you to the doctor – and she continued.

The doctor pretended to work in his laboratory, manipulating a glass.

– Doctor, you have visitors – she announced.

–Oh! "He is the grandson of the Duke of Luzard," he said, approaching and drying his hands on his apron.

– Yes sir. Son of Jean of Luzard.

– I know, I know. I knew your father. Come, young man, come, let's go to the office – he points to the girl.

– This is my grandson, by affinity, Jean.

-Jean?

– Yes. He has the same name as your father.

The young man extended his hand to her and she shook it.

– A pleasure to meet you friend. My name is Jeanpaul. But they always just call me Jean.

– What a coincidence! – He exclaimed smiling. – Three Jeans at a time.

– It's true.

– Come, go to the office – the doctor invited, leading them to the inner room, where he made them sit down.

– Don't worry, young man. It is in this room where my patients wait their turn to be treated.

– Do not worry sir.

– I met Lady Suzanne, your grandmother, I suppose.

– No she was not. But I consider her that way.

– She was a charming woman. And it's been seventeen years since he passed away. As time flies!

– My father sends greetings to you and my mother too.

– I appreciate their kindness. I know your mother succussed Lady Suzanne to everyone's satisfaction.

– Yes, of course – he answered, however without taking his eyes off Jean, sitting next to the doctor, with her legs crossed and playing with the hilt of her sword. She didn't take her eyes off him either – My mother continued my grandmother's work. She is much loved by everyone in the area and continues the same care.

– Thank God! And your father?

– He follows her. He is an exceptional man.

– Now that you have finished your studies, do you plan to return there permanently?

– How do you know that I finished my studies? – Jeanpaul asked surprised.

–Well, considering the time you were at the Academy, your age and the fact that another school year has already ended, it is easy to understand.

– I'm sorry.

– Young man, an old man like me has experience in these things.

– Sir – Lenoir began, entering the room and greeting the visitor with a smile –, you now have an appointment and the patient has already arrived.

–Oh! Yes, yes. It must be Mr. Silard... – and he stood up –. Please, young man, make yourself comfortable. I won't take long. My grandson does it for me sometimes.

– Don't worry, doctor. I will be comfortable.

The doctor left, leaving the two of them face to face. They looked at each other, moved in their chairs, cleared their throats, until Jeanpaul spoke:

– Are you studying, Jean?

– Huh? – She was scared. – I asked you if you studied, friend.

–Oh! Yes, yes.

– How old are you?

– Seventeen.

– Me too.

– I was born on September 8.

– Wow, what a coincidence! Me too, and on the same day?

– Yes, friend, yes. And look, how interesting: – my name is Jeanpaul, everyone calls me Jean. We are seventeen years old and we were born on the same day!

She smiled and uncrossed her legs.

– In fact.

– The only question that remains now is that if we were born at the same time.

– What time you were born?

– I don't know.

– Neither do I – They laughed.

– You are very kind, Jean. What do you want to do? What course did you take?

She felt embarrassed, but managed to respond:

– Languages, mathematics and sciences.

– Are you going to follow your grandfather's profession?

– No no. I barely know how to make a bandage.

– Do you know how to use a sword?

– Oh! I know, what about you?

– What I know is enough to defend myself.

–And what do you plan to do now that you have finished your studies?

– Well, ending would not be the appropriate term. There is still a lot to learn. You too, I guess. For now, I'm going back at my parents' house. Maybe join the king's army. Who knows?

– Yes... you are rich, from what I understand, grandson of a duke...

– Yes, but what does it matter?

– I hope to take it one day.

– Of course. Do you like hunting? Do you know how to shoot?

– Honestly, Jeanpaul...

– Just, Jean.

– So, from Jean to Jean, no, I'm not very good with firearms, but I like to hunt.

– Do you swim?

– Where, in the Seine?

–Oh! No, not in the part that passes through the city, it is dirty.

– Yes, I know how to swim.

– Do you play ball?

– No, I prefer bilboquet.

– Bilboquet? – And he laughed.

– *Diabolo*.

– I know, I know – and he continued laughing.

– Why are you laughing?

– I'm sorry, but these are games for kids or girls – She blushed.

– Are you calling me girl? – she asked, closing her eyes.

– Of course not. Don't get angry. I'm sorry, I didn't mean to offend you.

– I'm sorry too. There's no reason to bother me.

–Would your grandfather allow you to come with me to Alençon?

– Huh?

– I invite you to come with me. There we can hunt, fish, ride horses, swim and even duel for exercise.

– Are you inviting me, Jean? To go to your father's house? – He urged, leaning towards him, smiling.

– It would be great to have a companion there.

– Oh! Jean!

– I would love to, Jean.

– I'm going to talk to my grandfather, and when are you leaving?

– Tomorrow, early tomorrow. Until we get there it will be about ten days, but with you the trip will be more fun.

– Who is going with you?

– My grandfather.

– The Duke?

– Yes. He's a good old man, you'll like him and he'll like you.

– He may not approve it.

– If not, He won't go – They laughed.

– Tomorrow early?

– Yes very early. If you go, we will pick you up.

–Oh! That would be great!

– Talk to Dr. Girardán. I'll help you convince him. You won't be in any danger.

– Also, both of our birthdays are approaching.

– It's true. It's August 20. In ten days we will be in Alençon. Our anniversary will be a party.

– For real!

– Where do his parents live?

–Oh! They are poor.

– It doesn't matter. I hope he does not take long.

– Don't worry. He'll be right back.

They talked for more than half an hour, until Jean returned. She was blushing and laughing a lot.

– So? – Jeanpaul asked.

– He agreed – and hugged the doctor.

– Well well. How wonderful, dear! However, be careful.

– I'll take care of Jean – Jeanpaul said, putting his hand on his "friend's" shoulder.

– Very good. We talked and talked and you forgot to tell me the real reason for your visit, young man – the owner of the house recalled.

– Sorry, doctor, it was a simple courtesy visit, at the request of my parents. They asked me to convey to the doctor, renewing their feelings of friendship and appreciation.

– I will prepare a letter that I will ask you to deliver to your parents. So the trip is for tomorrow?

– Very early, sir.

– We will be waiting.

– Well, I'm going back to my grandfather's house. I'll give him the good news – and for Jean – And you're going to derust that sword. It will be useful there. We will definitely have a duel.

– *Oui* , sir! – She nodded, with an appearance of reverence – He smiled and extended his hand, which was shaken.

– Are you shaking? – Asked.

–Oh! It's natural – said the doctor –, it's emotion.

– See you tomorrow, Jean. And get up early –. And he left.

"Get up early," she said, dropping into the chair and taking off her hat and unbuttoning her blouse –. I'm not even going to sleep. Girardán laughed and, bending down, grabbed the girl's leg to remove her boots.

– Happy?

– A lot. But exciting.

– Did you like the boy?

–Oh! He's nice! He left me with the impression that I had known him for many years. It's nice!

–Mon *Dieu* ! – The doctor exclaimed.

– What's happening?

– Where have you ever seen a boy fall in love with another?

–Oh! You old man and I'm a boy?

– He knows?

– No, he doesn't. It's going to be difficult.

– I cannot do anything. I can only advise you, since you want to perform this pantomime.

– And what do you advise me?

– Do not sleep in the same bed, do not shower together.

– Now, grandfather, what would I do this?

– This is where your greatest difficulty will lie.

–Oh! – she whined –. What will I do?

– You had your menstrual cycle fifteen days ago. There are fifteen days left until the next one. Since you are healthy, try to remember that your own metabolism will let you know. Then you will know not to do certain things, such as swimming, horseback riding, swordplay or other games. And be very careful so they don't see the menstrual blood.

– How difficult it is to be a woman! – He exclaimed, putting his hand to his forehead.

–Your stupid father was responsible for this. By the way, how is he doing?

– For an old man, pretty good. Bochet is the one who no longer stands up. When I return I will take my father's place.

–Mon *Dieu* !

– I was prepared from a young age to carry out this mission, doctor.

– Darling, enjoy your friendship with young Jeanpaul and forget this nonsense.

– I can't – she responded convinced, while she got rid of the vest. Her youthful breasts bounced.

– Wait, I'm going to look for your clothes – and the doctor walked away, leaving her abstracted.

– I had the impression that I already knew the boy.

She unzipped her pants, stretching her shapely, strong legs. Dr. Girardán came back with women's clothing.

– Go to your room. The afternoon is coming to an end, take a shower. Lenoir will bring you the water.

– Bath, bath! – She complained.

– That's right, and don't forget to do the same in Alençon. Now I'm going to prepare your bags.

– What bags?

– I'm lending them to you. Let's put all your stuff.

– The dresses too?

– No, no. Only what is necessary and men's clothing. It was good to have bought it. Wear brocade blouses only on festive occasions, if possible. The rest are for daily use. And never forget that you should wear underwear. And the vest. Then I will write the letter to Jeanpaul's parents. Go, go to the bathtub. Lenoir already brought the water.

– Wow, too much baths!

– Go, boy – and he prepared to beat her up. She ran.

– Jesus! – He exclaimed –, what've I got myself into. A poor old man like me! Oh, if only I knew that Jeanpaul has been her traveling companion in so many incarnations! Why do I have to know everything? Sorry my invisible friends, I didn't mean to complain. Let it be!

✳ ✳ ✳

– What euphoria is this, grandson? – The old duke asked when he saw the young man burst into his office, taking off his belt with the sword and throwing it on an armchair, his face open with a smile.

– What happened? What miracle did the old wizard perform to dispel the moon's bad mood? And don't call me old.

– Oh! Grandpa, I found someone...

– *Voila* ! She must be beautiful, daughter of which duke? Or marquis? Would he be a baron or a count? Blonde?

– What is this, grandfather?

– You didn't just say...

– That I found someone?

– And then?

– She is not a woman, grandfather.

– No? Well... – and the duke looked at him seriously.

–He is a boy my age, grandson of Dr. Girardán.

– Now, look, I didn't know that the magician had a grandson.

– By affinity.

– And then, why all this euphoria? He must be a bootlicker, naturally.

– Grandpa, don't judge before you meet the boy.

– Meet? And will I meet him?

– Of course. I invited him to come with us to Alençon.

– What? – The duke got up quickly.

– That's what you heard.

– Oh! Naturally, you will share the direction of the carriage with our coachman. Do you know how to deal with horses? Yours is a good idea!

– It's nothing like that, grandfather. He is a friend, not a servant. He studies, is intelligent and very educated.

– Grandson of a Witcher.

– After you get to know him you will have another concept. He's a good man, he treats all those poor people with love, and the boy, you'll like to meet him – And he's coming with us.

– Gonna.

– You no longer want to be with your grandfather.

– It's not that, you should know that young people want the company of others and we are both the same age.

"Speak no more," the duke agreed. I understand very well. You will ride, you will hunt, you will swim, you will fish with him.

–And with you, crazy duke. There is no better hunter in the world than you... – and he threw himself into the arms of his grandfather, who, ashamed and moved, took him in. Afterwards, they both laughed and talked about what they were going to do.

– Okay, and when will we pick up this brat?

– Tomorrow.

– Will he be awake? We will leave before dawn.

– I even think, grandfather, that he won't sleep tonight.

– It's possible!

– Grandpa, I had the impression that I already knew this boy.

– But how? There is not the slightest possibility.

– I know, and that's what intrigues me. His name is Jean, he was born on the same day as me.

–Oh! So the celebration at your father's house will be double! Excellent! Along the way we will buy a few more cases of wine, Morriet wine, the best in France.

– There's no need. My father must have a full basement. But I wanted to give a present to my friend.

– Did you think of something?

– A sword and a pair of pistols.

– Doesn't he have a sword?

– He does.

– And then?

– It's old, one of those that soldiers use.

– Oh. But do not worry. I have some beautiful swords, as you know. Simply choose one that suits your new friend. How tall are is he?

– A little less than me.

– It won't be a problem. Come on, let's get to the armory. I think I have everything your friend could need.

In the armory, there were shelves protected by sliding glass doors, several swords and more florins, daggers, daggers, with their attractive cases next to them, as well as countless pistols and muskets – the duke said:

– You choose what you want – Jeanpaul walked around the room, examining the beautiful weapons. Finally, he stopped in front of one of them.

– Could this be it?

–Oh! Of course, but she's the twin sister of your weapon!

– For that very reason.

– You chose well. It is made of pure Damascus steel. The scabbard, like yours, is inlaid with gold. And look at the crossbar and the glass.

– I know, isn't it the same as mine?

– It's true. I'll clean it and put it in the case. I hope your friend knows how to use it.

– I'm sure.

– Yes, it really seems like you've known him for a long time.

– And the guns?

– I suggest you take these, which are also the same as yours. Light, short barrel, single flintlock key. They do not deny fire.

– That's what it will be like.

– Take that dagger too, as a gift from me.

–Oh! Grandfather!

– If everything you take is equal to what you have, complete it with the dagger. It is identical to the one you have.

SECOND PART

Chapter I
The Unexpected

Early in the morning, the carriage, driven by two beautiful horses and two more riding horses, tied to the back, stopped in front of Doctor Girardán's house. It wasn't even necessary to knock on the door. It opened and Jean appeared. Jeanpaul helped his friend gather his belongings, passing them to the coachman, who tied them to the roof and covered them with a thick tarp. The doctor appeared at the door.

– Don't worry doctor, Jean will return safely.

– I know, boy. And here is the letter to your parents.

– Come meet my grandfather – he took the doctor to the carriage window –. My grandfather, the Duke of Luzardo – presented.

– A pleasure – and the duke extended his hand, which was shaken by the doctor.

– May Our Lord Jesus Christ, the Son of God, grant you a safe journey, sir – he wished.

–Thank you– he thanked, somewhat frowning, for the way in which the nobles of that time treated the commoners.

– Can I make a recommendation?

– Me? Well, you can. Which?

– Avoid crowds. Eat plenty of fruit, especially apples and lean meats. Do not use fermented drinks. And that the meats are very well roasted, with the vegetables Only once a day.

– And why are you telling me this?

– By adopting this diet, you will no longer have the gout that torments you so much and that you keep so much secret.

– Interesting!

– Do this, Duke. It is medical advice. If you follow it, you will be free of this intermittent disease that bothers you so much, right?

– Who informed you that I have gout? – He asked in a low voice so as not to be heard and leaning towards the doctor.

– I see it in your eyes, do this and have a good trip. Did you memorize my recipe?

– Good trip sir. Recommendations for your child.

– Grandpa, here is my friend – Jeanpaul shouted, letting Jean inside the carriage. The duke exclaimed – He is a handsome young man! – Jean blushed, shaking his friend's grandfather's hand.

– Thank you.

–He looks like you, except he has black hair. – Oh! I liked you at first sight, boy!

– Thank you – she repeated in a low voice.

– Shall we go, grandfather?

– Yeah come on.

They greeted the doctor and Lenoir and the carriage trotted along the uneven cobblestones of Saint Germain Street, until it left the city through the north gate and took the road to Alençon. The comfortable vehicle had very soft padded seats, one in front of the other. In front, with his back to the coachman, was the duke. In front of this sat Jean and Jeanpaul. For her everything was new. She had never left Paris, she didn't know the countryside, the roads, other towns or cities. And she did not hide this detail. Her companion had the pleasure of explaining everything about the places they visited.

– When will we get there?

– Well, we haven't started traveling yet – observed the duke. – Are you anxious, young man?

– I confess that yes, sir. I never had the opportunity to travel.

– That's the way it is. Take advantage and see everything. If you're hungry, we'll have a snack. However, since I woke up early and I'm not your age anymore, I'm going to get some sleep. Can I?

– Well, grandfather, you always do this. Go, sleep, we won't bother you – he spoke to his friend – At noon we will have lunch at an inn near Versailles. Then we will continue until almost nightfall, stopping in Dreux, where we will sleep. From then on, there will be no place to spend the night. We will have to do it either in the carriage, or under the light of bonfires. I do not know if you like it.

– It's fascinating, Jeanpaul.

– Are you adventurous, like me?

– Of course.

– We have two horses back there – and he pointed to the bottom of the vehicle.

– I saw them.

– From time to time we leave the carriage there and ride. Is that ok?

– Completely.

– You are sleepy?

– I have never gotten up so early.

– Be honest. You have slept?

– Almost nothing.

– That's what I thought. Go, relax. You with your feet to my head, me, the same. Let's get some sleep. Lulled by the jolts of the carriage, they soon fell asleep.

✳ ✳ ✳

Meanwhile, King Francis was facing state problems. His relations with Charles V[23] were always bellicose. However, Gaudí, the latter's hometown, rebelled against him, which led him to ask his archenemy and rival for permission to pass through France to achieve his goals. The case was brought to parliament and soon one among the peers who did not agree emerged:

– Gentlemen, although obedient to the king, I do not conceive of this amnesty, allowing the greatest enemy of France to pass through our lands. Why not go directly to your destination? If he fights with Suleiman and the king has already made certain acquiescences with him. A heretic! We cannot do anything. Now Charles V comes to ask us for free passage to go quell a rebellion in Gaud! I am against. And I take my distrust to the king.

Sitting with his legs loose and stroking his beard, Francis limited himself to listening. When he saw the speaker return to his chair, he said:

– Lautrec has certain reasons. I didn't expect anything else. He is a great strategist and no one else would be appointed commander of armies. However – and he stood up – we will receive Charles V's entourage in Paris. His army will be contained in the periphery. With him here there will be no danger. I allow you to come. I will receive him with the honors of a great statesman. After all, he's just passing through. Please respond to Emperor Charles V

---

[23] King of the Netherlands from 1506 – 1555. Emperor Germanicus from 1519 to 1556. Enemy of Francis I

with my permission. He will be a guest from France. Don't you understand that he would be our hostage if he had other intentions? – And he abandoned the throne.

Outside his sister Margarita approached him.

– Brother...

– What? – He asked harshly.

– You threw Lautrec's pride to the ground.

– Now don't bother me.

– He is an iron man.

– I know – he turned to his sister –. And I also know that the soldiery hates him. He doesn't respect it. He thinks that only with force can everything be solved. I don't admit it. Charles V will be our guest and while he is here he will be treated as a head of state. And you, organize a tourist itinerary.

– Me?!

– Why the surprise? Who else? And quick.

– You are angry.

– In fact, I am. I want to marry you and you reject it. We live in a difficult situation, which requires a union between the kingdoms.

– That can wait.

– That's what I'm doing.

-Alright. What does your "friend" Charles V like?

– Churches, lots of food, parties.

– And women?

– Well, sister, this will be done in the blink of an eye. That is what is not missing, and with a gesture of annoyance he left, leaving his sister thoughtful.

* * *

When the coachman stopped in front of the Two Swans inn, he had to wake up the three passengers. They had to have lunch. When he opened the door, clouds of dust came out from inside the vehicle. The duke, getting up with difficulty, ended up waking up the two young men.

– Come on, dorks, do you just know how to sleep? – And he coughed –. They both stood up, a little scared. Jeanpaul asked his companion:

– You were in my dreams.

– And you were in mine – and they stared at each other for seconds –. The duke, already jumping, shouted:

– Come on, scoundrels, let's go, Mr. Thomas is waiting for us. To the bathroom everyone.

– Bathroom? – Jean asked.

– Yes, Jean. Mr. Thomas has a waterfall at the back of the house. It is a beautiful place, pure water. Let's get naked and enter that beautiful little pond. My grandfather and I do this all the time. *Voila* ![24] – And he slapped Jean on the back – And she thought – what now?

The owner of the inn, short and fat, with a huge hat that hid almost all of his scalp, dressed in that white, rather brown, blouse and velvet shorts that hugged his shins at the ends, was all smiles. After all, the duke was one of his most important clients. The establishment was simple, entirely made of wood, two floors, built entirely with raw materials from the forest. It had a large portico that surrounded it, a large room, divided into two; one for leisure,

---

[24] How about that.

reading; and the other, for meals, tables being arranged for this purpose. At the top were the bedrooms.

-What's that noise? – Jean asked.

– Well, *mon petit* [25]– The duke reported –, it is the noise of Thomas waterfall. It's the best we have here. This noise as you called it is like a lullaby. You will see it up close when you immerse yourself in those clear, balsam-smelling waters.

– *Merci*,[26] sir duke, *merci* – said Thomas, receiving the luggage, but only the one that contained ready-to-wear clothes.

– Come on, Jean, let's go up and change our clothes. Let's go swimming. She put her hands to her throat and coughed lightly.

– What's wrong?

– I don't know, Jeanpaul. I think the dust from the road affected my throat, I even had chills!

–Oh! Right now, Jean!

– I'm sorry – she apologized, forcing her voice to sound hoarse. – You know, I'm not used to traveling. Oh I'm very sorry.

– You have a fever?

– No, not yet, but I don't dare enter that lagoon. The water must be very cold.

-It's true. I'll talk to Thomas. While my grandfather and I bathe in the lagoon, you will wash in the room with hot water. And wrap your neck to avoid further problems. I warn you that, until we get to my father's house, we will have no choice but to splash some water on our heads. Therefore, clean everything and wear lighter clothes, since the rest of the trip will be longer.

– I know, I will do what you say.

---

[25] My little.
[26] Thank you.

– Come on, boys – they heard the duke call.

– We are coming, grandfather – and for Jean's sake – go, any room you enter will be yours. I'll talk to Thomas and he'll get hot water.

– Aren't you going to change your clothes?

– Of course.

– In what room? – The boy smiled.

– I don't need. I take my clothes to the waterfall. I take it off and go skinny dipping. Me and my grandfather. Thomas collects the used ones and takes them to wash, dry them on the fire and that's it.

– Oh right!

– You will miss something unforgettable. But, when we return, you will enjoy it – the duke called again.

– I'm coming, grandpa. Go, Jean, don't worry, your water will be in the room soon – and he walked away to meet his grandfather. He spoke with him and the innkeeper and they went behind the inn.

– Good, good! – said the duke –. Does your friend get sick at the best of times?

– Grandfather, it is understandable, the boy never left Paris. The dust...

– Yes, yes, but what is that light complexion? You just have to insist to get used to it.

– When he returns, he will be used to it. Let's change the subject?

– I'll beat you in swimming, stubborn boy – Jeanpaul smiled.

– Let's see if you ever beat me, old duke.

-That? – The grandfather reacted – Old duke? Wait, rag, when I catch you – and he ran after the young man. Meanwhile, Thomas had provided him with everything Jean wanted: warm water and even offered him an infusion of leaves, recommending:

– After the bath, son, gargle with this infusion. It is a sacred remedy for the throat.

– *Merci*, my friend Thomas.

– I am always at your service. Do you want something special to eat?

– Right now, what the others eat, I will eat too.

– *Pardon*. However, they always eat roast boar, with vegetables. If the boy, with a sore throat, wants chicken, vegetables...

– *Merci*. Whatever they eat is fine with me.

–When the duke returns, he usually stays here for three to five days. So yes, we have time to always improve the service. On the way to Alençon, I never know when it will happen. Sorry for the lack of comfort.

– Now, Mr. Thomas, are they complaining?

– No, no. But, since it is the first time that such a kind person visits us...

– Everything is alright. I'm going to take a bath, then I'll come down and we'll talk.

– Yes. If you need anything, call me.

Jean entered the room. She closed the door, locked it, leaned against it and sighed. She soon untangled herself from the threads of her blouse. Then she threw her sword belt on the bed, took off her blouse and vest, and was free. Then she instinctively massaged her breasts, with seriousness. She unbuttoned her pants, A took them off; then the boots, leaving only the shorts. She went to her suitcase, a kind of saddlebag, and took out another pair of shorts and a new blouse. Finally, she took out the last suit, examined it, and entered the tub with it. Bars of soap made from scented resins were close at hand. She was thoughtful while washing.

– How difficult it is to be a woman! It would be very easy to be there on the lake. But I'll move on. After all, I'm going to be the King of the Beggars. Oh! Jeanpaul, I seem to love you! Oh! God!

After bathing, carefully, since Jeanpaul had said that it would be difficult to bathe again from now on, she washed all her clothes, wrung them out, got dressed, and went downstairs. She was only wearing very thin leather pants. She was wearing a short-sleeved blue blouse with the inevitable vest underneath. She found Thomas setting the table.

– So? – She asked, still straining her voice. –. Oh boy! I think you will have to wait a long time. Those two, when they come here and go to the waterfall lagoon, they take their time. But you didn't put anything around your neck?

–Oh! – she exclaimed –, I think that I forgot?

– Wait. I have a handkerchief from my late wife, may God rest her soul! – She gave it to me. I'll bring it.

– Do not worry sir.

– Nothing, wait here, make yourself comfortable.

Jean remained silent, looking at the simple room of the inn in the middle of the forest. She had never left the Court of Miracles, or rather, the outskirts. Everything was different. She no longer cared about going out at night and stealing, climbing among the vines, to some balcony of a noble residence. After all, her community needed to live and she was the heir to the kingdom. At the same time she was reflecting, the farce she was living also came to mind. At the same time, she began to feel that she loved Jeanpaul. What to do?

"Here you are, sir," said Thomas, all smiles, with the red wool scarf in his hand. Consider it a gift. Please.

– *Mon père* – she exclaimed upon receiving the piece.

– Your father?

–Oh! I remembered him! He always uses one like this. He's already old.

– That makes me happier. Put it on and go, boy, meet your friends.

Who knows, maybe they'll be back soon.

– Hurry?

– No, no, the boy is going to travel so much... the sooner they leave, the better for everyone. Look, I made a bottle with that recipe for your throat. You will take it with you.

– *Merci, m'sieur.*

– It's no big deal. Go, see what you're missing, but what you'll get in return. Go – while Thomas prepares everything.

She left. There was a dirt road through the vegetation. She was guided by the sound of the waterfall. She hadn't arrived yet and she could already hear Jeanpaul and his grandfather laughing. She approached and, just after a turn, she came across an impressive landscape. The clear, foamy water fell from above, about seven meters, forming a small lake between the enormous rocks. For those who had never left the city, it was a moving sight. She was enthralled. And jealous of those two who swam. They threw water on each other, completely naked. She hid behind a thick tree and watched for some time. Since they were naked, she did not want to be seen. Then she decided to take a walk in the forest. Everything was new to her. She remained that way for some time. When she returned, the two of them had already returned to the inn. She tightened her scarf around her neck and entered.

– Well, well, so you went for a walk? – Asked the duke, who was drying his hair with a large, fluffy towel – Why didn't you go to the lagoon?

– I was there, sir. But I didn't want to disturb your fun.

– Are you better?

– This happens. It's just the throat. Where is Jeanpaul?

– He went to change. Let's fill our bellies and move on.

Soon everyone was having lunch. Jean would occasionally clear his throat, pretending to have a sore throat. But she ate, for she had never seen such a table, full of delicacies she did not even know about. And she ate well. Hurriedly, the duke, rising, approached Mr. Thomas and asked:

– Thomas, prepare a snack. I want everything you put on the table, you see, our visitor, although his throat hurt, liked it.

– Well, Mr. Duke, everything is already with your coachman and, if anyone eats like him...

– And where is?

– Ah, he ate a lot before going to the waterfall. He's still sleeping. After all, the trip is long and we had to rest.

– Yes, you did well.

– I will call him. The snack is already there in the carriage.

– Now we are going to sleep.

– We, who, grandfather? – Jeanpaul asked –. Us...

– Grandpa, you sleep. We will go ahead on the back of our horses.

–Oh! Yes, Yes! And I want to be like two young people!

– You are young... however, how do you eat, eh?

– Bootlicker! – The duke roared, taking some coins from his pocket and placing them in Thomas's hand, recommending: – I'm going to bring a wild boar to smoke. You will prepare it and we will stay here for ten days.

– A single wild boar, my grandfather? You eat everything in one day – Jeanpaul observed.

– Now, don't interfere. I eat ten, or more, what does it matter to you? Goodbye Thomas and thanks for everything.

– Don't forget, sir – the innkeeper said to Jean – to gargle with the bottle I gave you. Goodbye.

– But how are we going to go without the coachman?

– Oh! Wait... and he went to call the carriage driver, who; However, was coming already.

– Are you ready? – The duke shouted through the window.

– Yes, sir, I am ready.

It was already after noon when they left. At first they talked, but then they noticed that the duke began to yawn, moment by moment, and then fell asleep.

– See, Jean? He can't stand much. Shall we?

– What shall we do?

– Do you feel good to ride a horse or are you still sick to your throat?

– I will do it – she thought –. If she was pretending, everyone had already accepted it. Now; however, the time had come to prove her worth as a man.

– Let's go then?

–Of course, but aren't you going to stop the carriage? – Jeanpaul smiled.

– No, let's go out the door, go up to the roof, go down the back, pull the horses' reins and jump into the saddle. I always do this.

– *Mon Dieu* ! –She exclaimed.

– Come on, it's easy. Hold onto the horse's bridle and jump, twisting your body to fall forward into the saddle and simply untie the reins, we are free. Shall we?

– I do not know if I can.

– How not?

– Jeanpaul, my throat hurts.

– And what does the throat have to do with this?

– Well, I never allowed myself such acrobatics.

– Oh! It's true. I ask the driver to slow down. You jump. I do what I have always done. I untie the two horses and go with them to meet you. Good?

– Yeah.

Jeanpaul stuck his head out the window and asked the driver to slow down. Once this was done, he turned to Jean:

– There you go, Jean. Jump.

Opening the door, he looked for a moment at the rapidly passing ground. He had to jump. And he did it, successfully, running a few meters. He saw Jeanpaul leave through the door, climb nimbly onto the roof of the carriage and head towards the rear of the vehicle, which had increased its speed.

– Laurier! – She exclaimed walking.

Upon reaching that part, Jeanpaul stood up and quickly jumped into the saddle of one of the horses he had tied behind. In fact, he had to do a midair spin to land on the chair. He untied the ropes tying the animals to the vehicle and turned around, taking Jean's with him. Smiling, he stopped next to the girl.

– Come on, gentleman – he said smiling.

– Are all crazy people crazy like you?

– Come on, what a nonsense. Come on, ride.

Fortunately for her, she occasionally rode horses along the banks of the Seine. But she was far from being a good horsewoman. She mounted.

– Where will we go?

– Do you have your guns?

– No, just the sword. Why?

– Just caution. Come on, let's overtake the carriage – and he urged his mount, picking up the gallop. She followed him. They overtook the vehicle in which the duke was dozing and soon disappeared on the dirt road, among the trees. They rode freely for about ten minutes, happy, joking with each other. Sometimes Jeanpaul would ride in front of her and be the object of her admiration: she would stare at his shiny hair, fluttering in the wind.

– Come on – he shouted – you ride like a girl!

She thought to herself: "Oh, if you only knew how right you are!" – She made the horse run, pairing her with his friend.

– You ride well, but you remind me of *Captain Belle Rose*.[27]

– *Belle Rose*? – Smiling, he explained:

– They say that figure existed. Brave, excellent swordsman. Except that...

– Except that?

– She was a beautiful young lady.

–Hey... – she exclaimed, embarrassed. When he realized this, he apologized.

– *Pardon* . Don't get angry. Just kidding.

– And did this character really exist?

---

[27] *Captain Belle Rose* , one of the spiritual author's romances

– I don't know, they are certainly stories. When I was little I heard about her – and changing the conversation –. You like dogs, don't you?

– You will love Diana.

– How old is she?

– Mother Diana died at the age of fourteen. The current one, her daughter, is, I think, two years old. It's terrible.

– As? Fierce?

– No, no. Playful, friendly, although brave. She loves my father.

– You must have felt very sorry for the other's death, right?

–Oh! They even erected a mausoleum for her! And to never forget her, he named the baby after her – They punt their mounts next to each other, side by side, at a slow trot and were talking animatedly, when they heard a noise up ahead.

– Listen... it seems like a carriage is coming towards us.

– It's true – she agreed.

– Let's stay on the side of the road.

Soon a huge wagon appeared covered by a threadbare awning. Two men were in the front and two more were sitting in the passenger seat of the vehicle. When they saw the two young men, the cart stopped. The two drivers approached slowly.

"Unlock the sword, Jean," the young man advised, and she was immediately obeyed.

They were rude, ugly and dirty men. However, each one had a sword on his belt. One of them, fat, with a big mustache, came forward and asked loudly:

– Are you lost, gentlemen?

His companion, thinner but stronger, gave a small laugh.

– No, gentlemen, we are not lost.

– And what are you doing here?

– We preceded my grandfather's carriage.

– Oh! Is a carriage coming? Excellent!

– I don't understand.

– You will have to pay the Monastery fee.

–The Monastery fee? What monastery?

– Saint Michel.

– Well, Saint Michel is so far from here and monks are not known to have collectors.

– But they do, nobleman. And you have to pay. Look, our cart is full of payments: chickens, pigs, flour, etc.

– And you are collecting them along the way?

– That's how it is.

– And what payment do you want from us?

– Since you have no poultry, no pigs, no flour, gold is good for us.

– Oh! – Jeanpaul laughed. – Does the Abbot of Saint Michel know this?

– We don't have to give explanations. That sword of yours is very beautiful. It would look better on my belt. I will accept it as payment – and he jumped off the animal, accompanied by the other. Jeanpaul smiled, looked at Jean, and they both jumped up, swords already drawn.

– Oh! Do you want my sword then? Come get her, ruffians.

The men stopped in surprise. Then the burly man smiled, smoothed his mustache, jokingly:

– Well, well, aren't they two fighting chickens!

– And with spurs waiting for you, scoundrel.

– Let's get done with this, Joseph – shouted one of those left in the cart –. We are in a hurry.

– Calm down – the named man roared – this won't take long – and he drew his sword, like the other.

– We are going to cut off your combs, chickens – and he attacked. Jeanpaul stopped the blow. The other advanced towards Jean, who was looking for more space. He launched a thrust that was dodged.

– Come on, scoundrels, let's go – Jeanpaul urged. And for Jean – keep your back to the trees, Jean – the steel collided and the two of them were no longer playing, because they saw that they had been deceived by the two boys. Everything they tried was met with due force and they had to do everything they could to stop the blows. It was then that Jean confessed:

– Jeanpaul… I'm already tired.

– Tired! What do you mean, Jean?

With what she said instinctively, she became a little careless, almost being hit by the attacker's sword. But she thought quickly, attacking the man with fury.

– Didn't you call me *Captain Belle Rose*?

– So, the captain is "tired"? – what do you plan to do?

– As you see, they are two pussies. I'll finish mine soon.

– Yes sir. Do it.

The two attackers were sweating and seeing that they had encountered two worthy swordsmen, they were already showing fear, combined with the poor swordsmanship they possessed.

They used the sword in their daily lives to scare, without knowing the technique of how to use the noble weapon.

– There! – One shouted.

– What happened, Jean?

– I think a bee stung our friend's arm – the girl responded, while her opponent, dropping his weapon, held the shoulder that had been pierced. Jean kicked him out of the way and, circling the tip of the sword near the wounded man's face, continued:

– Do you want a close shave or a little closer?

The man groaned, blood passing through his fingers and down his immobilized arm. She turned to Jeanpaul and said:

–Captain Belle Rose has finished. And you?

– That's it, Jean – and he stopped a high blow, turning his body, letting the mustachioed man's sword slide against his, hitting him in the thigh. Another scream and blood gushed out.

– That's it, Jean, it's over. What a pity!

At this, the two men driving the car, seeing their two friends out of combat, jumped out of the car and ran forward. They had no swords, only thick staffs.

–Hey, Jean, two more.

When they were like this, the carriage appeared.

– Here, my grandfather! – Jeanpaul shouted. The duke did not hesitate to ask. He jumped up quickly.

– Jacob, the musket, quick!

The coachman threw the gun he had taken and then cocked it, advancing towards the attackers, who stopped.

-What's going on here? – Asked.

– These rascals tried to rob us.

– Rob?

Jeanpaul pulled a gun from his waistband and pointed it at the two men.

– Drop the batons!

They obeyed, fearful.

– They say they are from the Monastery of Saint Michel. They were charging us the abbot's mite.

– That? Yes, they are criminals. So, the abbot of Saint Michel would have rags at his service? Evildoers, that's what they are. And they attacked you?

– Yes, but look at the result. Jean hit one on his shoulder. I took out the other, on the leg. And these two charged with their staffs.

– Are you Ok?

– Clear.

– Well, ragpicker, stop the cart, quickly – and for the coachman – Jacob, bring ropes.

The men were tightly tied to the car. The duke looked at its contents and, taking a little pig, declared:

– This will be the duke's mite.

– Are you going to take it, grandfather?

– Well, when we get to the inn, it will become a beautiful roast – shouted the little pig.

–Oh! No sir, poor thing, he's so small, let him go – Jean asked.

– Drop it? If he does, he will be easy prey for wild animals and will be placed back in the cart – he returned to the cart, took a sheet of parchment with his captured weapons and wrote:

– *Mr. Provost. These men are highway robbers. Arrest them.*

He signed it and stuck it to the car. Then they moved it, putting it in a condition to continue, and continued their journey.

– The cart is coming after us, grandfather – said Jeanpaul, next to the car.

– That's how it is. The horses know that they are returning to their place. They will only stop on their destination. And they will be arrested. However, it is too heavy to reach us. Are you going to continue riding? Why don't you go up and rest a little? Let's go faster or the night will catch us on the road and I don't want that.

– Yes, it is better – Jeanpaul signaled to the coachman, who stopped the carriage. They dismounted, tied the two horses to the back of the vehicle and both got in.

– Are you really okay?

– Without a doubt, grandfather. And, like fencing, here is our *Captain Belle Rose* ... – said the boy, hitting Jean on the back.

– *Captain Belle Rose*? – The duke was surprised.

– It's a joke, grandpa. – This captain was a legend. I learned about it when I was a child.

– I know, my father told me.

–So, the boy really knows how to use a sword.

– You bet, grandfather! He immediately put the criminal out of combat.

– Yes, but if I hadn't arrived in time the other two would have given you a good beating with the stick.

– Which is nothing. My gun was ready for action.

– I will send an emissary to Saint Michel and tell the abbot everything. We'll see if those vultures use his name to stock up on the belongings of poor villagers.

– Tired, Jean?

– It is not normal.

– And the throat?

– Oh! It burns me a lot!

– Soon we will arrive at the inn. You will take a good bath, we will eat and then you will sleep until five in the afternoon, when we will continue our trip.

Chapter II
Friends Jean and Jeanpaul

In Paris, the population was scared and the army was on alert. Charles V's troops remained camped on the outskirts of the city, while the Emperor was received at the palace, with all honors. Tours and visits to churches, palaces, etc. were organized. And as was always the style of Francis I, the evenings followed one another. The people; however, they only breathed a sigh of relief when Charles V left the city with his troops.

– Don't you think it was reckless to allow such a visit? – Margarita asked.

– I think so. Let him spend his troops. And on top of that with Sulimán –. The weaker he gets, the better for us. Now, dear sister, I think I am going to spend some time in the country. A little hunting will be good for me.

– What about the Witcher?

– What Witcher?

– The doctor, Girardán.

– Now, my sister, leave the poor man alone.

– Never! – She roared –. I want it at the stake.

– I have a lot to worry about, my dear sister – He made the guest list and left.

The king's sister's hatred towards Dr. Girardán was linked to his refusal of a blatant and dark request. An abortion. Then a mad hatred broke out towards the good doctor, who helped care for the needy in the poor area of Paris. But this is a story that has already been told in the previous book.[28] We return, therefore, to the passengers of the carriage, who arrived, without further mishap, to the land of Jeanpaul's father.

The vehicle entered through the enormous gate opened by two servants and rolled along a paved path, which crossed a large, well-kept lawn, until it stopped in front of the stairs that led to the residence. The owner of the house and his wife were already there, smiling, and a small army of assistants. As soon as the vehicle stopped, the young man opened the door and jumped to the ground, running towards his waiting parents, arms open and faces lit up by wide smiles.

– Father, Mother! – He shouted hugging himself and being hugged and kissed by his parents.

– My son! – Paulette exclaimed moved –, you are a man now.

–So, how were your studies?

– As always, father, as always, your son was the first in the class.

– Oh! Glad to hear it!

– Father – he said looking at the people who were there –. I don't see Pierre – and he looked seriously at his father.

– Don't worry. Pierre is already in his eighties and is ill. You will soon see him in his room.

– Mary! – The boy exclaimed, throwing himself into the arms of one of the servants, who hugged him smiling and crying.

– *Mon petit* – said Mary.

---

[28] *Love is Eternal*, from the same spiritual author

– *Mon petit* ? I am a man, Mary.

– Yes, yes, I know. I won't be able to bathe you anymore.

Everyone laughed, Jeanpaul greeted everyone and then, turning towards the carriage, he shouted:

– *Grand pére* !²⁹ Old duke, are you still sleeping?

A curse was heard, the carriage door opened and the duke, already jumping to the ground, shouted:

– Old Duke? You'll see when I catch you, you stuck-up brat – and he started running after the young man who had taken refuge behind his father, who was laughing with amusement.

– My father, you look great – they hugged each other.

– Paulette! Always exuberant like the flowers of the field, the duke greeted her, hugging her and kissing her. This brat needs to be put in shackles. He doesn't miss the opportunity to call me old.

– Oh! Father, mother! – The boy said solemnly – the couple hugged him – I have a surprise – and headed to the vehicle – Get off, Jean. – She obeyed.

–Oh! Who is it?! – Paulette asked, admiring the stranger.

– He is a friend. He is the grandson of Doctor Girardán.

– Girardan? Excellent! – And they advanced towards Jean, who made a careful bow to Lady Paulette, kissing her hand. Later he greeted the noble lord of Luzard.

– It is a pleasure, young man, to have you in our house.

– Grandson of Dr. Girardán?

– By affinity, madam.

---

²⁹ Grandfather.

Paulette examined the boy's features so thoroughly it made him blush.

– So, mom? Love at first sight?

– Don't doubt it, he is a beautiful young man.

– And brave. We chased away four criminals who robbed us.

– *Mon Dieu* ! – And Paulette put her hands on her chest.

– What are you saying son? Did they rob you?

– Well, Jean – said the duke –. Four criminals.

One of them will not be able to use his arm for a long time; the other will not be able to walk.

– Did you duel? – Jean asked with his mouth open.

– No, dad, we just trained.

– Oh! I want to hear everything.

– Not now. Can't you see we just arrived? Tell us to carry our luggage. We'll talk later.

– Madam – Jean said, taking out a crumpled roll of parchment from his vest and handing it to Paulette – this is a letter that Dr. Girardán sent you.

–Oh! – And he received the letter.

– I'll read it later. Thank you. What is your name, young man?

– Jean, ma'am.

– Wow, what a coincidence! My husband too. And my son Jeanpaul.

– And we were born on the same day, mother.

– Good omens. But come on, let's get in.

– And Diana, father?

– Oh! She has grown beautiful. Worthy of her mother. You will see her later.

– Mom, I want another bed in my room. Jean will stay with me.

– Yes naturally, son.

Jean lowered his head.

– And now? – She thought. Paulette, mischievous as she had always been, noticed the change in Jean's face. They climbed the well-kept marble stairs, with red guides, which contrasted with the white of the steps.

– I will show you the room you will stay in.

– Isn't it mine?

– Of course, but your friend doesn't know the place. And it may need cleaning.

They reached the hallway, lined with doors, to a large balcony that formed a spacious living room. Paulette opened a door. They entered. A spacious room, with a comfortable bed in the center, mahogany wardrobes, bright. Hanging on the walls were some hunting trophies and a bookshelf full of books to complete the decoration. A large window, which opened, revealed the gardens at the back of the majestic estate.

– Here we are. Just add another bed and you're done. Well, I'll be calm. Your belongings will arrive soon. I have to give some orders.

– See you later, mom.

As if on intuition, Paulette took the parchment from her chest and entered the room that had belonged to Mrs. Suzanne and which was preserved intact. There, on the dresser, were still the medicine bottles and the personal effects of that long-suffering woman. Even her slippers could be seen next to the bed. Paulette treated that room as a sanctuary and went there when she wanted to meditate or when she felt melancholy. In front of a large painting depicting the former housewife, she was sitting in an elegant rocking chair. Daylight illuminated the room, entering through the diaphanous curtains. She broke the seal on the parchment and began to read. And her face changed as her eyes scanned the text. She put her hand on her chest. She read and reread the letter. After that; she dropped it onto her lap and stared at the portrait.

–Oh! Mrs. Suzanne, what do I do? Certainly God wants something from me, since chance does not exist. When I looked at the boy, I suspected it was a girl.

My eyes as a woman and as a mother do not deceive me. But where is the certainty? And now, Mrs. Suzanne? What do I do?

Suddenly, the soft scent of wildflowers reached her nostrils.

– This perfume – she murmured, lifting his body in the chair – was her favorite. Lady Suzanne – she asked – are you here? Please! – And she started to cry, with her eyes closed –. At that moment, she felt a gentle pressure on her forehead, as if an invisible hand was touching her. She remained motionless. The perfume vanished into the air. She opened her eyelids. A dewy flower lay on the bed. She got up and went to bed. It was a huge lily. Carefully, she picked it up. She smiled. "You were here," she said happily. Thank Miss.

She raised her head, composed herself, and quickly left the room, going to call her son's room. The luggage was already there. Jeanpaul had taken off his shirt and was preparing to do the same with his pants. From the window, Jean pretended to contemplate the landscape.

– Jean – she called, entering.

-Mother! What's happening? – He asked, wrapping his torso with a towel he picked up from the bed.

– Son, your friend Jean can't stay with you in this room.

– Well, why not?

– The thing is – and she looked for an excuse – that we don't have more beds.

– And in the other rooms?

– They are bolted to the floor.

– Well, mom, unscrew one.

– No, Jeanpaul – the girl intervened –. Why give work? What does it matter if I stay in another room?

– Now we could talk, make plans to hunt; After all, we talk about topics that we cannot discuss openly.

– Come on, Jean – said Paulette – let this grumpy man change his clothes. – Well well. You go, but I protest – he roared –. Change your clothes and let's go take a bath.

– He'll do so in the bedroom, son.

– Fine...

– The throat, Jeanpaul... – Jean lied.

– Go, go, before I challenge you to a duel.

– And who would win? – He asked jokingly.

– Well... at most we would tie.

Paulette took Jean to a room next to her son's. She ordered her belongings to be brought to her and, sitting on the bed, with the door closed, she said, smiling:

– Now, can you undress, daughter!

– Daughter?

Paulette, looking at her laughing, exclaimed:

– Ah, Planchet! What a fool! How inconsequential!

– Planchet?

– Of course, your father.

– Lady....

– Come here, sit next to me, girl – She obeyed.

– So?

– So what?

– Do you hope, like your father, to deceive everyone? Until when?

– Madam, I...

– Do you love my son...?

She gave her a sideways glance.

– I know you love him, but you are bound by an oath. Come here, crazy – and she pulled the girl to her chest. Jean started to cry.

– Cry, cry, it's okay.

– What do I do now?

– Nothing. I will help you, although I know that if my Jeanpaul knew the truth, he would love you, which he cannot admit now, because to him you are a man.

– Madam, how do you know all this?

– It is a long story.

– Do you know my father?

–Oh! Lady, you can bet.

– But...

– Your father was always a scoundrel, although deep down he was a good man. Planchet and his most beloved assistant, the fool Bochet.

– Lady! – Jean exclaimed surprised.

– I belonged to that community, my girl.

– The Court?

– Not only the Court, but the sewers. The king of the beggars, Planchet, was a great friend of mine. When my Jeanpaul was born, you were born too. But your mischievous father always had daughters and needed an heir. However, what was born to me was a man, but since he had a reputation for "only making women," they didn't even bother to check my baby.

– Jeanpaul, is he my brother?

– No, no, calm down. Planchet had a reputation as a great stallion and they soon attributed my motherhood to him.

– Did you know everything?

– No, I only found out about the birth of Planchet's son. But I soon left there. Only now I understand everything. Dr. Girardán let me know in the letter you brought.

– Oh! And what will you do, madam?

– Take it easy. I have already started acting. I took you out of my son's room.

– Aren't you going to tell him?

– I'm not going no. You will do it yourself someday. If you managed to deceive him and others, until then, let's see if you can continue the deception for long. You took too many risks. You could lose Jeanpaul.

– How, madam?

– He is a man, he can fall in love with a girl, since for him you are the same sex.

– What are you saying? – She remained thoughtful for a moment and then declared:

– I swore an oath to my father.

– Unreasonable oath, how unreasonable his idea was. Think about it. Now I'm going to ask for hot water. In the letter they wish you both a happy anniversary. I'll bring you some things that only women use. Let's see how you do. Come on, girl, get rid of those clothes. At night, before you go to sleep, I will give you a good massage, just as the doctor asked me to.

– Thank Miss.

– It is your responsibility. I know nothing. Think carefully, since you love my son. You just have to lose, or everything to win. I'll be back soon... – and he left. Alone in the room, she sat on the bed, taking off her boots and thinking. Indeed, she lacked Jeanpaul's greatest affection. Sometimes she wanted to confess everything, but then she remembered her people, who were also deceived by her father. She thought that if Planchet died, her people would not have an immediate leader, a fact that would result in true chaos for the Court of Miracles. The beggars, without leadership to guide their steps, would begin to act on their own and this would surely lead to the death of many. A contingent of well-armed soldiers would be enough to exterminate them. And this massacre did not occur before, due to the strict control that Planchet exercised, avoiding excesses. And her father was at the end of his life. And everyone knew he had a successor. No, she couldn't fail them. On the other hand, she loved Jeanpaul. Fatally, she would lose him if she did not confess her status as a woman. She recognized that she was going through a real dilemma.

Then, there was a knock on the door, waking her from her thoughts. She got up to answer. There was Paulette, with two mistresses. One of the servants carried in her hands a large enameled basin and the other two large amphorae filled with water. Paulette carried fluffy towels with her. They entered.

– I hope this hot bath makes your throat feel better, son – she said.

–Oh! Ma'am, you shouldn't have bothered.

– It's no big deal. You can now bathe calmly.

The maids left the room, smiling at who they thought was a boy. Paulette sat on the bed and watched her undress. She helped her take off her vest. Jean, dressed only in her tight shorts, smiled sheepishly at the lady.

– What a waste, my daughter! – He exclaimed –. You're cute! Oh! Planchet! You deserve a big beating! Go clean up. Then put on a very loose blouse in the front.

– Jeanpaul is waiting for me to go to the lake to swim.

– I will take care of stopping him from doing it, but I don't know for how long, naughty girl. And put on the scarf. Remember that you have a sore throat.

– I haven't forgotten, ma'am.

– The day after tomorrow is your birthday.

– And Jeanpaul's too – and she frowned.

– What happened?

– I have nothing to give him.

–Oh! I'll find a way! Do not bother yourself. We'll have a little party. Now go, take a bath.

Sometime later, already on the front porch of the house, Jeanpaul seemed anxious.

– Mom, where is Jean? How long it takes!

– Grandson, wait! The boy, besides having a bad throat, is not like us. He will come soon.

– But, grandfather, are the wild boars waiting?

– Ah, naughty! I know where to find them, calm down.

– We'll have to go without him.

– That's not necessary – said Paulette –. Here is the young man who arrives.

Jeanpaul ran towards him.

– What's wrong, Jean? If you're not feeling well, we understand. But I really wanted you to go hunting with us.

Jean smiled.

– And did I tell you I wouldn't go?

– But you took your time.

– I'm not at home. I had to pack my belongings.

– And you missed the bathroom.

– I cannot right now.

– Throat.

– Yes. But, who gives me a gun? After all, are we going to hunt or not? – And she winked at Paulette.

– Well, everything resolved. Release the dogs. Come on! – roared the duke. Jean – son of the duke –, mounted on a beautiful black horse, shouted:

– Let's all go, old duke.

– That? You too, unnatural son?

– Grandpa – Jeanpaul called.

– Yeah?

– Do you see that it is not just your grandson who calls you the old duke? – And he spurred his mount.

– Rebels! – The duke roared with an indignant air –. Wasn't a son and now a grandson enough? Paulette, Paulette!

– Yes, my father-in-law?

– It's your fault, I'm going to kill one and the other.

– You are going to kill them, but – and he raised his index finger – bring the skins, old duke!

-What is this? You too? Is it a plot? Arrogant! All that's left now is for Jean to join the trio! – And leaning over the chair, he kissed Paulette.

– They are going to pay me.

– Come on, father-in-law, you are a better hunter than them.

– And you will have your punishment, maiden.

– Which?

– I only eat what your hands make. You will have to work. If someone else touches it, I don't eat it.

She smiled.

– Guide Jean. Be careful, old man.

– Come on boy. Be a man like the duke.

They waved at her and trotted away, following Jeanpaul and his son. These, already far ahead, rode side by side.

– Son, I really liked the friend you brought.

– Oh! Father, I have never gotten attached to someone in such a short time.

– I know, I feel him needed.

– It's true. He is a poor boy, he didn't even know his parents. I wanted to take him to them, but I noticed he was avoiding me. You know how it is. However, we were talking about astronomy, general knowledge, mathematics and he responded.

– I know, son, but I notice a certain caution in him, as if he were always on guard, a shyness...

– Oh! Dad, you should have seen him fighting criminals. I thought he was very good with a sword, but Jean is equal to or better than me. He's brave, the boy. I confess that I was afraid for him when the robbery occurred. But during the fight I lost my fear. He really knows how to use a sword.

– He is a handsome boy. Who knows, maybe he needs a push to get into the Military Academy?

– Oh, father! Leave the Academy aside. I really don't want it...

– ...and you will be captain right away.

– Father, I am a person of peace.

– But France is about to go to war. And our monarch, although a great statesman, is not a strategist: he joined forces with Suleiman, the heretic.

– I know, I know, but all this is to ambush Charles V.

– And is Charles V a Court jester?

– And this interests us, father?

– But of course, Jeanpaul! We are French.

– No, I didn't make it clear, does this matter now? And the wild boars? Look, the "old man" is already coming with Jean – The father smiled and stopped his mount.

– The "old man" – you say –. This man never ages. He will always be a child... seventy-eight years old.

– Hey, idiots! – The duke shouted as he approached –. Let's go hunting. If I don't bring a wild boar for Paulette to treat, cook and roast, I will be the one roasted.

– Another bet, my father?

– She, like her son, called me the old duke.

– And?

– And I promised to bring her a wild boar, for her, Just for her, to gut it, skin it, boil it and roast it. And she will do it, word of the duke.

– What do you say, Jean?

– It's a family dispute, sir – replied the young woman – although it is fun, I can't take sides.

– You're doing well, boy. It really is an old fight, but believe me, to this day my father only brings partridges or wild turkeys. Paulette never bothered to do what he said with a wild boar.

– That? With these muskets from Spain I won't have a single wild boar left. And she will treat it, but she will, very well. And if you doubt it, you won't eat it – and the mount advanced, followed by the hunting dogs, who ran quickly, but still without smelling the smell of the game.

– Pure boasting, Jean – said Jeanpaul, joining them –. However, he was once a great general and is adored at Court for his always decisive attitude in favor of poor and needy creatures.

– Is it still active?

– Although not so much anymore, yes. He simply cannot tolerate the king.

– How so?

– Francisco is dedicated to the festivities and, in the middle of big decisions, he stops and goes hunting, leaving everything in the hands of his ministers. His sister and mother help him a lot. He knows; However, what he does, but my father does not admit it. The king, for him, has to be in charge of everything. And, as you may know, France is not so safe. The king's adventurous character greatly worries the population.

– Dad, let's leave politics for the balcony, soon. What matters to us now is not to let grandpa hunt wild boars.

– Because?

– Well, then my mother doesn't have to treat him, according to the terms of the bet.

– It's true, son – the father agreed –. And how we do it?

– You and him will go one way. Me and Jean, on the other.

– Good. You know the rules.

– Yes – and turning to Jean – we will only shoot low or high game. Never in a horizontal direction.

– I understand – said the girl –. We could hurt each other.

– Indeed.

They reached the edge of the forest. The duke joined them.

– So?

– You, father and I, on the left. Jeanpaul and Jean, on the right. Do you have the bugle?

– Of course, son.

-And you?

– Yes father.

– At the touch the hunt ends. Take your dogs. We, ours. You only kill what we can eat.

– And good hunting! – The duke shouted.

They separated. Jeanpaul and Jean entered the forest, to a certain point, when the boy, stopping his mount, dismounted, shouting:

– Come on, Jean.

– As? Shall we stop here?

– Yes. The horses, in this part, would only get in the way. Let's leave them tied with a long rope so they can graze. There is no danger for them.

We will go on foot. Do you have the guns? '

– And loaded.

– The musket?

- Ready.

– Then have gunpowder and ammunition on hand. Never shoot when I shoot.

– Because?

– If we shoot together, we will have to reload. And, if necessary, one can defend the other. Do you understand?

– Yeah.

– So, if I shoot, even if I miss, don't shoot. Wait until I reload again and then the next shot will be yours.

– I understand, friend.

– Let's see if you are as good at shooting as you are at fencing. And be careful, we have to prevent the "old man" from making my mother want to prepare the wild boar.

– Yeah.

– And the throat?

– Oh! – And he put his hand on his neck.

– I'm getting better.

– That's good. Listen, dogs bark.

– Far.

– What do you want? We have to run towards the barking. But those are not signs yet that they have found the piece. Come on, let's run so they don't get too far away.

– What if the hunt comes this way?

– It will not appear.

– How do you know?

–The dogs came through here, Jean, and they didn't find anything.

– Oh right!

– Come on. Curve your hat over your forehead to protect your eyes from the branches. Let's hurry – And there were two shots in the direction of the barking dogs. They came to see them when, suddenly, they ran through the forest.

– Now this is it, my dear Jean. They smelled big game. Put sebum on your pimples. Let's go back – And from there it was a constant takeoff with precise speed, among the vegetation, sometimes having to put on knee-high boots, to keep up with the dogs. Jean was sweating, she felt pain in her upper body, squeezed by the vest, but she did not give up. She followed Jeanpaul. The barking became more insistent and fixed.

– They cornered it – he said.

– What?

– It can only be a wild boar. They always go in groups. But, when attacked, one offers resistance so that the others flee. Do not speak. Save your breath. Runs.

Finally, they arrived at the place. The three dogs, barking furiously, kept a beautiful specimen of wild boar next to the trunk of a tree. The animal, snorting, dug the ground with its front paws, staring at the dogs. Huge fangs protruded from its jaws and it growled menacingly, all bristly.

– Look – Jeanpaul said, cocking the musket and taking aim. Slowly.

– Shoot!

He lowered the gun.

– No, you are the visitor. You shoot.

– But...

– Quick, Jean. It will not be at your disposal.

Jean raised the gun to his shoulder, took aim, and fired. The beast growled, rose to its knees, and then fell to the side.

– Bravo! – Jeanpaul shouted, hugging his "friend." –. Good shot!

– We saved your mother's honor – she said, loading the gun again.

– It's true – and he approached the sacrificed animal. Jean wanted to touch him when he shouted:

– No, no, Jean!

– He is dead.

– First, we have to be sure. Never approach an animal of this size without first making sure it is dead. Even mortally wounded, the instinct of self-preservation gives the animal the strength for a last attack that could be fatal.

Certain that the animal was indeed dead, they tied its legs and Jeanpaul put it on his shoulders.

– This is the worst moment of the hunt: loading the corpse.

– I will help you.

– There's no need. Your throat.

When they returned, they heard two gunshots in the distance.

– Did they kill another one?

– Who knows? Jean, there are two locks on the bugle.

– Eh? – The bugle, play it. Twice.

Jean tried and only managed to puff.

– Oh, Lord God! – Jeanpaul roared. – Hold the corpse on my shoulders and give me the bugle – she obeyed and two high notes and one low note came out of the instrument.

– There you go, Jean. We are going now. there

– Are you angry?

– I? – The boy smiled –. No, until you turned out okay. Didn't you kill the boar?

– It could have been you.

– Forget about this detail. We are a team.

– I just hope Grandpa doesn't hunt a wild boar.

– Yes. It would be very unfortunate. But we'll see.

They reached the horses. Jeanpaul tied the boar to Jean's saddle, saying:

– Glory to the hunter. Come on *mon ami* , let's run, because if they kill something, the glory, in reality, goes to the one who arrives first.

And they galloped down the ravine, with the dogs barking behind them, demonstrating the mission accomplished. They arrived early. They delivered the piece, the dogs were taken to the pound. Mrs. Paulette brought refreshments and the two sat on the porch, waiting.

– Jeanpaul, my son – his mother told him – they will be surprised.

– Mom, the honors go to Jean. He was the one who shot the wild boar.

– Didn't we work as a team? And weren't you the one who let me shoot? The honor is ours.

– They are coming, madam – a servant warned.

– Oh! I hope they don't bring another wild boar.

When they dismounted, each one with a wild turkey in his hand, they arrived at the porch with the look of a victor – at least the duke – who stepped forward, lifting the enormous bird by its legs:

– Good hunting! We'll have turkeys for dinner.

– Why do you think like that, grandfather? – Jeanpaul asked, sitting down and with his legs stretched out:

– Well, I don't see what you hunted.

Jean Sr. went out to his wife, suspicious, and hugged her, noticing in her eyes that something had happened, and he waited.

– Did you hear the bugle, grandfather?

– Yeah.

– Did you hear our shot?

– Yes. Did you hear ours?

– Yes, I heard it, so...

– So, what, brat?

– So, Monsieur Duke – said Jean, getting up, Lady Paulette won't clean the boar.

– What boar? – The duke complained –. Now, "old" duke – said Jeanpaul, getting up and running after his parents, whom he hugged –, the boar that Jean killed.

– What? – He roared.

– The shot you heard... BOOM! –, and the boar fell. We play the bugle. Shortly after we heard two shots, two turkeys! And I don't even know if you shot one or my father shot both.

– I still kill this boy, Jean. This is a revolution, it is a lack of respect, an uprising. I cannot stand it! – And everyone laughed, including him.

– So, it was you, young man, who killed the boar?

– I did it, sir. And, if you all allow me, do you want to say what you would do, in relation to Mrs. Paulette, if you were the hunter who shot the beast?

– Well – and the duke scratched his head.

– Say it.

– She would clean it, gut it, cook it and roast it.

– Well, it's quite the opposite.

– How so?

Mrs. Paulette intervened:

– The wild boar, which must weigh about thirty kilos, is in the kitchen.

– Well...

You'll do it, sir, everything you wanted her to do – said Jean.

– Now, brat, do you come here to dictate rules?

– There are no rules that my friend dictated. You established them. Go, grandfather, take care of the hunt and cook it well.

– *Sacre Coeur* ! – And turning to Jean –. I don't like you and this son of mine seems to have no aim.

– It's true! – said Jean (father) –. I shot the first turkey, killed it. While it took a while to cock the Spanish musket, I quickly loaded mine and fired the second.

– Glad to know.

– My gun jammed. What the hell! I'm going to the kitchen, ragbags – As he passed, he stroked Jean's hair.

In the afternoon, still early, Jeanpaul went to visit old Pierre. He was accompanied by his parents, the Duke and Jean. The old servant, lying on a spacious bed, welcomed them with the desire to get up.

–Hey, Pierre, calm down. Get up, for what?

– Sir – he expressed himself, with a trembling voice –, I feel useless here in this bed.

– Well, old man, whoever is here is worth it.

– Who, sir? – And he turned his face from one side to the other, but his eyes could not see well.

– Me, Pierre.

– Huh?

– Me, my old man.

– Oh! The boy Jeanpaul. Oh! God! What joy! – He exclaimed, taking the young man's hands in his –. Oh! Lady Suzanne, here it is – Those present looked at each other, the patient continued –, here it is, did you bring her, my lord Jeanpaul?

– Who, my good Pierre?

Paulette intervened:

– No, Pierre, not yet. He won't turn eighteen until tomorrow.

—Oh! – And without letting go of Jeanpaul's hand –. I know, I know, but Lady Suzanne said he had found his kindred spirit. I don't think I understand it, I'm sick, weak.

– He brought a friend, Pierre.

– A friend. It's always good to have a friend. Where is he? At a signal from Jeanpaul, Jean approached.

– Is here. Take his hand – Jean let the old man take his right hand, without letting go of the boy's. The old man remained thoughtful for a while, then spoke. Daughter, take care of him. They love each other.

Jeanpaul looked at Jean, smiled, but she remained serious. Paulette intervened again:

– Rest, Pierre. She will take care of him, I promise you – and he removed his hands from the old man's.

– Try to sleep, Pierre – advised the Lord of Luzard – and they left the room.

– Poor! – The duke commented –. He doesn't know what he says anymore.

– It's true, he took Jean for a young woman. Forgive him, Jean.

– I don't have to forgive him. In its state it is understandable.

– That's right – added Paulette –. He wanted to see Jeanpaul married.

– It's true.

– Really, in his condition, senile, it is a shame that all of us, with age, have to go through this – commented the duke.

– Everything that is born must die one day – exclaimed Paulette.

– Yes, we know it, but we never get used to it.

They went down to the hall, amply lit with enormous candles, arranged in several chandeliers, and they stayed there for a while talking, commenting on the hunt, hovering around each other.

– What did you think of the wild boar, grandfather?

– Good...

– Only good?

– I like it better when I hunt it myself.

Jeanpaul laughed.

– What are you laughing at, rascal?

"So," the boy continued, "it will take you a long time to eat something you like." Everyone laughed.

The duke ended up laughing too.

Then he stood up, stretching and announced:

– Well, the hunt was exhausting. I'm going to retire. How about a morning ride tomorrow?

One by one they left the room. A servant began to blow out the candles. Jeanpaul went to his room and so did his father. Under the pretext of giving some orders, Paulette went to the kitchen, stayed for a while, and then headed to Jean's room. At the exact moment the door opened and she entered, Mr. de Luzardo appeared at her door, watching her enter Jean's room.

– What is happening? – He thought, suspicious –. He entered, sitting on the bed, thoughtful.

Jean had taken off all her clothes and Paulette began the massages prescribed by Dr. Girardán.

– Poor thing – he lamented – taking risks like that, without need. Your chest, even your navel, is swollen because of the vest. Tomorrow I will put give you another one that does not harm circulation – After about fifteen minutes, she said goodbye to the young woman and left. She entered the room and found her husband sitting in a large chair.

– No sleep, dear? – Asked.

– And you?

– Falling down...

– I do not think.

– Because?

Jean of Luzard stood up abruptly and spoke angrily:

– I saw you enter young Jean's room. And during the time you were there, I kept wondering what you were doing – Paulette became serious.

– Come on, say it – he almost shouted, harshly.

– I gave him a massage – he said calmly.

– What?! – He became exasperated, taking her arm.

– Calm down, Jean. You're hurting me.

– Explain yourself, Paulette.

– Yes, there is nothing else to do. Come, sit down and I will tell you everything – The husband obeyed, distrustful and expectant.

– Jean, dear, it's a girl.

– As? – Jean of Luzard was startled –. What are you saying?

Paulette then began to inform her husband of the entire situation. Then she went to a closet, took out the parchment, and handed it to him.

– Read – she asked, bringing a chandelier with a candle. He did so, frowning.

– My God! – He exclaimed.

– And you, distrusting me.

– Sorry, sorry.

– You are not doing wrong.

– And now what, Paulette?

– You are one more person to know the truth.

– Now I understand yours, I mean her, in a distant way.

– That's how it is.

– Planchet is crazy! Poor little girl! What will we do?

– For now we will keep the fact a secret. We'll see what happens. And Pierre...

– What's wrong with Pierre?

– "Daughter, take care of him...", remember? – he made the reference, taking her hand.

– I remember it, yes.

– God! And I thought I was a fool. He got it! But how?!

– He sensed it, dear.

– It can only be!

– Do you see that lily in the glass of water?

– Yeah.

– How was it on Lady Suzanne's bed, if when I entered the room, with this parchment, it was empty? Suddenly appeared. I felt her presence at that moment.

– Poor Suzanne!

– Poor! She is happy and in her own way tries to understand us, help us.

– Help us now with what to do with the girl.

– That's what I'm also asking. We better go to sleep.

The next day, while they were having breakfast, Jeanpaul asked Jean, dressed in a striking white lace blouse, very loose; His black hair, just below his nape, shone, well cared for:

– Are we going horseback riding?

– Of course he will – said the duke, nodding for her.

– How do you decide on the child, my father? – Lord of Luzard asked, cutting a fruit.

– Now, wasn't this already decided yesterday?

– Jean is not coming today – Paulette announced – The girl looked at her surprised.

– Can I know why? – Jeanpaul asked.

– Yes, of course son, tomorrow is your birthday, as you know, his is too. And we're going to welcome some people. Jean, not being prepared for the event, asked me for help choosing some clothes in town.

– Now, Jean, forget about this. Only the villagers come here, none of them will notice anything. If we were still in Paris...

– It is decided, children – added Lord of Luzardo –. Your mother consulted me and I approved the idea. After all, being your age will also help you choose your gift.

– What a gift, dad...

– Besides – Paulette continued – he has to get even more handsome, since our neighbors' daughters will be here.

– Oh! Soon I saw that there was a woman in the middle.

– And the trip can be postponed until the day after tomorrow. You will go with your grandfather.

– Is it your taste, Jean, to do what these two want? Jean smiled.

– Yes, Jeanpaul. This is an emergency.

– So, let it be as you want. We will go, won't we, grandpa?

– But of course, buying clothes, bah!

– Well, before we go, could you at least lend me Jean?

– What are you going to do?

– Introduce a great friend.

– Oh! Diana!

– You guessed correctly.

– Very good. – It must be a beautiful *chienne*.[30]

– Then – concluded the duke – while you take her to the kennel, I will go to the stables and harness our horses. And should you carry the musket?

Who knows, maybe some beautiful wild boar will cross our path.

– The only thing you think about is eating, grandpa?

– No, no, but you know...

– My father will prepare a musket. This way you won't have to return from the stable. Right, father?

– Of course, son. He will leave here complete.

– Complete, father?

– The wild boar is still missing. If you thought about giving it to me tomorrow, I'll be left without a gift. Come on, Jean, let's let this old man boast.

– What, whippersnapper? Squire, come, I challenge you to a duel. "Choose your weapons, brat," the duke roared jokingly as he stood up.

– Do I choose weapons?

– Yes, rebellious boy.

---

[30] Female dog.

– Well, I choose, wild boars – and he left, pulling Jean.

– Come back, ragbag!

– Calm down, my father.

– Madam, Lady Paulette, I am still going to let this son of yours rest. The rascal does not respect a duke like me and you, Mary, what are you laughing at?

"Sir," said Mary, putting both hands to her mouth.

– May sir, not even half a sir, come here, have his piece of temptation, or rather, all of the temptation. Your name is already Mary, imagine if it were Magdalena – Mary, suspicious but smiling, approached.

– Come on, come closer, woman.

Close to her, he put his arms around her waist, made her bend down and spoke in her ear, loud enough to be heard:

– Is there anything left of yesterday's wild boar?

Mary began to laugh, accompanied by the others.

– That remains, Mr. Duke, that remains. Do you want it?

– A little – and he explained to those present – I am a carnivore par excellence. These fruits don't stop my appetite.

– I'll bring it, sir.

– No, Mary, you won't. Ask them to bring you, belonging to the family, Mary.

– Mrs. Paulette... – she whimpered.

– Paulette is right, Mary. You ask one of our assistants to bring you what you want.

– Well, when you decide, I will no longer have an appetite – the duke complained.

– Madam, I kept it and only I know where it is... I already knew that he – and pointed to the Duke – was going to ask for it. So since yesterday I reserved a piece, already in advance.

– There!

– And he, of course, knew it!

– By the wounds of Christ! – The duke responded –. Okay, Mary, go.

When the woman left, Mr. Luzard turned to his father, who had been meditating, and said:

– Tell me how much you like this creature, father. Why the pretense?

– What? – He freaked out, shaking the beautiful wig he had put on, and banging his fists, in whose hands a knife and fork were ready, on the table, making the plates jingling –. Do you want to play with the Lord? Duke Antonio Dambrose of Luzard? Peer of His Majesty Francis I?

– It is true, lord Duke – Paulette added – do you confess or not?

– Is this torture? Why torture a hungry man's stomach in this way? Let me at least try a little of the refreshment I asked for, gentlemen – he spoke as if he were among his French peers, in the Palace –. Later, with our hunger satisfied, we will talk about the case. Good?

– Let's leave it, honey.

– There's really no need to – Paulette said, kissing her husband's forehead.

– Stay there, glutton!

– Are you going to leave me alone, in the clutches of this woman who went to look for me the wild boar?

– Yes. Let's walk around the garden for a while.

They left. Through the spacious and well-kept garden, hand in hand, they began to walk, at first in silence, until the Lord of Luzard broke the silence:

– Honey, now, after what you said, I see how beautiful she is.

– It's natural. You didn't pay much attention to her before because you thought she was a man.

– It's true. This Planchet is really stupid!

– Not so much. He wanted to free her from the promise. She didn't accept it.

– Maybe she'll accept it now.

– I don't think so. Why do you think that?

– Knowing Jeanpaul and loving him, what is left for her to do?

– I don't know, honey. She seems decided to succeed her father no matter what... it seems like an obsession, my God.

– And we, we have to be accomplices.

– Even so. Today she enters, if she has not entered yet her menstrual cycle. I already have everything prepared, according to Dr. Girardán's suggestions. She shouldn't effort too hard.

– And she was going to ride.

– That's how it is. It was providential that you said she would go to town with me.

– Indeed.

– Well, you know, we will actually go.

-You're going?

– Yes, I need some things for her. And the gift for Jeanpaul.

–I already have mine.

– The Arabian horse?

-That. With all silver harnesses.

-It's nice.

– That's why I hid it.

– And hers?

– Jeanpaul already has them.

– Do you know what it is?

– A sword like his, a dagger like his and a couple of pistols.

– Bi-idem – Luzard completed. – All offered by my father.

-How you know?

– Now, Paulette, when it comes to beautiful and rich weapons, my father has to be in the middle. Naturally, Jeanpaul told him about his friend's birthday and he, of course, immediately thought of weapons.

Paulette smiled, amused.

– That's all. Our Jeanpaul told us. And, indeed, the gifts are precious.

– But, for the girl...

– For now he is a boy – and shaking her husband's hand, resting her head on his shoulder, as they walked –. Ah, Planchet! You clever old man! I would like to see him now! And pull those big ears.

– Which? The real ones or the bloody ones he uses?

– Jean...

– Would you have the courage to go back there?

– Of course, as I hope to do one day.

– What? – The husband was startled.

– Everything tends to end someday, darling. Who knows, maybe bring some to work with us.

– What?

– Well, they are fruits of the environment where they live. See our lands, on the north side, are virgin, without us being able to explore them due to lack of people. We will found a town, each with a small piece of land.

– Dreams, my love.

– It was Lady Suzanne's dream.

– Why do you always call her Lady Suzanne?

– Oh! Dear – and she squeezed her husband's hand even more –, I was very afraid when you brought me here. You were married, and I was your lover. Oh! Lady Suzanne... what a heart!

– She told you everything.

– Yes, she said, but then I trembled, not out of fear, but I did feel guilty, after all, normally she didn't deserve that and she became my friend for the short time she lived.

– She still lives, dear.

– And how! I always feel it. And you have to go into her room, Jean. She is there.

– Don't you always go?

– I'm do, nothing changes there. Her slippers are arranged accordingly, so that when a person lies down in bed, when she gets up, her feet immediately find it. Her clothes, her jewelry, everything, everything is as if she were there. That room is cozy. You should go there, Jean.

– I'm will. Don't worry.

They sat on a bench in front of a small lake, where ducks and geese were swimming.

Meanwhile, Jeanpaul and Jean, at the kennel, freed the beautiful, shiny black-furred dog from forced and comfortable captivity. What a joy! She jumped as soon as she saw the boy. Jean walked away, fearful.

– Calm down, Jean. It's just love. Let her smell you and soon she will be your companion.

–How beautiful!– Jean exclaimed, while the dog ran and barked, jumping again on her owner.

– Stop! – He shouted –, and she sat on her hind legs, obediently,

– Give my friend your hand to kiss and kiss his. – Go, Jean, without fear and ask for his paw.

Jean approached a little scared and asked:

– Diana, the paw, my kiss – and the dog held out her paw to her, she kissed it, then she licked her face. It was an exchange of kisses.

– Dear! – Jeanpaul shouted. – Come! – And he ran away, followed by her.

– They played for a few minutes.

– How are you?

– She is pretty! And how sweet she is!

– She also knows how to be brave – and he stroked the back of the dog's ears.

– She's going with us today, on the walk, it's a shame you can't go – Jean lowered her head.

– What's wrong ?

– Nothing, nothing. That's what Mrs. Paulette had promised...

– Take it easy. All good. Tomorrow is our anniversary. And the neighbors who will surely come, you'll see, they are beautiful! Michelle is a lovely blonde. She loves Me very much. Françoise, a spectacular brunette. I will be afraid...

– Fear? About what?

– That they both prefer you over me.

– Jeanpaul... I don't even know them.

– I don't know, Jean… but, give me one, okay?

– Which of the two?

– I really like Michelle; to my parents too.

– Then she is yours. I don't like blondes.

– Are you angry?

-I? Oh no! You have to go for your walk and it's already late. I'm going out with Mrs. Paulette. Come on?

– Sure. Come, Diana, let's go home.

The beautiful animal ran away, stopping occasionally to wait.

– I can't live without her – said the boy.

– She? Michelle or Françoise?

– Well, Jean, Diana.

– Isn't that a lot of love for a dog?

– I don't know, a dog friend is better than several dog friends.

– *Mon Dieu* ! What are you saying?

– *Pardon*, I remembered the Court.

– Look, your parents.

–Oh! They were dating! – Diana ran towards the two.

– Diana is going with us, father.

– With us? – Mr. de Luzardo was surprised, while he was petting the dog.

– Yes, me and grandpa.

– Oh! Yes! Yes! She needs exercise.

– And father, although she is very comfortable in that kennel, I want her to be released from now on.

The Lord. of Luzard looked at Paulette and nodded:

– Okay, whatever you want. But you see, she was never mistreated.

– Now, dad, it's not about that. It's just that she is far from everyone.

– I know, son, I know.

– You can even sleep in my room.

– But she takes care of the entire property.

– No, she is part of it. Mastiffs do guard work.

– But they work for her!

– I know. From now on they will have to do without it. After all, she is a lady!

– Oh! Son, you do the same as your father with the other Diana.

– My grandmother Suzanne loved her.

– That's true, but she screamed when she jumped on her bed.

– I know. But just for fun. Didn't I sometimes sleep with Diana? – the Lord of Luzard shook his head.

– Yes, yes, this happened. Sometimes I would go into the bedroom and there would be Suzanne and Diana hugging. My God, my Diana!

– And Mrs. Suzanne? – Paulette asked.

–Oh! Of course, I didn't want to make comparisons. We talk about dogs.

– I know, love, I know.

– Tomorrow, Jean, our Jeanpaul will take you to the two mausoleums that I love the most.

– From Lady Suzanne – Paulette clarified.

– And Diana's – Jeanpaul completed –. Come on, ragbag! – The duke shouted, leading two beautiful horses by the reins –. Let these weaklings play *diabolo*. – Let's go!

– Go, Jeanpaul. The old man is angry.

Jeanpaul looked at Jean. She lowered her head, wanting to shout that she wanted to go too, that she was a woman. But he remained silent.

– See you later, Jean – he said goodbye.

– Go, Jeanpaul. I'm going to buy your birthday gift.

–Oh! But, fool, I already brought yours from Paris!

– That?

– Grandpa, tell him.

– Do not say anything. Isn't tomorrow your birthday? – Come on, brat, I can't stand holding these animals anymore.

They mounted and galloped away, with Diana running behind. Jean began to cry; the Lord of Luzard hugged her.

– Girl, beautiful girl!

– Huh? – she was startled.

– He knows, Jean.

– But, Lady Paulette...

– He saw me enter your room and felt jealous. I had to reveal everything.

– *Mon Dieu* ! – And she hugged the Lord of Luzard against her chest, letting her tears fall in torrents –. What do I do? I love Jeanpaul. Please help me.

– Forget this silly oath, Jean.

– I can't, I can't. My father needs me.

– He freed you, darling.

– I know, Mrs. Paulette, but deep down he wanted a man to be his successor. And if now I say loud and clear that I am a woman? My father doesn't deserve this. I'll move on.

– Even if you lose Jeanpaul?

– I don't know how to answer – and she burst into convulsive tears and her body softened, Jean de Luzardo carried her in his arms.

– Poor thing! – He exclaimed, walking towards the house. Mary ran, helpful, with other servants.

– Nothing, Mary. The child suffers from the throat. This dust.

– Oh! I have some drinks!

– I know, come on, I'll take him to his room. Everything is alright.

– Mary, prepare some hot tea and take it to his room.

– I will do so, ma'am.

In the room, lying down, under the care of Paulette and her husband, Jean began to show signs of recovery. And she started crying again.

– My God – said Jean of Luzard –. Why, my daughter, is all this? I want to tell Jeanpaul everything.

"No, sir," she cried, getting up halfway from the bed and taking his hands. Please no!

-Take it easy. I won't tell him– and for his wife -. Loosen her clothes – he said. Paulette spent the rest of the day going back and forth to Jean's room. The girl felt cramps derived from her feminine state. In the afternoon Jeanpaul and his grandfather returned. They brought some partridges. Diana, full of feathers, which stuck to her fur.

– Son...

– Father, look what beautiful partridges we brought.

– Naturally, you killed them.

-No.

– No?

– I didn't take my musket.

– So, it was my father?

– Well, in a way, it was… with the help of Diana.

– Vulture ! – The duke roared.

– Are there bullets or bites on these birds?

– Dad, dad, no fights. These birds were helpful.

– Because?

– Son, your friend Jean had a sore throat.

– Now!

– He has been lying down until now. A partridge soup will surely relieve you.

– What a complicated boy, this friend of yours, Jeanpaul! – The duke exclaimed –. Don't you count on him at all?

– It's not like that, grandfather. We fought thieves together, remember? And so. But...

– Dad, forget it. He is our guest and the least we can do is provide him comfort. Let's see if you understand it.

– I understand. But don't call me "old man" – he responded, pointing his finger.

– No, no, grandfather, he didn't call his old father old – and he ran away.

– I still kill this brat – and his son –. How is the boy?

– It's OK now.

– Tomorrow is the party.

– Yes, father – and he put his arm around the duke's shoulders –, it is tomorrow.

– You're worried, I'm sorry. What's happening?

– Do you remember the date Suzanne died?

– Well, son, of course. I just couldn't be here.

– I know, dad, I know. What date was it?

– Well, September 8th, there is no way to forget it.

– And Jeanpaul and Jean's birthday is precisely September 8th.

– Oh! Son – and the duke hugged him –. I understand you! Sign two extreme moments in your heart: joy and sadness.

– More or less.

– My son, Suzanne, wherever she is, is happy, content and want us to be happy too. Lift your head. We go to the town, talk to the priest and order that a mass be celebrated.

– No, no. Go get him and we'll go to the oak tree. There he will say the prayers that I cannot.

– I will surely go early, my son! Get happy. You have a son who, if not from my dear daughter-in-law Suzanne, was accepted by her. And look at the beauty of celebrating, the day she gave her soul to the creator, your son's birthday. Oh! Who knows, maybe she'll be sitting on a cloud, watching and applauding at this party.

– Father...

–By the way, did Paulette go to the villa with Jean?

– No, they didn't go.

– So, you didn't buy gifts for my grandson?

– And Jean?

– He will give Jeanpaul one of ours, as if it were his. It's a secret, old man.

– Old? You too? – Jean of Luzard smiled.

– Well, the brat took the birds.

– Let's go dad. You take a bath and we'll have dinner.

– I'm hungry and I'm tired.

Night had fallen showing, in a clear sky, a huge full moon. On the porch Jeanpaul, his mother and Mary were talking.

– You are eighteen years old, Jeanpaul. You are educated. What are you going to do now?

– I still don't know, mom. I'm thinking of joining the king's brigade.

– Do you want to be a soldier?

– That's more or less.

– Then you will have the rank of captain.

– I know. Captain and grandson of the duke.

– Will you have time to decide and how is our doctor Girardán?

– Oh! Mom, the good doctor is misunderstood! In fact, there is a case against him. They think he is a witcher.

– Witcher? Doctor Girardán?

– My grandfather is more aware of the details than I am, but it's true.

– Poor Dr. Girardán!

– And you, Mary, when do you get married?

– Me? – And the servant put her hands on his chest –. Wow, Jeanpaul, I'm old now!

– And? However, my grandfather never takes his eyes off you.

-Jean Paul! – She exclaimed blushing –. What are you saying?

– Do you see it, Mary?

– What, madam?

– Nothing escapes my son.

– Mrs. Paulette...

– You're not that old.

– My lady...

– Will I always have to warn you not to call me my lady?

– Look, here comes Jean – Jeanpaul warned, ending the discussion.

Jean was on the porch. She was wearing a lush velvet blouse, long sleeves, tight at the wrists, white pants that reached below her knees, and black shoes with a high plate in the middle of the foot.

– Good night! – Greeting.

–Oh! Jean, how are you?

– Better.

– Excellent. We waited for my father and grandfather to have dinner.

– Sorry, I'm not hungry.

– Oh! But you're going to have partridge broth with vegetables! – Paulette said.

– Lady...

– Yes, you will, and then go to bed. After all, tomorrow is a big day, you have to be strong.

~ 140~

– And the girls will be here – Jeanpaul observed – Michelle and Françoise... they are beautiful.

– Which of the two do you prefer? – Jean asked, sitting down –. Michelle is beautiful, but don't worry, Françoise doesn't stay behind at all. She will like you.

– I hope so – she said, looking askance at Paulette and crossing her legs.

– Who knows, maybe you will leave here married?

– I doubt it, Jeanpaul, I doubt it – she replied.

The duke and his son arrived. They were talking animatedly.

– Paulette, I was telling your husband that we eat better when I am here: wild boar, partridges, deer.

– Wow, what a pretension! – Paulette reacted to her husband's smiling face.

– That is very pretentious, my grandfather – Jeanpaul intervened – Well, look: we ate the wild boar that Jean killed. As for the partridges...

– What happens to the partridges?

– As far as I know, Diana was the main hunter.

– Come on, brat. What Diana. So what trigger did she pull?

Diana, feeling like the target of the argument and hearing her name, barked twice, raising her head, ears pricked.

– You see it? She claims one half. Yes, you should give her one.

– Now, have you seen it yet? A dog eating partridges at the expense of a duke?

– Old duke...

– You rascal! – And, as always, they ended up laughing. Dinner was served and they enjoyed pleasant conversation. Then, sitting on the porch, they continued talking, until Paulette came forward firmly:

– Jean, you should go to sleep now. You didn't have a good day. Mary will bring you some infusions that will be good for you.

– It's true – he stood up –. Good night.,

– Good night, Jean. Sleep well, because tomorrow is our day – She smiled and left.

– Mom – said Jeanpaul – you are so affectionate with Jean, so affectionate...

– Oh! Son! And wasn't it supposed to be like that? After all, he is your friend and our guest.

– The scoundrel is jealous – added the duke.

– You're jealous, grandpa. It's just that she treats it almost mathematically; It doesn't look good for a boy to be spoiled like that.

The Lord of Luzard intervened:

– Your mother is like that. She wanted so badly to have another child to keep you company.

– As far as I know, she wanted a girl.

– It's true. And who knows, maybe it will.

– With forty two years? It doesn't seem possible to me.

– Who knows? Well, I'm going to retire. Tomorrow we will have a lot of work.

– It's time to let the old corpse rest.

– He calls himself old and he doesn't like to be considered that way.

Mary appeared, coming from the kitchen, with a glass vase on a tray.

– Wait, Mary. Give it to me, I'll take it. The duke wants to talk to you.

– Lady...

– I? – The duke asked surprised.

– Isn't that what you told us? Sit down, Mary. Talk – And she left with her husband.

– Why did you do this?

– Well, your father only watches over Mary. Let's see if he has courage in front of a woman. She knocked softly on Jean's bedroom door, while her husband headed to theirs. The door opened and she entered. Jean was wearing a nightgown.

– So, miss, how are you?

– Well, I didn't feel pain anymore.

– Have some tea. And sleep.

– Thank you, Mrs. Paulette. And forgive me for the inconvenience I'm giving you.

– Oh! Girl – and she hugged her – go to sleep. May God give you good and beautiful dreams.

She fell asleep.

Early in the morning there was a general stir. The kitchen was almost packed. Some sacrificed pigs, others pheasants and chickens. Paulette and Mary giving orders and also working. The duke, dressed in a dressing gown, approached the door and roared:

– Can't someone sleep peacefully in this house? Otherwise, I'd stay in Paris.

– Well, stay, father-in-law – Paulette agreed, handing him a roasted leg of pheasant.

– Then I won't stay any longer. "It was the best good morning I have ever received in my life," he observed happily, biting into the bird's juicy thigh.

– What time did you go to bed?

– Early, right after you left.

–And why does Mary have those dark circles?

– Huh? Make sure you respect me, ma'am – she responded awkwardly.

– Old duke!

– What?

– I'm going to talk to your son.

– Now, stop talking nonsense. We just talked a little.

– Only a little…?

– Simply, yes, pimp. I'll talk to my son, witch.

– Come here, give me...

– Give what?

– The thigh of the pheasant. You won't eat anymore.

– Now, beautiful creature, goddess of Olympus, this old duke adores you, even more so, this bird of paradise that you offered me, Lady Luzard – Paulette couldn't stand it, she laughed, while the nobleman walked away biting his thigh.

– See you soon, beauty. But we'll talk later. I am going to bring the Holy Inquisition upon you, you will see.

– Go, go.

✳ ✳ ✳

In Paris, more precisely, underground, the story was different. Planchet was very ill. He felt the end was approaching. And he wanted to see his "son." Without his strong pulse, everything was in complete confusion. Safeth, a Turk who had found accommodation there, took the reins of the community, exercising, with his evil and strength, the functions of King of the Beggars. He was not well liked, only tolerated for his fierceness and threats, and had even eliminated some. Little by little he took control of everything. He was a troublemaker. Everyone feared him. Planchet was dying, more from grief over what he was told about Safeth, and promised that they should wait for his son to arrive to restore order to the community. Safeth smiled. Completely bald, with his almost one hundred kilos spread over a height of almost two meters, he boasted:

– Now, what will an eighteen-year-old boy do with me? Come.

Planchet had sent a messenger to Dr. Girardán to tell him what had happened and ask him to notify his son. The doctor, alone with Lenoir, reflected:

– To do?

– Warn the boy, master.

– What boy, man? It's a girl, don't you know?

– Oh! It's true. Still, we have to warn her. Her father dies.

– This is a reality there. However, if she comes, what will this Turkish dictator do? I fear for her.

– If you are a friend of the duke's grandson…

– Oh! Lenoir, who will go to Alençon?

– I can look for someone, doctor. The street vendors of the Saint Denis square.

– Yes, go see if you can find one.

Not only in the Court of Miracles was the situation tense. France itself lived under the sign of fear. It turns out that Henry

VIII[31] of England and Francis I wanted, at all costs, to remove Charles V from the fight for the imperial throne, after the death of Maximilian. Their objective was to end the preponderance of the Habsburgs in Europe. In Madrid, the news was the most disconcerting, if not disturbing. The main peers of the kingdom decide to negotiate their votes with the best payer. Then, they send word that Francis has already offered a fortune in gold. Immediately, Carlos calls his advisors. Candidate for emperor, he did not have the financial aspect of the matter. There was no money in his coffers, since gold from the newly discovered lands was very scarce. It was then that a great statesman, Gattinara, announced that there was a solution.

– What is the solution? – Carlos V asked.

– The bankers – Jacó Fugger from Augsburg, who runs a chain of banks.

– This idea of yours is interesting. But can you tell me how we are going to repay the astronomical sum we need?

– Sir, bankers don't want money lying around.

– And what does he want then?

– A concession from His Highness.

-Which?

– Property rights and sovereignty over the port of Antwerp.

– What? – The monarch shouted. – This is our main port. If I accept, they will have all of our control in their hands.

– Take it or leave it.

– I have no other choice. I have to secure power over Europe.

---

[31] (1491 – 1547) King of England from 1509 – 1547. Founder of Anglicanism.

– Augsburg bankers financed two-thirds of the lost amount. What was left, Carlos, with great sacrifice, took from the nation's coffers, paying it to the main voters. And there was no difficulty. Gathered at a large table, the voting begins, which soon ends with the election of Charles as King of Spain, Emperor of Rome and Supreme Dignitary of the Holy Roman Empire, taking the name Charles V. The bells ring, telling the world the great news.

In France, upon receiving the news from Frankfurt, Francis was desperate. The rivalry between the Habsburgs and the Valois dynasty went back many generations. With the election of Charles V to the empire, France was surrounded by the enemy. To the north, the country of Flanders; to the east, Germany; to the south, Spain. And with only one authority: the Habsburgs. Thus threatened, France began to prepare for war.

✳ ✳ ✳

At the Luzard's magnificent property, everything was already prepared for the party. The immense crystal chandeliers, adorned with large, thick candles, began to light up. The porch had been transformed into a living room. There was a long table covered with a bright white linen tablecloth, on which cutlery was placed. Several chairs with soft cushions were scattered around the porch. The duke, dressed to the nines, with a beautiful coat sewn with gold thread, a little hat on his head, blue velvet pants with genuine leather sieves, a huge gold chain with his insignia, and at his waist a wonderful sword with a hilt encrusted with precious stones. All the awards paid to him were displayed on his chest, showing that he was a man of the kingdom. He appeared on the porch, petulant, with his head held high, looked, paced back and forth, stroked his mustache, and then headed into the kitchen.

– What do you want here? – Mary asked – Are you the first to change clothes?

– Oh! Goddess! While the other guests don't come, why don't you change your clothes too?

– Wow, my father-in-law – Paulette shouted – we are working. We will go together to make ourselves beautiful: me, for your son; Mary, for you. Do you understand?

Mary chuckled. The duke, naturally, did not want to face the evidence and avoided it, finding a way out:

– And Jeanpaul and Jean with the girls who are about to arrive.

– Father-in-law, go, I think the first carriage is arriving. Go, please.

– I'm going, I'm going.

Sure enough, a small carriage was approaching, driven by a single horse. The butler helpfully went down the stairs, opened the door and, with a solemn air, to the astonishment of the duke who was alone at the top, announced:

– The Count de la Croix and His Excellency his wife, Milene de la Croix, with their daughter Françoise.

– Huh? – The duke shouted. – Are you introducing me to the guests?

– Lord Duke of Luzard – the butler continued – The Count of...

Stop, stop, Santelmo. I know... they are our neighbors – he shouted, in front of the butler's big face.

– I know, I know, the count... come, come up.

–Sir, you should go greet them... – Santelmo tried.

– Shut up, you scoundrel! – He reacted in a low voice. – Why do I have to go down? They are younger than me, let them come up and stop that. We are not in Paris. Go, go to the kitchen. Bah! Do I get out of there so as not to subject myself to labels and you repeat them to me?

– Oh! Mr. Count! You can upload. My gout prevents me from getting there – he lied . – Excuse this poor old man – and he opened his arms –. My son and grandson will be arriving soon.

Jeanpaul appeared, dressed in white. Feather hat of the same color. The blouse, which at the waist formed an upward visor, with pantaloons of the same color, with a huge gold chain at the waist, on which was girded a majestic sword, in a black sheath, inlaid with gold. His boots, which shone so brightly and reflected the light of the candles, looked like black mirrors.

– Gentlemen – he greeted, kissing the countess's hand, and then addressed the Count de la Croix, with the same respect:

– Lord Count, how much time has passed!

– Boy

– Boy?

– I'm sorry, today you turn eighteen, you are a man.

– Correct, Lord Count. Have a seat. Soon my father will be here. In the meantime, my grandfather will attend to you. Isn't that right, grandfather? – And he looked at his grandfather with an ugly face.

– Oh! Yes, Mr. Count de la Croata...

– Croix, grandfather, please – Jeanpaul corrected.

– Ah! Time is running out here, forgive me! I don't even know who I'm talking to anymore, Count de la Crota...

– Croix, grandfather.

– Yes, yes, Monsieur le Count de la Croix. I haven't seen you in a long time. You know, yesterday I killed five wild boars and eighteen partridges.

– Grandfather...

– Well, two wild boars.

– Grandpa, I'm going to look for Jean. Did you remember the present?

– Well, I already have it there, on that shelf.

– Grandpa, don't lie, just do it; I want Michelle, no, Françoise, you understand, you old fool?

– What?

– Calm down, it's my birthday.

.– And?

– Along with the gifts we brought to Jean, I want to include this brunette.

–Françoise?

– Exactly. Keep them there.

– Oh, oh, Mon Dieu!

– Make sure you understand, grandfather – and turning to the couple.

– Forgive me. I was talking to my grandfather about something about the party. Make yourselves comfortable.

Jeanpaul ran towards his mother as she entered the room.

– Mother...

– Oh! Son! What's happening?

– Jean...

Where is Jean? Françoise has arrived, I have to introduce her to him.

– Son, you know the night didn't go well. Wait. It'll be there in minutes, I promise. Go back and take care of your grandfather. Go.

Paulette did not enter her room. He went directly to Jean, knocked on the door and announced himself:

– It's me, Paulette.

– It's open – the door opened.

The girl jumped on her neck, crying.

– Dear...

– What do I do, what do I do?

– Calm down, girl, be strong. After all, it's only your fault.

– I never imagined going through a situation like this.

– And you're going to have to get over it. Come on, finish dressing. One of the invited families has already arrived.

– Who's there? Michelle or Françoise?

– Francoise.

– Oh...

– Well, you have to court her. Jeanpaul is eager for you to appear. Your clothes are the same as my son's. Just don't use the sword.

– Well why? Without it I feel naked.

– You will soon know why.

He helped the girl put together the details of her outfit, adjusted the feather hat on her head, looked at her and, without holding back:

– What a waste!

– Come on, come on, Mrs. Paulette, or I won't be able to go out.

– You just go. I'm going to the room to change.

– But...

– Go, Jean.

She took a deep breath and walked towards the porch. Jeanpaul saw her arrive, smiled widely and went to meet her.

– You took your time, friend! You are handsome!

– "And you are beautiful, my love" – she thought.

– Come, I will introduce you to our guests.

Françoise, in her flowy dress, with a very tight bodice that outlined her shapely chest, had her black hair curled in elegant braids that fell over her back and shoulders. The immense black eyes shone in the charming face, forming a beautiful set.

– These, the marriage of the Count de la Croix. – Jean kissed the matron's hand, bowed to the count, who reciprocated and added:

– It's a great pleasure.

– And this is their daughter, Françoise.

"Delighted, miss," said Jean, taking the young woman's hand by the tips of her fingers and bringing it to her lips.

The Lord of Luzard appeared with Paulette. They were elegantly dressed. They went to join the group. Wine was served and they sat down to talk.

– Excellent wine – commented the count.

– Coming from you, sir, it is a privilege, since you are a great wine connoisseur.

– It's a Morriet, right?

– Precisely.

– It is a pity that the Duke of Morriet no longer lives. And his son Philippe is not interested in cultivating the vineyards.

– I met him once in Paris. He is a handsome young man.

– That's right, but very arrogant. He almost killed the duke's son, Colby.

– I knew about it. They say he is an unbeatable swordsman.

– And he is. He learned from Mr. Fontein and the foundryman Cellini.

– Excellent teachers. But look who arrives.

A carriage had just stopped in front of the house. Jeanpaul quickly left and went down the stairs. Jean realized this and instinctively lowered her head.

– It is the Marquis de Ville.

Jeanpaul opened the carriage door and offered his hand to the marquis' lady, who got out, then to her husband, and then to her daughter, a blonde of unusual beauty. Jeanpaul's eyes were shining and Jean, from above, was observing everything.

– Calm down, honey – Paulette warned in a low voice. She turned around and, looking at the lady, said:

– I can't stand it.

– I wanted to? – and took her to a secluded corner.

– You can't take it anymore, what?

– Jeanpaul melting because of that shamelessness.

– Jean! – Paulette complained – Are you a man or a woman?

– I am a woman and you know it.

– And Jeanpaul is aware of this? The others too? This is a scam, Jean, you're going to lose Jeanpaul. He gave you Françoise because he doesn't love her, you understand? He stayed with Michelle and introduced you to that one. He doesn't know that you are a much prettier girl than those dowry hunters. However, you remain uncompromising. There's still time. Take off this man's clothes in the middle of the room. My husband and I will protect you and take care of everything. My son will love you.

– Can't.

– So, daughter, look and be consumed by jealousy. I cannot do anything.

– Would you take me to my room?

– No, no, remember that you have gifts to give, others to receive. Continue, gentleman Jean. Jean of what?

– Jean... from the Court of Miracles?

– Jean!

– I don't have a last name, only Jean.

– It's... Jean de...

– Of what, madam?

– And what do I know? I'm thinking for a last name.

– So...

Paulette held her chin, thought, and then her face lit up.

– Jean... Jean de Susanpierre.

–Susanpierre?

– And why not? Susan, from Suzanne, and Pierre, from our dear Pierre.

– But...

– Go, Monsieur Jean de Susanpierre! And act appropriately.

– I tremble just looking at those spirited creatures.

– You're going out with one.

– And she will never forget Jean.

– What are you going to do?

– In a way, the same thing a man does to a woman.

– Jean!

– And isn't that what they expect?

– Jean!

– I will scare them both, if possible.

– Look, girl

Jean smiled.

– Keep calm. I have nothing to hurt them with.

– I don't like this sewer language.

– Weren't you from there?

– Yes, but I left.

– Well, I left and I'm coming back there.

– Girl – Paulette became exasperated –, at least respect me.

– Oh! God! Yes, I respect you, Mrs. Paulette. But I'm living a farce, aren't I? And I have to keep Jeanpaul's suitors further and further away – Jean lamented, pouting.

– Don't cry, go on, pretend as you want.

– If I had my sword!

– Would you kill everyone?

– No, is not that. I already said that I feel naked without her.

– Come on, miss, before I give you a good beating in front of everyone.– It's the sword you want, come on! – And she pushed her.

– Jean! – Jeanpaul shouted, when he saw them arrive.

– Were you always there?

– Your mother asked me to help her.

– Look, this is Michelle.

He cast an absent glance at the beautiful blonde, bowing deeply before her to appear as polite as she should. So much so that the visitor's little hand, understood, was not touched.

– Hello! – she exclaimed indifferently, turning to Françoise who had approached.

– Are you coming with me, Françoise? – He asked, offering his arm, which was accepted.

.– See you later, Jeanpaul – He looked at him, smiled, without realizing anything.

– Of course, go.

But Paulette, mischievous and vigilant, applauded, attracting everyone's attention.

– Gentlemen, my father-in-law asked me to inform you that it is time to deliver the gifts to the two birthday boys – and he told me. The Duke of Luzard, at that moment, was attacking a large piece of pheasant breast, with a huge napkin on his chest.

– Father! – Jean called him.

– Huh?

– Someone is calling you.

– Well, I'm not for anyone, son. Say I'm sleeping.

– Father-in-law! – Paulette's voice resounded.

-Hey?

– Are you going to distribute the gifts or finish off the pheasants?

– But how can I get rid of the pheasants if I haven't eaten a whole one yet? What's happening? – He responded wiping his fingers with the napkin.

–The count and I do the honors.

– The count is on the other side, my father-in-law.

– Oh! So he left me alone!

– Only not, with the pheasants.

– What do you want, oh unnatural daughter-in-law, to interrupt the meal of a hungry old duke?

– Gifts...

– Now I know that those present are our neighbors.

– The gifts, old man, from Jeanpaul and Jean.

– The gifts, ah! Yes, Yes I understand!

– Father!

The duke stood up, stamped his feet, smiled and headed to the anteroom, returning later with a servant, smiling, leaving some wrapped packages.

Well, I'm honored to pass it into the hands of a new family friend, Jean de...de...

– de Susanpierre, old man – Paulette whispered to him.

– From... Jean de Sarsaparilla...

There was widespread laughter. And the Duke cried out in pain when Paulette pinched him.

– What happened?

– Jean de Susanpierre, father-in-law – she said out loud.

– Sorry, the Duke is an eternal joker. I'm sorry, Jean.

– You're welcome, ma'am.

– Here, son. It's all yours. Open it...and he handed a beautiful leather case to Jean. She held it, under Jeanpaul's watchful eye, and opened the case, putting both hands to her mouth, in a feminine gesture, but one that only Paulette understood.

.–How beautiful!– She exclaimed, taking the beautiful piece out of the case, holding it and manipulating it as if he were in a fight – How beautiful! – She repeated.

– Just like yours, Jeanpaul!

– I know buddy. I chose it for you.

– Thank you. Thank you so much.

Paulette stepped forward and wrapped her sword around the girl's waist.

– You see? Now you have a sword.

– Understood.

And the duke shouted.

– There's still more! – And he gave the "boy" two cases again.

– Two guns! – And opening the other –. A dagger! Jeanpaul, is everything the same as what you have?

– I insisted... my grandfather and I.

She was very excited, almost betraying herself. Paulette, holding her in one arm, said:

– Calm. Here is my and my husband's gift to you. And here, your gift for Jeanpaul.

She opened the small case. There was a gold cameo encrusted with precious stones and his name engraved: "To Jean, with much love." He hugged Paulette, who whispered to him:

– Take it easy! – He approached Jeanpaul and handed him the other small briefcase. This one opened it. It was a duplicate of his, but written: "To Jeanpaul, with much love."

– Well, *mon ami* – and she was about to cry, but her "guardian angel", Paulette, caught all the attention to herself:

– Now, the gift from the father to the son.

– That potato? – Jeanpaul asked, expectantly.

The Lord of Luzard reached the porch railing and shouted:

– You can come, Alex.

Everyone ran towards the railing. And they saw the servant Alex leading by the reins a magnificent chestnut Arabian, all black, adorned with an elegant saddle and a silver harness.

– Father! – Jeanpaul exclaimed happily, while hugging the Lord of Luzard.

– He is the son of Tigger, the Duke of Morriet's Arabian stallion.[32]

– From Nantes?

-Yeah. I left him at the estate of the Comte de la Croix, who has taken care of him until now.

– It was a great pleasure, *mon ami*.

– Oh! Dad, if it weren't night and I would ride it right away! – And turning to Jean –, tomorrow, Jean, let's ride. I give you the priority of riding it before me.

– Not at all – she replied. – I'm going with you, but you ride it. It's yours.

– Jean...

– Friend, I understand your courtesy. However, I decline such an honor and if Françoise accepts my invitation, naturally, with the approval of the family, we will go for a walk together. What do you say, Françoise?

– I accept, Jean.

– Approved – the father agreed.

– And what do I do? – Jeanpaul asked.

– Well, go out with your stallion – Jean continued.

– Alone?

– And Michelle? She looked at her parents.

– Yes, you can go – the father agreed.

– So?

– Then, let's all go.

– Me too? – Asked the duke.

– You, my grandfather?

---

[32] Character from *Love is Eternal*, by the same author.

– And why not? I could take my new Spanish musket.

– We are not going to war, grandfather.

– But what if a wild boar appears?

–Jean kills him for you, with your Spanish musket.

– This child has no manners.

– No – The Lord de Luzard responded, laughing with pleasure –, my father will go out with me. What do we old people want by interfering with the young?

– It is true – the Marquis agreed – when we were young and, by the way, if Lord de Luzard can consider himself that way.

– You are too kind, sir. I'm over forty.

–And we at sixty did so many things. Those were good times. Today everything has changed. It seems that the world is not like that anymore.

– You are getting better, dear marquis – said the count.

– Not long ago, Spain discovered new lands and Portugal was not far behind. They have now found and explored vast regions, giving us great comfort since the world was becoming smaller and more populated.

– In a way I agree, but I think of us, here in France, eternally at war between the Habsburgs and the Valoises. Until when?

– From what I have heard, our monarch is declaring war on Charles V.

– Gentlemen – said Lord de Luzard – as a general rule we avoid talking about politics in our house. Let's change the subject. I will have your rooms ready. They will stay with us tonight. OK? Our children are no longer here.

In fact, the young people were nowhere to be seen.

– It's true – commented the Duke –. Only we are left.

– You can go out too, father-in-law – Paulette suggested.

– As?

She approached him.

– Mary is always looking at you. Come on, old man, cheer up the poor thing.

– If you weren't my daughter-in-law, I would order the Holy Inquisition to set you on fire, witch.

Jean was walking with Françoise and, a little apart, Jeanpaul and Michelle. Jean couldn't take their eyes off each other. So much so that she caught the attention of her companion, who asked:

– What's wrong with you, Jean? Are you upset about something? You don't speak, don't even take your eyes off your friend.

– Oh! It's no big deal! – Jean lied, forcing a smile and shaking the young woman's hand.

– Tell me about you. What are you doing?

– Studied. Now, like Jeanpaul, I still don't know what to do.

– According to what my father told me, France is preparing for war.

– I don't know, I didn't hear anything.

– And your parents?

– My father has a business establishment – he lied.

– Oh! And what is the activity?

– Well, jewelry, watches, bracelets, all kinds of merchandise (in a way, the truth was true). I'm supposed to be in charge of his business soon.

– Leave me your address. I'll look for you in Paris in the summer.

– With all pleasure. I expect a messenger from my father at any time if he needs me – he lied, not knowing; However, a man was running towards him, at the request of Dr. Girardán.

– It's a shame that we meet only now!

– I feel the same – and looking at the fence next to her, she saw Jeanpaul put his arm around Michelle's waist and pull her to kiss her. The blood rushed to his head and he screamed:

-Jean Paul!

Frightened, he let go of the girl and turned to his friend, looking stunned.

– What happened, Jean.

– What happened? –Françoise asked.

She felt embarrassed for a moment. But, regaining his calm, he hid:

– Sorry, I thought I saw a snake on the fence.

– Snake? We don't have snakes around here, Jean.

– Sorry, it must have been some reflection of the moon, I don't know! It seemed to me that something was moving on the fence.

– Well, Jean...

– It's getting late, Jeanpaul. And with the drink I had my throat hurts. I'm going back to the house.

– But Jean...

– I'm sorry friend. I feel fever. Stay, if you want.

– No, we will all return. Don't we have a ride tomorrow?

– True.

– So, let's go. You should feel better after a good night's sleep – They went back.

– Forgive me, Françoise – Jean apologized, already on the porch, taking her hand – The truth is that I don't feel well.

– I noticed, you looked strange.

With a gesture, Jean called to Paulette, who came over to help.

– Madam, my apologies to this beauty for having forced me to repeat my throat – and he put his hand on her neck.

– Oh! Son, are you worse? Sorry for our negligence. We will keep you longer than necessary. Go inside. Françoise forgives you – and to the young woman –. He has a sore throat. Look, he has a fever... and he put his hand on Jean's forehead.

– I understand, ma'am. Go, Jean, go rest. We'll see you tomorrow – Jeanpaul approached.

– Do you need to go to the doctor, friend, do you always feel bad at the best of parties?

– Relieve me, please.

– Come on, Jean, I'll take you to your room.

-Thank Mrs. I know the way. Don't worry. Tomorrow everything will be fine – and she left with a firm step – Paulette followed her with her eyes, shook her head and turned to Françoise:

– Poor thing, he must be suffering a lot.

– It is a pity! – She agreed.

Late in the evening, after enjoying a joyful gathering of food and drink, the servants led the visitors to the rooms reserved for them. Once this was done, they began to blow out the candles. Jeanpaul sat in a chair, placing one leg stretched out over the other.

– What do you have, son? – asked Lord de Luzard, with a glass of wine in his hand.

– Nothing, father, nothing.

– Tired, at your age?

– No, no. Just thinking.

– In Michelle?

– No.

– Don't you want to trust me with your thoughts?

– Father...

– And I do not? – Paulette's voice was heard approaching.

– Well, it's something quite personal.

– I know, but no matter how personal it is, who knows if the three of us will be able to clarify it?

– Yes, it's about Jean.

– What's wrong with Jean?

– It's difficult to explain and I don't want to be unfair to him.

– Explain your doubts – and the parents sat in front of their son.

– I don't know how to start – and he ran his hand through his hair, then unbuckled his sword belt, placing it on the chair. He looked at the expectant parents.

– Well, they both know and know about my masculinity.

– Son – The Lord of Luzard was surprised – and did anyone doubt it?

– No, father, no.

– What's wrong with you, Jeanpaul? – Paulette insisted.

– Jean...

– Why are you reticent? You already know that the matter involves your friend Jean. Open your heart.

– Yes... yes, but I'm ashamed.

– Ashamed, how?

— I don't know, whenever I need him there is an excuse. The throat, always the throat. He seems to run away from me.

— Son...

— Wait dad, let me vent. However, on the way, with those thieves, he behaved bravely, wonderfully and defended well. However... it seems he doesn't approve of my romance with Michelle!

— In what way?

— I think he's looking at me. I was going to kiss her today and he screamed, saying later that he had caught my attention because he had seen a snake. We don't have snakes here!

— It could have been a lizard.

— Thats not all. The worst is coming now.

— Say it.

— I don't feel good being away from him. I even think I was looking at him too! I'm a man, dad, what's wrong?

— There is nothing strange — and the couple looked at each other — he is your friend.

— Another very strange detail is the feeling that I have known him for a long time!

I almost love him, as a woman! Because I know I am a man.

— *Mon Dieu* !

— Son, you love him very much.

— Dad, do you know how many friends and classmates I had at Fontein Academy?

— Several, I suppose.

-So then? This child appears to me at Dr. Girardán's house and here he is with me. Have I ever brought you any son of a duke, count or marquis?

– No, you never brought anyone.

– And now? I don't even know who his parents are, I don't know them and I invited him to spend some time with me! Yes, there is something I don't understand.

– Jean... Jeanpaul...

– And more – he interrupted –. His name is Jean. You call me Jean. My father's name is Jean. We would celebrate the same day, we just need to know if the time was not the same.

– Son, your grandmother Suzanne always told me that we don't really die. We spend time here, we love, we suffer, we live, we have children, then we return there, where we take a break. Then, we go back to correct something wrong we did. Who knows, maybe you've met Jean somewhere.

– Oh! Mom, if that were the case, how can we be sure? And if you're right, it should have been a woman.

– Or vice versa, son.

– Mom, I'm serious.

– Your mother too, son, it's just a hypothesis.

– Maybe. But where does this take me?

– Wait until tomorrow when you go out riding.

– I almost bet he will make an excuse not to participate.

– What about Michelle and Françoise?

– They didn't bring riding clothes.

– So, in this case, there won't be riding.

– No, there won't be. But nothing stops me from challenging Jean to a race. They will love it.

Paulette looked at her husband.

– No competition, son.

– I know what to do – he decided, getting up.

– And what will it be?

– Oh! Tomorrow morning you will see it!

– Look what you are going to do!

– Do not worry. Just wait. Now I'm going to bed – he kissed his parents and was about to leave, when he stopped, turning around – where did the old goat go?

– Your grandfather?

– And is there another one?

– More respect for your grandfather, boy. He should be sleeping.

– And Mary too?

– Jeanpaul, what are you implying?

– I? Nothing – and he walked away laughing.

– It's true, where is my father?

– Wow, there – and Paulette pointed – in the garden with Mary.

– This old man!

– Leave him alone. This encourages him.

– A seventy-five-year-old man shouldn't expose himself like that, dear! And apparently you encourage it.

– Jean, there is no age for love. And that can only do him good, or does it bother you that Mary is a servant?

– Oh! No, no. And she is no longer a servant; It's already part of the family.

– However, he is a noble, she is not.

– Paulette, these are just outbursts of old age, they will soon pass.

– Could be. But come on, let's pull ourselves together. I'm tired.

– And what about what Jeanpaul revealed to us? – He asked on the way to the room.

– He is quite worried.

– We could end this whole pantomime with a snap of our fingers.

– Oh! No, let's wait a little longer. Who knows, maybe Jean herself will decide to tell everything.

– Yes, let's see what happens.

They entered the room. They had not yet fallen asleep when they heard loud footsteps in the hallway. It was the duke who arrived. The morning was radiant, with the sun shining in a clear sky and a mild temperature.

–Has Jean already left the room, mom? – Jeanpaul asked, before greeting the guests who were having breakfast at the table.

– Jean? He ate some toast, drank some juice, and headed to the stables.

– Now! Apparently, he woke up ready. He sat down, ate a snack, while asking the two young women:

– Do you like horse racing?

– It's excellent – said Michelle.

– It is even more so to participate in one.

– Listen, naughty boy, weren't you planning a walk? – The duke asked, nibbling on some toast.

– That's it; You said it right, grandpa. But, since our guests had no riding clothes here, I decided to compete with Jean.

– But he doesn't like horses, he rarely rides them.

– He must have gotten used to it by now. And, grandfather, you will be the judge.

– He already knows it?

– No, no. I will inform him now – He apologized and left.

The stalls were set up very far from the house. He was going fast and found Jean riding a white chestnut horse, leading by the reins the thoroughbred that his friend had received as a gift the day before.

– Oh! Sleepyhead! – He greeted her happily. She was wearing a short-sleeved blue flocked blouse. Riding pants went into shiny boots. From her waist hung the magnificent sword she had received. Jeanpaul smiled.

– You thought well about going to prepare the animal – and he mounted it agilely.

Side by side, he looked his partner in the eyes, without saying a word. Jean felt ashamed, but, with an effort, she held that gaze that penetrated her intensely.

– What's happening? – He managed to ask. He smiled.

– Nothing. But there was change of plans.

– In what way? – He asked surprised.

– There will be no horseback riding.

– Well, then what?

– I challenged you, in front of everyone, to a race.

– What? – She almost screamed, incredulously –. Without consulting me?

– I thought you would accept. After all, it's just a joke.

– Oh! Jeanpaul, you know I'm not as good at dealing with horses as you are.

– You ride well, don't worry.

– Well, but I will do my best, on one condition.

– Which?

– After the race, I challenge you to a duel.

– Duel?

– Just kidding, I want to try the sword you gave me.

– So be it. It's fair. Come on, they're waiting for us.

– Will there be assistance?

– Of course, and judge.

– "Something is happening that I don't know what it is" – she thought, but remained silent.

They arrived at the stairs of the farm. The porch held a group of very interested spectators. The duke, solemn, said:

– Gentlemen! See those two stakes stuck in there? – And he pointed to the place where two sticks that measured about two meters were separated by about three meters, parallel –. It is the arrival.

The two nodded their heads in understanding.

– Well, go now, at a natural pace, to the edge of the forest. It should be about 1,500 meters from the arrival point.

Line up there. And when you hear the sound of this hunting horn, begin. And may the best win.

– Very good, Mr. Judge – Jeanpaul agreed, turning his mount and trotting away, accompanied by Jean.

– This grandson of mine arranges each one! What do you want to prove? Which is better, gentleman? We know this. And with that Arabian horse...

– Let's wait and see.

Jean paired his horse with Jeanpaul's and they headed towards the beginning of the forest. Upon reaching the starting point, Jeanpaul jokingly asked:

– Do you want to give up?

– I am not one of those who abandons any effort. Much less of a challenge. And she smiled.

Ready, with the reins secured, their feet resting on the stirrups, tense, they waited. Suddenly the bugle was heard. The restless horses, at the command of the two, took off. At first, Jeanpaul managed to get ahead, but Jean followed close behind.

– *"Mon Dieu"* – she thought, I have to put up with these obstacles. Everything seems to be loose inside. And how well this madman rides! She pushed the animal even further as she got closer, gaining distance, until they were almost even. Jeanpaul looked at her. She was leaning completely forward and didn't take her eyes off the road. Jean managed to pair up. Her horse was also very good. They stayed together for some time. They approached the goal, already seeing the two challenges they would have to overcome. Now much closer, the Arabian horse took a head start and crossed the finish line. They walked a little further and dismounted at the stairs.

– Phew! – Jeanpaul moaned, addressing Jean.

– You won – she said, blushing.

– But how difficult it was! – And he hugged his friend, who instinctively moved his body away, but hugged him back.

– What's happening?

– We are dirty, Jeanpaul.

The palm trees echoed on the porch. The two went up holding hands, while a pair of stable boys led the animals.

– Very good! – The grandfather shouted, hugging his grandson –. The winner.

"Close up," said Lord de Luzard. Our Jean rides very well. His victory was fair. I couldn't win. Without disparaging my horse, yours is phenomenal.

Paulette hugged Jean and led her to a table on which several vases of fruit juices were arranged.

– How do you feel, girl?

– Oh! It feels like everything is loose inside.

– You didn't need to accept the challenge.

– How not? I have rejected so many that he might suspect.

– And that's it, dear – and he handed the girl a glass.

– What? As?

– I don't know, but this is natural. Some gesture, a feminine attitude, I don't know...

– So, I have to act. In fact, two.

– Which?

– You'll see, ma'am. Give me a glass of juice, I'll take it to the winner.

Paulette, without understanding anything, obeyed and followed the girl. Jeanpaul went to sit with Michelle and Françoise on the side. She approached and offering him the glass, said:

– To the winner!

– Oh! Jean, thank you.

– You are welcome sir. But you beat me in the race. This doesn't give you the right to stay with the two beauties that visit you. And before the surprised look of the boy and his mother, who had approached, while the others present were talking animatedly, he held Françoise by the arm. waist, saying:

– At least, unhappy in the game, happy in love. And the runner-up deserves a kiss from this beautiful young woman, and, hugging the girl, he kissed her for a long time on the lips – Paulette covered her mouth with her hand to avoid laughing and Jeanpaul was perplexed.

– Thank you, miss, I hope to live up to other similar ones.

Françoise was static, showing her astonishment through the glances that passed from one friend to another.

– Well, the first place winner did not receive such a precious gift.

– You will be rewarded when you deign to fulfill the agreement, Jean replied.

– And what did we agree?

– Was it the condition for the race?

– Oh! The duel.

– Yes, and now.

– Already? Aren't you tired?

– Because? A little race like that?

– What is this about, anyway? – Paulette asked.

– A challenge.

– A challenge? Are you crazy?

– Leave it mom, he wants to use his new sword – and he stood up. – Very good sir, let's go down.

– You won't get hurt.

– Don't worry, mother – They took position.

– *En garde* ![33]

And the irons collided. The clang of metal in action caught the attention of the rest of the staff.

– Devils! – The duke roared. – What is happening? They fight?

– They just train, father-in-law.

---

[33] On guard.

–But, with bare swords? Don't we have florins for dressage?

– Paulette, did you know about this madness? – Lord de Luzard asked seriously.

– Right now, darling. They had agreed.

– But they could get hurt!

– I don't think so.

In silence, everyone remained watching the confrontation. Jean was a skilled fencer. She had learned in the sewers of old Bochet, who was also one. She had not attended academies, but she had observed a lot with her friends in the Court of Miracles, some of whom were fearsome swordsmen. She stopped and applied successive blows, forcing Jeanpaul to use all his technique to defend himself. They fought for about fifteen minutes, when Lord de Luzard decided to end the game. He went down the stairs and shouted:

– Enough! Stop! – He was soon obeyed.

– What nonsense is this, son?

– We were having fun, dad.

– Fun like this is done with blunt guilders.

– We weren't going to get hurt.

– One stumble, one bad defense and we would have someone injured!

– I'm sorry, Lord de Luzard – Jean said, sheathing his sword.

– Get up, let's go. And as for you, Jean, I think my wife wants to talk to you. Please look for her.

– Yeah.

Once on the porch, Françoise approached him and, with a huge smile, greeted him:

– How well you fence, Jean!

– Will I receive another kiss? – Jeanpaul looked at her out of the corner of his eye.

– Soon – the young woman promised. Jean went to Paulette.

– Do you want to talk to me, ma'am? Your husband sent me to look for you.

– Oh! Yes, yes, come here – and taking her to a corner – Go to your room and examine yourself. There is a very large vase with water. You understand, right?

– Yes, I understood.

– It was a lot of effort for just one morning and change clothes – Jean smiled and without saying anything, headed to the room.

– How well you fight – the marquis praised, putting his hand on Jeanpaul's shoulder.

– Thanks my Lord.

– Your friend is an excellent swordsman – added the count – He should be in the French army.

– So what? – the Duke intervened – They are just two children. No army for now.

– But, congratulations. I have seen them fight, there were twelve thieves on the road, and they wounded eight, making the remaining four flee.

The two nobles looked at each other.

– True? – One of them was startled.

– Jeanpaul can tell you, gentlemen.

The young man faced the duke, smiling, and tried to alleviate the phenomenal aspect with which he had illustrated the fact.

– Well, gentlemen, my grandfather exaggerates. The thieves had limited sword-wielding skills.

– Even so, it was an act of bravery.

– Well, Jean and I understand each other. He fights very well.

– And with what elegance.

– It's true. Now if you allow me I'm going to wash.

– Calm down, young man.

– Old liar! – Jeanpaul said, when they were far away – What twelve thieves were those?

– You were angry? If they were, they both would have ruined everyone.

– Grandpa, how did Jean do?

– Magnificent!

– He is very good. I would never want to have him as an enemy.

– Yes, it reminded me of a pirate, a privateer, that I once knew.

– Don't tell me fables.

– No, no, it's true. It attacked our ship, on a trip to England, about six years ago and what a coincidence!

– Which?

– That pirate was called Jean.

-Jean? – The young man marveled.

– Yes, yes, Jean Ledusk. What a sword!

– Did they steal everything?

– No, we didn't have anything of value that he wanted. He only learned later that he wounded several officers, including the commander. Nothing important, it just hit him in the arm. He was a gentleman with us. He only took a gold watch and a few more louis that, he declared, were for his men. And he let us continue on our way.

– Jean Ledusk...

– Yes, a feared privateer and a knight.

– Is there honor among thieves?

– In its own way, yes.

–And what was the purpose of this pirate?

– As far as I know, it remains in the seas.

– I would like to meet him.

– Oh! – And the duke hit the boy on the back –. Do not bother yourself. Next birthday I'll invite him and his entire band of filibusters. You will see! Now go wash up. The blonde has her eyes on you.

– Did you see the kiss that Jean gave Françoise?

– Son, I see everything around me.

– What a kiss! It left the girl speechless!

– Well, you do the same with the other one.

– Have you already done it with Mary? – He said and ran.

– Vulture, come back here, you beardless brat. Respect your grandfather, ragged, or you will feel the weight of my sword.

– What's wrong, my father-in-law? – Paulette asked, approaching with her husband.

– What's happening? – He shouted – This brat of a son doesn't respect his elders.

– Be careful with gout, father.

The duke began to laugh.

– I love this child – he observed.

– Well, well!

– You seemed so angry that you were about to strangle him.

– He is an idiot. Each one says! He asked me if I had already kissed Mary, with Jean's enthusiasm for Françoise.

– Between you and me, father-in-law, now?

– Unnatural mother! The son's pimp... oh! I have seen that he is as uneducated as you! I'm leaving – And he walked away with strong steps. He hadn't walked far, he stopped, turned around and confessed:

– I'll try it today.

– Ah, old man!

Resuming, Jean found himself in the hallway with Jeanpaul.

– Have you washed yet? – Asked.

– Everything – Jean responded.

– All? – He was surprised, smiling.

In an instant, he recovered and repaired:

– All the clothes, including... you do it too.

– I? Well, we have people for this. Go, Jeanpaul, go. Françoise is waiting for me.

– Slow down, boy.

– Don't worry. I know how far I have to go.

– I'll wait for you on the porch.

✳ ✳ ✳

Paris was regurgitated with people from all the cities and provinces, swelling the army that would go to war against Charles V. Lenoir, Dr. Girardán's assistant, had met a traveling salesman a few days ago who was heading to Alençon. He sent him to the doctor's house, who wrote a letter to Jean, giving him news of Planchet's condition and what was happening in the Court of

Miracles. He rewarded the merchant with some coins, asking him to hurry up, trusting that it was a matter of life and death. The man kept the letter, said goodbye and left, with his cart, an assistant and several pack animals.

– I don't know if Jean will find his father alive! – He said thinking –. The trip to Alençon is long.

– And there is still a way back.

– That's how it is. Let's pray to God that everything turns out well.

✷ ✷ ✷

On the Luzard's property life was quiet and fun. The visitors had returned to their farms three days ago. One day, Jeanpaul invited Jean for a walk.

– Where we go?

– To remove the ivy from Diana's grave and put flowers on her grandmother. Do you want to go?

– Naturally. Wait, I'll put my boots on.

– I'll see you downstairs. I'll go look for the animals.

Jean entered the room and was already walking down the hallway when Lord de Luzard called her.

– Yes sir?

– Are you happy, Jean?

– Yes, sir, yes.

– When are you going to tell my son everything?

– One day, sir. It's just that I have a job to do and if I told him everything now, Jeanpaul wouldn't let me do it.

– In the Court of Miracles?

– Yeah.

– And when do you plan to start this task?

– Soon. I'm thinking of going back.

– I fear that...

-What are you afraid of?

– Have you realized that Michelle has already sent two emissaries to invite my son to her house and you know what that means.

– Commitment?

– He couldn't refuse this, dear. And we have become so attached to you, that we have even become your accomplices.

– I have to take a risk, sir.

– Very good. Do what you want.

– I'm going to put on my boots. I'm going out with Jeanpaul. We're going to Lady Suzanne's mausoleum and we will lay flowers.

– And clean Diana's – he interrupted.

– That's right.

– Go, Jean, go.

During the walk to the edge of the property, Jeanpaul noticed the gloominess of his companion.

– What happened, Jean? You remained silent...

– It's no big deal. I get like this when I visit cemeteries.

– But we are not going to any cemetery.

– I'm sorry.

– Well, whenever I go to those places I do it with great joy. It's like visiting my loved ones.

– You're right. Let's go... – and she spurred the animal on.

They soon reached the gigantic oak tree that stood towering, like a sentinel next to the tomb of the former owner of everything.

Jean de Luzardo had ordered the construction of a small and simple chapel, which contained the body of his first wife. Jeanpaul opened the iron gate and entered. There was a small altar with two candelabras. He lit the candles. Under the altar was the tomb with the inscription: "We will never forget you, Suzanne." Jean, Paulette and Jeanpaul." And the dates of birth and death. The boy knelt and prayed, as did Jean. Then they went out and picked wildflowers which they placed on the tombstone. They left the place closing the gate. Not far away, a small marble tomb with the inscription... "To you, Diana, who made my life so happy. Jean." Below, the design engraved in the marble of a beautiful specimen of a shepherd breed canine. Jeanpaul began to remove, with his hands, the ivy and grass that insisted on hiding the tiny grave. Jean helped him.

– She must have been beautiful, right?

– Yes she was! And what a friend!

– Do dogs have souls?

– Of course they have it. God would not put His creation into the world without a soul. Now it should be in the place intended for them. But let's get back to it. I'm afraid this place will make you depressed.

– No, I don't feel depressed.

– Anyway, let's go back.

– Why the rush?

– Michelle may send me another invitation. And this time I can't escape.

– And why not?

– I do not want to be rude. And Francoise?

– She asked me to visit her when she said goodbye.

– What a kiss, huh?

– Well, I have kissed so many – he expressed the lie with the greatest simplicity.

– I guess.

– Do you like Michelle so much that you would commit to her?

– It is a difficult question to answer. I almost have no choice.

– And in Paris you didn't have girlfriends?

– Nothing serious and my studies prevented me from attending parties, evenings, etc.

–So, you have decided to go visit Michelle.

– I think so. I can't delay it any longer.

Jean remained silent, looking at the grass the horse was walking on.

– Now then, you subjected me to the real interrogation and now you remain silent? And you, what do you think of Françoise? Or do you have a girlfriend in Paris?

– Some, but nothing serious. I think, before making a decision, consider what to do in life. As you know, I don't have the resources. My father is poor, I am not the grandson of any duke and life in Paris is hard.

– Don't talk like that, Jean. You are my best friend, you are the brother I never had – Jean looked at him seriously. She saw herself reflected in the boy's eyes. Her eyes filled with tears. Jeanpaul noticed.

– Don't be like that, friend. I will help you with everything you need. She lowered her eyes. With difficulty, he said:

– Come on, let's go.

– Look! – And the boy pointed out smiling. She looked in the indicated direction and smiled too.

– Diana! – He exclaimed – She found us!

The beautiful dog came like an arrow, and when she approached, she began to bark acrimoniously. Jeanpaul dismounted and patted her.

– Hello friend, did you miss us? – The animal put its paws on the young man's shoulders and licked his face, moaning with joy.

– It's okay, you already kissed me. Now, Jean's kiss. The young woman leaned completely to one side to receive the dog's caresses.

– Good morning, dear – he said, caressing the head of the animal that had placed its paws on the horse's belly. – You look pretty – Jeanpaul got on the horse and they returned to the house with her barking behind.

Chapter III
Leonardo da Vinci

Planchet had gotten worse. He no longer remembered that strong and iron man whom everyone respected. Lying on a pallet, he was cared for by women who took pity on him. And his situation worsened when he learned of the excesses that turk Safeth was committing. He spent almost all his time sleeping, but when he woke up he only asked about his son. In his old age, he had even forgotten that she was a daughter.

One day he sent for Dr. Girardán. He felt deeply weakened and wanted to talk to the doctor. He didn't have to be begged; he went to the smelly den. Some knew him, as he was the one who healed their occasional wounds. Others looked at him suspiciously. One of them, a brute, almost bald, came forward and asked:

– Are you going to see the future deceased, doctor? – The doctor looked at him, smiled and responded:

– I don't know who you're talking about, future deceased?

– The Planchet.

– Oh! And Planchet is the deceased's candidate?

– Well, we all know that he is on the verge of death.

– I don't know, son. However, if you must know, you seem more like a candidate to me.

The onlookers laughed, enraging the evil-looking individual who punched the one closest to him and threw him away.

– Tramp! – He roared.

– Calm down, man, calm down – the doctor tried to calm him down. – Think about what I told you. Your son is about to arrive. He won't like what you do.

"The brat?" And he laughed. I will break him in two with one blow.

– Careful. The Duke of Luzard is his friend.

– And I, Safeth, am I afraid of the dukes or the children?

-Wait and see. Sorry... – and he walked through the underground points, whose fetid air hurt his nose. A woman recognized him.

– I'll take him to Planchet, doctor.

When they arrived, the woman took him to the cot, where the man was lying. The smell of incense and herbs filled the place; that is, one of the tunnels through which all the rainwater of Paris passed. Construction designed by Leonardo da Vinci who, of course, would never have imagined that it would serve as shelter so many people, like rats. The doctor stopped in front of the dirty bed, remembering the dying man's past, when he was the center of everything. Several statues, stolen, of course; weapons suspended on the walls, some paintings, all decrepit like the owner.

"King" – he called, taking one of the patient's hands.

– Huh? – He opened his eyes and recognized his friend.– Doctor Girardán!

– Yes, I am the one who comes to answer your call – he said.

– Doctor, my son?

– Yeah?

– Where is he?

– I don't know friend.

– How come you don't know? I gave you...

– You gave me a girl.

– A young man? And who did you give my Jean to?

Girardán soon realized that the dying man was not in his best days. He had mapped out in his mind everything he had planned. The daughter was a son.

– Don't worry, friend, your son is coming.

– Oh! Doctor, my good doctor! He will kill everyone. None of these unfortunates will be left alive. I am Planchet, the King and he will avenge me.

– I know, I know, Planchet. Calm down though.

– How can I calm down, doctor, watching that hairless monster do what he does? He is a murderer. If the number of crimes in Paris has increased, he is to blame. It is attracting too much attention from the authorities. Everything bad that happens in this vile city is charged to the account of the Court of Miracles! What will happen to us? Is there no more honor between us?

Girardán chuckled.

– But my son will come and put an end to all this. Safeth doesn't lose waiting.

– I know I know. I will prescribe you some medicine.

– I don't want medicine, what's the point? My wife is already gone. Bochet, the same. They are waiting for me, I don't know where. I called you to confess.

– Confess? To me? Why don't you call a priest? Planchet coughed, wiped his mouth with the back of his hand and replied:

– A priest? And would any of them come here? Those vultures only want money, but without sacrifice, except Olav.

– Not all, friend Planchet, as you said.

– It's that same thing. However, what I want to confess are not my sins, doctor. There are so many that only an army of priests could hear them. And if that were the case, it wouldn't work.

– And why not?

– Because? Well, I would be absolved for one sin, but not for another, and so on. The result is that I would die without reaching a common agreement.

Girardán smiled.

– So? What do you want to confess to me?

– Ah! I'll tell you – he coughed again. – A woman approached and asked:

– Do you want water, King?

– I want, I want, bring her and leave us alone.

He cleared his throat as the woman filled a clay cup with water from a jug and handed it to him. He drank and shouted:

– Now go, I want to talk to the good doctor – he waited for the woman to leave and continued –. I have a fortune in gold, which no duke has – he coughed again –. Do you know the banker? Thomas?

– Yes, the Swiss.

–Well, I have so much money with him that no nobleman could get his hands on. It's all my son's.

– Now...

– That's right.

– And what do you want me to do?

– A document, which I sign, so that everything remains in the name of my son Jean.

– I understand. But...

– But what, doctor? Planchet is dying, I know it. I can't go there and take away his fortune.

– But your son is not a son... he is a daughter.

– Huh? – and Planchet tried to get up, coughed again and fell back onto the pillow.

– It's true, Planchet.

– Really – he said, after a few seconds of reflection. – Yes, I am Planchet des Foiers. Everything is in the name of Jean de Foiers.

– What about sex?

– Wait. Take a small suitcase out from under this bed.

The doctor bent down and took out the tiny wrought iron suitcase.

– Open it.

– How? In addition to a lock, it has three padlocks.

– I have four keys hanging around my neck. Please take them from me – Girardán obeyed.

– The biggest is the lock. The other three, try them.

The doctor tried several times; He finally managed to open it. It contained many coins and various papers.

– At the bottom there is a closed envelope. Look for it – he said –. Open it.

The doctor did so and read it. He smiled.

– You have been sensible, Planchet. You put this entire fortune in the name of "my daughter" Jean de Foiers. Thank God! And what fortune! Planchet, you didn't need to end your days here. You are rich.

Planchet smiled, coughed and took the doctor's hand, declaring:

– We planted a tree... a small sapling. We water it every day. It grows. Meanwhile, the gardener withers, dies... yet it remains. I planted Jean. I passed her off as a man, because I always wanted to have a son. Now I die. Isn't it fair that everything is yours? To make up for what I went through? She's rich now, she won't need to stay here like me.

– How should I act now?

– Make a document, granting a power of attorney to the banker, in my name, which I sign, transferring all my assets to my Jean.

– Yours?

– Mine... and for now, doctor, right now.

Girardán opened the suitcase he had brought and took out a sheaf of papers, wrote it down and gave it to the man to sign.

– I do not know how to write.

– So...

– There is a stamp on the suitcase. It's mine alone, the banker admits. Paste it to the document. Once completed, the doctor put everything away and asked:

– And this money? There are even diamonds, what will you do with all of it?

– Take some for yourself; The rest – and he coughed again – is for my three wives –. You will have to list them.

Planchet laughed, causing another coughing fit.

– King?

– Well – he confessed as soon as he recovered –, I want to see them fight over the jewels, like they used to fight over me.

– Planchet...

– Now go, doctor, go, I'm tired.

– Your daughter will arrive.

– I'll wait for her. I won't die without seeing her. Go away.

– Now I'm going to the bank. I will do everything you asked of me. I'll bring the banker.

– I know doctor, I don't know, but tell me something. When I die, will I really live anywhere else?

– Of course, of course. Only the body withers and dies.

– I'm doomed.

– What, doomed?

– Will we meet those we knew there?

– Yes, Planchet. They are waiting for you.

– *Mon Dieu* ! – And he put his hand on his forehead –. Imagine, doctor, me arriving there.

– And?

– All those women waiting for me, each one demanding something! I don't want to die anymore, help me – Girardán laughed, amused.

– I can't do this; only there.

✷ ✷ ✷

Alençon, although very far from Saint Michel, on the ocean, received the iodine effluvia from the sea. Hence the heat and salinity that the wind brought to that town at that time.

– Shall we go to Michelle's house? – Jeanpaul asked Jean, sitting opposite each other on the porch, with his father, his mother and the duke playing chess. Lady Paulette, who was watching the match that, naturally, had been without a winner for months, intervened:

– To Michelle's house, son?

– Mom, this is the third invitation I have received and I have not responded. It's impolite.

– Impolite, or you don't want to go? – Jean stood up and said:

– And on top of that she invites me to go there. If you want to go, Jeanpaul, go, if Françoise were also there – she pretended, anxious so that the boy would not go. However, he himself did not want to go. Paulette, vividly, advised:

– No, it is not advisable to go alone. And as for rudeness, I forgot. I'll find a way. Don't worry, besides the night is coming.

Diana, who had crouched at Lord de Luzard's feet playing chess with her father, suddenly stood up. He sniffed the air and barked loudly.

– What's wrong, beautiful? – Asked the duke's son.

– What a fox – said the latter, fixing a mistake on the board, out of his son's sight.

– Diana! – Jeanpaul called and she responded bristling. – father!

– What? This tower was not here.

– How not?

– Father...

– I don't cheat... Always complaining! If it wasn't there, it was your dog that shook everything and the piece changed position.

Diana barked loudly again and went down the stairs.

– Someone is coming – said Jeanpaul.

– Release the mastiffs – Paulette reminded.

– For what, mom? We don't even know what it is.

– But Diana...

– He is warning us. Let's hope – And he went down the stairs, with Jean.

– What will happen?

– A rabbit, perhaps?

– No, she's used to it – she shouted:

– Diana!

The animal responded reluctantly, with all its attention focused on the road.

– Do you think then that she is possibly seeing or hearing something?

– But of course. Look! Diana runs.

– Someone comes and look at the dust. Go up, call my father. Someone is definitely coming. Take your guns, after alerting my father.

– I'm coming.

Left alone, Jeanpaul shouted again:

– Diana! Here now! – And the dog responded. Holding her by the hair on her neck, he tried to calm her down. Calm down, friend, calm down, someone is coming on horseback – and, looking at the railing, she saw her father, her mother and her grandfather. Soon the employees appeared. Jean came down with the guns.

– What's wrong with you, son?

– Someone is approaching, father. And he doesn't come alone, there must be an army behind him, do you see the dust?

– Here – Jean said, handing him the pistols.

– And you?

– I have mine.

– Devils! All this dust. How many will there be?

– How many what?

– I don't know, I remember those thieves.

Finally, the cause of the uproar became visible. Diana was contained. It was a small caravan made up of a cart pulled by two horses and driven by a man and an assistant. Behind, several pack donkeys, carrying boxes and trunks.

– Good afternoon! – He greeted the stranger, jumping out of the vehicle, and introduced himself –. I am a traveling salesman, a door– to– door salesman in this country and in others – .Lord de Luzard and the Duke went down the stairs, since there were only his son and Jean downstairs, holding the dog.

– Good afternoon – replied the duke –. What do you want?

– Water, since we ran out of water.

– There is a river nearby, why didn't you get some water?

– Forgive me, sir, and you can take your hands off the guns. And don't let your men mistreat us.

– Speaks.

– We go to a monastery, but we stop in many towns, villages, cities.

–And you stopped here to drink water? Nobody has ever done it before – answered Lord de Luzard.

– No, sir, no. We wouldn't even stop to sell you what I bring.

– So?

– Give me water.

– Do you just want water?

– Sir, I went out of my way, leaving the main road of Alençon, just to do a favor, carrying a correspondence, and yet I find myself the target of distrust?

The duke man shouted.

– What correspondence? Talk later. You must be wrong.

The peddler reached into his leather doublet and pulled out a roll of paper, raising it into the air.

– Come on, Vulture.

– Dad, wait.

– It is addressed to a certain Jean. Jean, grandson of Doctor Girardán.

– Me! – said Jean –. It's me! – He ran towards the car –. Give me the letter – The man handed it to him. Jean opened it with enthusiasm.

– *Mon Dieu* ! – And he staggered. Jeanpaul ran, but Lady Paulette stopped him, speaking incisively:

– Give shelter to these men. I'll stay with Jean.

– But mom...

– Go, Jeanpaul! Take care of the horses.

– What's happening? – Asked the duke.

– Nothing, father, nothing. Do the house honors. I help Paulette.

– *Sacre Coeur* ![34]

Jean was taken to the porch.

– What's wrong with you, daughter?

– My father needs me. I have to return. Dr. Girardán asks me. I'm going right now. He is dying.

– Daughter – Lord de Luzard reflected – it is almost night.

– Go. Lend me a horse.

– Horse? I will give you a carriage.

– No, it would be too slow... a horse.

---

[34] Sacred heart.

–But what about Jeanpaul?

– My God, don't let him find out, except when I'm gone. Help me, please – and she started crying.

– what do we do? – Paulette asked.

– Nothing. She has to go. "I trust her," replied Lord de Luzard. Come on, let's go to your room – there, Paulette, helping her put on a riding outfit, put some clothes in the saddlebag, put the two pistols in the belt with the sword, a hat and left.

– Please, Mrs. Paulette, do not reveal anything to Jeanpaul. I will do it someday.

– Keep calm, daughter.

Lord de Luzard was waiting for her in the room.

– Here, Jean. You're going to need this – and he handed the young woman a bag full of coins.

– It is not necessary, sir.

– It is. Take it.

She accepted. He hugged the owner of the house, crying. Then to the duke.

– I'll see you in Paris.

– Without a doubt, my daughter. We will be there soon.

– The horse is ready, sir – announced a servant.

– See you soon – she said goodbye and ran down the stairs, going up quickly. Jeanpaul was arriving. She blew him a kiss, surprised, and galloped away, soon disappearing.

– What's happening? – He asked, oblivious.

– He's going to Paris, son.

– Paris?

–His father is very sick.

– Si what? And you just let him?

– He wanted it that way.

– But it's almost night. What recklessness! I'll go after him.

– No, you will not.

– But, father...

– He knows what he's doing. God will guide him.

– He blew me a kiss! I didn't understand!

– It was an instinctive gesture, son.

– Dad, you could have at least sent one of our assistants with him.

– Don't worry so much, son – Paulette tried to reassure him –. I know it will be fine. And, on horseback, you will complete the journey in less time than using a carriage.

✳ ✳ ✳

In another dimension, a beautiful young woman, holding the hand of a handsome young man, walked through an extensive orchard, among singing birds of varied colored plumage. She was dressed in white, a one– piece garment, tight around her body to the waist, when it widened, going down to her feet, almost dragging across the grass floor. A golden belt, in the shape of a large Y, surrounded her waist, letting the end fall in front of her body. Her thick black hair fell over her shoulders. The young man, tall and thin, was wearing flocked shorts and a white blouse. She wore shiny leather leggins that reached to her knees and shoes with a large square buckle.

– I love this peace, Fernand – she said, inhaling the aroma of flowers and fruits.

– It's a shame that we have to return to the physical body soon.

– It will still take a while. Our parents haven't even gotten married yet.

– And they are young.

– Yes, blessed divine providence. I waited for you so long, Fernand. How long!

– Yes I know. I took winding roads, I almost lost sight of you.

– While I was a man, you were also, as a woman, the same in terms of the norms of each region, what could we do?

– It's true. But now here I am. I wasted so much of your time.

– But, you already learned, that's what matters.

– Suzanne, although we are the children of Jean and Jeanpaul, being twins, we will be separated.

– Because? Won't we be siblings?

– Yes, yes… but not husband and wife.

– This detail is secondary. We are fulfilling one more task. You chose to be a priest. You will remain celibate and pay your debts. I will be reborn in a female body, to help you have a church. I will be your dear sister, until the next incarnation.

– I will be destined to be a Catholic priest.

– Apostolic and Roman – she added smiling.

– That's what it will be like.

–However, we must help Lord de Luzard and Paulette. She became my ex– husband's wife on the physical plane.

– Help how?

– To better understand the potential they have, spiritually, to also support others.

– How many times have you been there?

– Some. They remember me constantly. I can't explain why and I'm going to consult our mentors. However, the fact that, in my honor, they kept the room that was my bedroom intact, in that house, as if I were still there, and they almost venerated my mortal remains, next to the oak tree, attracts me, and I can't help but be there when they need me.. A while ago Paulette was there, when faced with any concern, she goes to that room, as if she were going to a temple, worried about Jean. I compared him, gave her a magnetic pass and also gave her a flower that I got from here.

– And the girl who will be our mother?

– The selfless Dr. Girardán will help her naturally, as we and our mentors intuit, but only in what is essential, without privileges.

She will suffer a lot, but she will also learn a lot.

– Have we found the right family?

– Don't have any doubts about it. However, remember that we were the ones who chose. They didn't impose anything on us. Since they have free will, let's just vibe so that everything goes well.

–This habit of hers of pretending to be a man...

– Before reincarnating, when she was still here, she wanted to animate a male body, as it had been, on many occasions, a woman's. She rebelled in vain, since the body matters little to the spirit. The father, who, in turn, had only had daughters, hid the sex of his daughter from everyone, making them believe that she was a man. And only later did she understand the importance of that lie in her life. She simply accepted to live in that condition until he met Jeanpaul. Now she finds herself between a rock and a hard place.

– Was this a punishment?

– No, it wasn't. Just a coincidence, but somehow it served as a lesson.

– It's true. Nothing is done with the intent to harm. We have the right to choose and try to do it well. The fault for everything, for the successes and the mistakes, is always ours.

– So, it is dear. See how much time we wasted?

– In our case, the fault was only mine,

– Ours, brother, ours. Now I look at my spiritual body and I no longer see the physical defect that I had while I incarnated. Isn't this wonderful?

– Praise God.

✸ ✸ ✸

Six days later, covered in dust, tired and hungry, Jean arrived in Paris. He went directly to Dr. Girardán's house, where he was warmly received by the old doctor and his assistant.

– My daughter! – He greeted the doctor, hugging her.

– I'm dirty, doctor – she said, but returning the hug. Then he went to hug his friend Lenoir – I missed you all! How is my dad?

– Wait, calm down, we'll talk after taking a good bath.

– I'll bring your water, girl. "Wait a moment," Lenoir warned.

– How is my father, doctor? She asked again, uneasy.

– Alive, if that's what you want to know. But come, have a juice.

Jean accompanied him to the kitchen. She loosened the belt, put the pistols and sword in a closet, then opened the blouse, sat down, and stretched out her legs.

– Six days practically in the saddle. Everything hurts.

She received a glass of juice which she drank.

– After the bath I will give you a good massage with an almost magical ointment that I have. You will feel like new, with your strength recovered, while you sleep.

– Sleep, doctor?

– Yes daughter. You are tired and you won't be able to do anything. Furthermore, the afternoon almost gives way to night – and looking at the sword –. Beautiful sword!

– Oh! It was a gift from Jeanpaul. It's just like his.

– How was everything there?

– Wonderful, doctor, wonderful. Lady Paulette, Monsieur de Luzard, the old duke, they are exceptional – and she threw her head back, thinking.

– And Jeanpaul?

– Oh! Doctor, I love him! How gentle, fearless and loving he is.

– With you? A man?

– Me? Man?

– He knows?

– He ignores it. How difficult it was, my God! If it weren't for Lady Paulette and her husband.

– It must have been really difficult.

– Doctor… the horse?

– Don't worry. If I know Lenoir well, it must have been unsaddled and fed. Do not be worry.

– It's just not mine. Lord de Luzard lent it to me.

– It was reckless, darling, to come alone.

– He put a carriage at my disposal. I rejected it. It would take a long time. I rode during the day and only stopped at night to rest.

We, the horse and I, are crippled.

– The water is ready, Jean. "Come, let me help you take off these boots," Lenoir announced when she arrived. Your horse is in the yard. There is a lot of grass there. Then I'll give it a good brushing. Your saddlebag is in your room.

– Thank you, Lenoir.

– Go, daughter. Get rid of all your clothes, put on a sweater. In the meantime, I will prepare something to eat and the ointment for you. Go, Lenoir will help you with your boots.

She stood up, stretched, and followed Lenoir. After taking off her boots, he left the room recommending:

– Leave your dirty clothes, tomorrow I will wash them.

– Thank you, Lenoir, thank you very much.

Bathed, perfumed, she put on her nightgown, combed her hair and went out. She felt light.

– Oh! What a relief! – Thought. She went to meet the doctor in his laboratory. He mixed some substances in a small porcelain vase.

– Now you are different!

– Do I look like a person?

– You look pretty. Sit down. Lenoir is preparing you something to eat.

– Thank you. Now tell me everything.

– No, not today. Tomorrow yes…!

– Doctor, I'm anxious.

– I know. And that's why I won't say anything. You need to relax. Your father is alive, although very sick. Tomorrow, calmly, we will discuss the matter.

– What is that smell?

– Oh! It's the ointment I told you about. It is an herbal compound with camphor and myrrh. It rejuvenates the skin, causes a certain lassitude in the body and the perfume helps decongest the respiratory tract. You will sleep like an angel.

– How can I repay you so much, doctor?

– But you are already repaying me, dear.

– How?

– Giving me the opportunity to serve.

– How old are you, doctor?

– Around eighty.

– Eighty?

– Do you think it is not enough?

– No, no… there are so many people who have much less and who do nothing else – He smiled.

– It's true. They don't know that work also brings us fun. You should never stop working.

– I admire you so much!

– Now tell me everything you did in Alençon.

– Oh! I even kissed a girl on the lips.

– Kiss? A girl?

– What a horrible experience!

The doctor laughed out loud.

– And why did you kiss her?

– To show Jeanpaul that I am a man.

– And he doubted it?

– No, no. He got me that girlfriend.

– Oh! I know… on the lips…

– What a terrible thing!

– And Paulette?

– She is a lady. She doesn't even seem to come the Court of Miracles.

– And Heavenly Father always does the right thing. Lilies also grow from mud.

– Oh! Jeanpaul... I miss him!

– Calm down girl. Everything will be fine.

– Come, girl, come to eat – Lenoir appeared calling her –. A good soup and pieces of roast chicken.

– What a beauty! I'm going.

Lenoir took her to the table, served it and recommended:..

– Eat everything. Fill that little belly. There's juice in that jug. I'll leave you alone – and he left. The girl eagerly threw herself into the food.

– What did you think, doctor?

– She is okay, look at her. She found love but, poor thing, she can't enjoy it. At least for now.

– I could accompany her tomorrow, to the Court of Miracles. I would protect her.

– I know, my good Lenoir, I know. But she will have to resolve this issue herself.

–But what about that Turk?

– It's a danger. But she will be fine.

– Did you say something to her?

– No, no. I'll do that tomorrow.

– Now she is a rich girl.

– And yes, Lenoir! Planchet knew how to manage his fortune.

– Are you going to tell her?

– Not yet. I have already settled everything with the banker, but I cannot inform her about this now. Disguised, here she comes again.

– Oh! Doctor, it looks like I haven't eaten in years! Thank you Lenoir. You are a great cook.

– Stay with the doctor, girl. You have a lot to talk about – and he left.

– Here it is, your ointment. I'll have to massage you. Are you ashamed?

– No, of course not, doctor.

– Well, when you go to sleep, just wear shorts.

– Doctor, you also need to rest. I can use the substance myself.

– I know, but you can't give yourself massages. Then I'll do it. And rest assured that you will not see the end, since you will soon sleep.

– Very good. Do you want to tell me something now?

– No, no. Tomorrow. We have time.

– And France, doctor? I heard rumors of war.

– Yes it's true. Francisco is in dispute with Emperor Charles V. He has already left with the army. France is going through bad times. We hope everything ends well.

Jean yawned.

– Come on, let's go for a walk. You are sleepy.

– And !

He shook the young woman's hand and walked her to her room.

– Lie on your back. Are you wearing shorts?

– Yeah.

– Excellent.

The young woman took off her nightgown, lay down and let herself be massaged. In fact, the smell of the ointment, combined with how sleepy she felt, caused her to fall asleep immediately. The doctor finished the work, covered her, adjusted the pillow and kissed her forehead.

– Sleep well, girl. May God illuminate your dreams – he blew out the candle and left for the laboratory, to prepare the medicines that he distributed to the poor of Paris.

– How is the Turk Safeth putting thing upside down, then? – She asked, still in her nightgown, biting into some toast.

– He is the one who takes care of everything. Everyone is afraid of him. He became accustomed to breaking into houses to steal, something that was rare before.

– It's true. We only pretended to be beggars to get alms. We rob, yes, some unsuspecting people, but breaking into houses, no.

– With this, all the blame lies with the Court's community. Soon they will send in the King's Musketeers and there will be a massacre.

– I have to go there.

– You have to be very careful, daughter. This man is a brute. And it's huge.

– I know Safeth. But, doctor, "the bigger the tree, the greater the fall."

– And he has henchmen.

– Let him have them. I'm going to get dressed... – and she left.

– From what I have heard, doctor, it is decided.

– It's true. Tonight, I prayed a lot, asking my sister Suzanne, who is closer to our mentors than I am, to protect this girl. And I trust that everything will turn out well for her.

It didn't take long for Jean to get ready. She was wearing the same clothes in which she had arrived at Dr. Girardán's house; That is to say, worn clean pants that clung to the body, the tips of which entered into her boots that folded just above her ankles, loose white ones. Blouse, but closing at the sides, cuffs. However, at her waist she had the beautiful sword she had received, in addition to the daggers. On her chest was the cameo that the Luzard couple had given her. To tie it all together, the hat with the feather.

– I'm ready, doctor. Pray for me. The old doctor looked at her.

– Jean, get rid of anger, hatred. I notice it in your face...

– It is not anger or hatred, doctor – the girl interrupted –, but justice. And justice will be done. I will not kill anyone, as long as they do not make an attempt on my life. I would never baptize this sword –and she took it halfway out of its sheath– with someone's blood, except to defend myself. Keep calm. First of all, I just want to see my father. Let's see what happens next. Will you give me your blessing?

– Oh! Daughter, of course. God bless and protect you. Oh, Mrs. Suzanne, my friend.

– I'll send you news, doctor – and she left.

– You will walk?

– Clear. Those there usually eat horse meat and I have to return the horse.

– Yes, yes, it will be safe. Don't worry.

She put on her hat and walked down Saint Germain Street, dirty, full of puddles of water, always leaning on the walls, avoiding frequented places. This is how she arrived at the Court of

Miracles. Several beggars were preparing to go out into the street. Some fixed the "wounds" on their noses, others wrapped their legs in bloody blankets, etc. All to fool passers – by looking for coins.

– Put this bandage over your eye higher up – she recommended to a fat woman covered in soot.

– What? Who are you to teach me?

– Don't you recognize me, Blanche?

– Huh? How do you know my name, brat?

– Take off the blindfold and look at me with both eyes.

– Well – and the woman did as she was told. A while passed and her face lit up with a big smile.

– *Mon Dieu*! You are Jean, son of Planchet.

– Yes, it's me.

– Oh! Honey where have you been?

– Here and there.

– Your father is sick, boy.

– I just found out and came to see him.

– Oh! Boy, this is about to die!

– Will improve. I came to take my father's place.

– You, Jean? Safeth has already done it.

– But he cannot. I am the son of the King of the Beggars.

– Boy, don't mess with the Turk. It's no use, it's an animal. Go, visit your father and leave.

– I'm not one of those who run away, Blanche. I am the heir and I want my title.

– It's reckless!

– Come on, Blanche, put on the blindfold. See you later» I'm going to see my father. Is the Turk there?

– He is still sleeping after having drunk a lot. Be careful, Jean.

– I will . See you later.

She walked to the mouth of the stairs that led to the Paris metro, the sewers of the big city. Soon the nauseating smell of rot affected her nostrils. It was a familiar bad smell, but now it repulsed her. All she had to do was stay outside for a few days, breathing fresh air, to feel the difference. She walked between the platforms, where, below, the fetid waters of the city flowed. There was a kind of plaza, from which several sewage pipes branched off, and above it, connected by wooden stairs that led to a kind of niches that served as "houses." She stopped and climbed the steps of one of the stairs. He came to a tunnel lit by torches and fire burning beneath a large smoking copper vat. She saw some figures sitting and talking.

– Hi guys! – Greeting.

– Who is it? – A voice sounded.

– Jean, son of Planchet.

– Jean?

– Yeah!

Soon the crowd surrounded her and the hugs continued.

– Suzette, how is my father?

– He's not here, in his old office, boy. He fell ill and moved at the request of the witcher Girardán.

– Witcher? – She asked.

– That's what everyone says – said the woman with an air of disdain.

– Yes, yes, but where is it?

– You passed by there.

– How?

– Right at the entrance, Paulette's old house.

– Paulette?

– Yes – added another, the one– eyed one –. I don't think you ever met her, since you were little.

– At the entrance? Where?

– Outside, in the Court.

– Well, I met with Blanche and she didn't inform me.

– That doctor thought he should get out of here and get some fresh air. Look, he has always lived here, now it hurts him – a laugh broke out.

Jean didn't want to talk, he just asked:

– How do I get there?

– You just had to ask, naughty.

– I'll take you there.

– And the Turk?

– Oh! This one is sleeping.

– Tell him that Jean, Planchet's son, has arrived to take his father's place.

– You? Against Safeth? You're crazy! You better go back to where you were. Safeth will kill you, *mon petit*.

– We'll see. Inform him that I have come to stay.

– Well, the fighting cock – and new laughter.

– I'm going to look for my father, stupid people. And all of you will come to me – and she put her hand on the hilt of her sword –. Does anyone want to try it? You who offered to take me, okay?

– Yes, yes – the crowd silenced the noise.

– Do not forget. He warns the criminal that Planchet's heir, the Beggar King, is here to claim the title and put him to rest. Shall we go?

– Yes, boy, yes – the old man agreed, taking the initiative.

* * *

– So, Fernand – asked the entity that had incarnated Suzanne's body –, what do you think of all this?

– I'm in the learning phase, honey. From what I see, you are always in demand.

– That's how it is. The good doctor Girardán, who will soon be with us, but in another area, since he is a saint on earth, invoked me to support our future mother.

– I understand; However, other things escape my reason.

– Which ones, dear brother?

– We chose it because of our parents, two young people who did not even get married, nor did they have any physical contact that would serve as a vehicle for us to be born. There are two kids.

– I could answer you, but let's talk to our mentors. They will dispel all your doubts.

– I know, Suzanne, you are much more evolved than me. You wouldn't even need to return to the terrestrial orb. You will do it for me.

– Dear... – and he hugged the young man –, true, you wasted a lot of time, you made me wait so long! But we love each other and I always wanted to be by your side. I just waited and prayed for you. You see?

– What?

– You are by my side; you finally came back to me.

– I could return alone, fulfill my regenerative mission and return to you.

– I know, but I want to go back to you.

– But we will not be husband and wife.

–Does it matter? We will be brothers and I will help you win, thinking about the next incarnation, when we will have the right to love each other in body and spirit.

– I will be a priest!

– Yes, you will. You have a debt to redeem.

– Yes... I killed Monsignor Lavigne.

– With refinements of cruelty.

– But he attacked my family.

– Driven by religious fanaticism. In a way, he cannot be considered guilty at all. All their practices were carried out in the name of religion.

– He ordered my family to be burned at the stake and we had a six– year– old girl.

– Have you already forgiven him?

– Yes, I did, after eliminating him and hanging his body upside down from a tree, tearing off his skin in strips.

– And then salt the body.

– At that moment it was not enough. But where are my relatives, consumed by fire? I have never found one.

– Remember! My dear brother! Family is not always our family.

– Apparently, I need to learn a lot.

– And so, you will, being a Catholic priest. You will study and live precisely the opposite of your disaffection. Keep in mind that in all human activities there is always someone who disagrees. The fact should not incriminate everyone. Not generalizing is the right thing to do.

– And my question?

– Come darling. Our mentors will enlighten us.

– Us?

– Of course, I also have a lot to learn.

–Suzanne, wait. Tell me... – and he put his hands to his forehead, smoothed his hair and only then continued:

– If we, the spirits, can see better than the incarnated ones, why not help them?

– And don't we help, love?

– No, listen: why don't we solve crimes and keep quiet about so many things? Sometimes, a person sentenced to death is innocent and we are aware of it; that person dies, when the real culprit dies in bed, not infrequently, like a patriarch. We can't do everything, right?

Suzanne smiled.

– Let's wait, honey. They will explain everything to us.

– All these enigmas of the world, my dear, without solutions, only presupposed by embodied minds, can we not act to help them unravel them? Hypotheses multiply without reaching any convincing conclusion.

Suzanne smiled again.

– Wait, they will clarify it for you soon.

– Why do you smile?

– Because I am enjoying your inquisition. You will be a great priest. Come on, let's go with our elders – and hand in hand, stepping on the soft grass that looked like a carpet, they passed by a charming lake, where swans and waterfowl swam happily.

– Is all this a mirage or do these birds and animals have spirits?

– Everyone has a divine spark. They are not just here to make us happy.

– Let's leave this for later.

– I think so. Let's keep looking for our mentors. Some buildings come into view.

– Do we have to make an appointment?

– There is no need. They are already waiting for us. They always wait for us. Don't worry.

They met many people who greeted them warmly. The suits were uniform. The groups chatted animatedly, children ran and played under the care of beautiful young women. The buildings, almost all three floors, except one, which looked like a palace, larger in size, with stairs and columns in the wide porch. That's where they headed. They climbed the stairs, crossed the long courtyard, and entered the building. A large room, several doors. They went to one of them and opened the door. A room like any office. A young woman and a young man were sitting behind a table.

– We wanted to talk to Brother Licínio – said Suzanne.

– Sure, sister. He's waiting for you – the smiling young woman informed –, you can come in.

– Thank you.

They crossed a door and came across a smiling figure, sitting behind a beautiful table, with the papers organized. There were two chairs next to the desk. The room was simple. A huge bookshelf containing an appreciable number of large numbered file cabinets; In a corner, a small table with a device reminiscent of an old typewriter. The man, almost completely bald, stood before the two's entrance.

– Greetings, brother Licínio – Suzanne greeted.

– Greetings, brothers. Sit down – they responded. He continued:

– I know where you come from. There is no need for questions, except those that are out of context. So let me explain.

Naturally, you can accept it or not. After all, I'm here because I've had similar questions before. Can I talk?

– Of course, sir – said Fernand.

– Sir? No, just brother. Listen: First of all, our sister, incarnating the body she previously possessed, paid, at her request, for the harm she had done to another person, winning after the paralysis of her legs, a cause that previously caused the current sister Paulette , incarnate., whose soul mate he tried to attract to himself. Therefore, our sister asked not to encourage the harm that was done to her immediately after birth. She went further, she chose a period of life in which everything was beautiful, happiness, being relegated to bed, paraplegic. Praise God! And, furthermore, it united two people who, in fact, loved each other, even allowing the union of others, in this case Jean and Jeanpaul. Her life, her suffering, redeemed her from practically all her crimes. However, she will return to her physical body, once again for love. He loves you, boy, who walked away, along obtuse paths, ending up ending the life of a Catholic priest. He also, in turn, asks to be reborn and be a priest, with the aim of fixing everything he did wrong – he crossed his arms and smiled –. His will be done. That's what it will be like. Only you will have the woman you love, as a sister, not as a wife.

Regarding one of the questions that you asked and that is recorded here. Of course, we know, nothing escapes us about what happens on earth. If we solved all those questions and other mysteries, what would happen? They would have nothing to do, they would not need to study to be lawyers, judges or even police officers. It would be enough, as is always done in any problematic situation, to look up and try to figure out: "Who killed so– and– so? Or who stole it?" and, with the answer, they would arrest the culprit, ending the case. It would be too easy, let's face it. However, I tell you that there are cases where we really help. They are rare, but they happen. Do you understand, brother?

– Yes – Fernand agreed, surprised by the prompt clarification of his dilemma.

– And as for being the children of the still teenagers Jean and Jeanpaul, our sister Suzanne asked. These are two spirits without much fault, who love each other and belong to the same spiritual family. She always wanted to liven up a male body, almost degrading the female one. Now she embodies the body of a young woman, but she has to pretend to be a man. And she is suffering for it. It will surely give greater value, from now on, to the feminine manifestation, God's reliquary to perpetuate the species. Did you assimilate it?

– Yes, yes, brother – Suzanne smiled.

– Well, you chose to be a priest. Naturally, you have already thought about the enormous responsibility that will fall on your shoulders.

Being a priest means lending the word of God to others. It is acting like Himself. It's not just about wearing a black habit and walking through the streets with the holy book in your hands. It means enduring the steps of Jesus on his way of the cross at every moment. It is sharing with the poor the little bread you will have. And be humble, friendly, loyal and celibate, as required by the laws of the Catholic Church. It is difficult to be a priest, brother, because, as such, you will always have to be up to date with everything that seems new, even if you have the Bible in your hands, which you will have to read, not memorize it, but understand it. Being a priest means breaking down your entire body for the benefit of others. If you want to be a good priest, do what I tell you, because there are others who are worthless, like doctors, lawyers and even kings. Perform your duties properly. You won't be doing yourself any favors.

– And will I be successful?

Brother Licínio smiled.

– I don't know. It will depend on you.

– I will help you, brother.

– You will be fortunate to do so, since your parents will be rich. It's another challenge. However, I trust you. Sister Suzanne is permitted to connect with her loved ones who are on the physical plane. Everything answered?

– Yes, Yes.

– So, continue taking your Theology classes. You are in contact with priest teachers. Thus, when you incarnate, you will have the vocation you have asked for. Don't let them down. See you soon, brothers.

Chapter IV
The Death of Planchet

The old man guided Jean out of the sewers. In the immense square of the Court of Miracles, on the corner of Les Clerc Street, the guide pointed out a small exposed brick house, almost in ruins.

– It's there, young man. You can go alone. The light hurts my eyes.

– Thank you – and he headed to the house, knocking on the door. His heart was also beating faster. A woman opened the door halfway.

– Who is it? – He asked suspiciously.

–It's me, Celina.

– Me who?

– Do not you recognize me? I'm Jean.

– Jean? – And the door opened wide –. Jean, boy! Thank God you showed up – and she hugged the girl in his arms and she responded –. He's in a good mood. Come, come see Planchet... and she pulled Jean's hand, closing the door.

– How is my father?

– Ah, *mon petit* ! It is coming to its end. Even more so when that damn Turk prevents us from buying medicine and food. Come, come, he only talks about you.

It was a small house: Celina opened a door, stood next to it and told Jean to enter. The smell of the medicines damaged his sense of smell. In that room, well lit, although it was still morning, Planchet was lying on a bed.

– God! – Jean was startled when he saw the emaciated figure, with long white hair, lying on that pallet. The old man had his hands on his belly, fingers intertwined. Closed eyes. The girl walked over and knelt next to the bed.

– Father! – she called softly –, and took the patient's bony hand –. Celina was at her side. The dying man, whose breathing was barely noticeable, opened his eyes and turned them towards the young woman. His lips stretched into a smile.

– Dad! – She spoke again, stroking his hair. The hand she held put light pressure on hers. Two large tears fell from his eyes, running down the lines of his face. He opened his mouth a little and closed his eyes. Planchet had given his soul to the creator. Jean leaned over him, sobbing. Celina ran to get a candle she had lit and placed it at the head of the bed, making the sign of the cross. Jean sobbed.

– Poor! – Said the woman, moved to see her again. He died happy; he was just waiting for you.

Jean remained there for a long time, remembering the figure of his father, who had been so strong and feared. Now, that emaciated body, almost skin and bones, lay on that pallet.

– Come on son. Do not you worry about anything. He left instructions for Doctor Girardán on what to do after his death. Come, let's go out and let the community know that the King of the Beggars is no more.

Jean stood up. He looked at the woman and declared:

– Yes, he is, Celina.

– But how, son? Planchet is dead!

– However, I am alive. And I am his heir. I am the King of the Beggars!

– *Mon Dieu*!

– Go and tell everyone that Planchet died, but his son remains in his place. I'm going to the doctor's house. I will be back soon.

And he stomped away.

– *Mon Dieu*! – Celina repeated –. There's going to be a storm here. Poor! So young! Safeth will kill him. Then we will have two funerals.

Virgin Mary!

Some time later, Jean returned to Dr. Girardán. The little house was full of old friends and curious people from Planchet.

As she passed, Jean was greeted by those who grew up with her.

– Welcome, Jean.

– Thank you, Antoine.

– My deepest condolences, Jean.

– Thank you Pedro.

He had to respond to countless greetings and feelings of regret. He managed to enter with Dr. Girardán. They had spread a sheet over the body and lit more candles. The doctor examined the body and then asked:

– Do any of you know Father Olav?

– The one in the church of Saint Denis?

– That one.

– I know him, doctor.

– One of Planchet's wishes was that Father Olav, to whom he paid a lot of attention, would put his body in order. Can you go warn him?

– With pleasure, doctor.

– Then go, son.

Celina approached Jean, carrying some of the dead man's belongings.

– Jean, here are your father's things – Jean looked and examined. An ancient sword, two daggers, a bronze chain that he wore around his waist, holding the sword, and a kind of silver necklace, with a small crown. It was the emblem of the King... King of the Beggars. Jean smiled and put the necklace around her neck, to everyone's surprised looks.

– King dead, king ready! – she declared loud and clear.

His childhood friends applauded, while the older ones became taciturn. Jean examined the sword. Suddenly, altered murmurs of voices broke the respectful silence in that improvised burial chamber.

– What's happening? – she asked.

There was no need for any of the spectators to give explanations. A boy entered the house, blushing:

– It's Safeth! He wants to enter at all costs to get the king's necklace.

– What? – she asked, instinctively putting her hand on the small crown attached to the necklace – and smiled –. I didn't expect it to be so soon.

My father hasn't even cooled down yet – and for the doctor –. When you die, doctor, does the spirit remain there?

– Good son...

– Answer please.

– There are no strict rules. Sometimes yes.

– So, let's pretend my father was present – and he left.

A crowd was pressing in front of the house. Standing out in the middle of it, a burly man, with his shirt open over his hairy and powerful chest. He was bald, had a dirty black beard, and had bloodshot eyes from alcohol consumption. Jean calmly led the way and stopped a few steps from the man.

– Hello, Turk! – Her voice sounded harsh, as she crossed her arms in front of her chest. Her gaze was fixed on the brute's eyes, hard, cold. – What do you want?

– Nobody calls me Turk – he shouted.

– And you're not? Tell me what you want?

– Planchet died. I am the king now.

– Who told you?

– It's my right. Now I'm the leader.

– Do you have more rights than me, the legitimate heir of the King?

– Now stop joking, *petit*. Give me this necklace and you can go back to your father's funeral.

Jean uncrossed her arms.

– You want to get the necklace, son of a whore from the banks of the Seine, so come and take it! – And he took a step back.

The big man turned red with anger. He snorted like a cornered bull.

– Don't play with me, brat. I can cut you in half.

– First you will have to catch me. The crowd was tense. They hated the Turk, but feared him. And they were perplexed by Jean's courage.

– Come and take it – and raised her hand to the hilt of her sword

– Oh! The chicken shows its spur... too bad it's a toy sword.

– Celina! – Jean shouted, without taking his eyes off the antagonist

– Yes?

– Bring me my father's sword.

The woman obeyed. With the weapon in her hand, Jean unbuckled her belt and handed it and the sword to the frightened woman.

– This is the King's sword. With it, I will drive you out of here, stray dog. Everyone stay away. And you, animal, on guard!

– Astonished, the Turk gave a half – smile. After all, he had a beardless boy in front of him.

– Oh! Do you want to play, boy? Well, soon your innards will be serving food for the vultures in Market Square– and he drew his sword.

The mob ran to defend themselves, staying behind walls or carts. People flocked from all sides. Disputes of that type were commonplace in the Court of Miracles. However, now it was different. It was a son claiming the right to succeed his father as leader of that community. The news spread. False beggars, carrying crutches and running quickly, blind men taking off their blindfolds, others, with red meat patches that imitated huge wounds, one–armed men that freed their perfect arms from their vests, huddled together to watch the fight. And they even bet. Doctor Girardan, despite being pale, was calm. The irons clashed. Safeth's first attack and Jean parried, retreating. He had his left arm thrown back, balancing his body. Swords clanked. Jean studied his opponent, who continued to smile sarcastically and attack. She just defended herself. After all, the man's strength was considerable. She just let the opponent's blade slide past hers to the guard that protected her hand and, agilely, deflected the blow. She hadn't attacked yet, waiting for a mistake from her opponent. She remained serious and never took her eyes off the competitor. Sometimes she would jump and run, sword drawn, forcing Safelh to chase her. So, she defended another blow and another, always jumping to avoid a cut and then attacking. But, she didn't let the man stop. She occasionally criticized him:

– Come, you, son of an angry bitch... come, you stinking Turk. – and the man became more and more angry. The bystanders were silent. Safeth began to sweat. His head shone in the sun, covered in sweat.

– Come on, mangy dog! – she shouted – This is my father's sword, filthy carcass, the King's, animal.

Safeth, addicted to alcohol, began to feel tired, which had an impact on his performance. A little oversight and Jean superficially pierced the muscle of his shoulder. He roared, but she didn't give him time to recover, attacking quickly to stab his throat. He dodged. His shirt began to turn red at the point of the cut. That infuriated him once and for all. And he began, not to fence, but to use the sword as a club. With each sword strike, Jean either jumped or ducked, but when she had to parry the blow, her hand hurt on the hilt of the sword. She parried it again. She always let him attack, in disarray. In one of those arcing sword strikes, aiming to cut off her head, she bent down and quickly pierced her opponent's thigh, almost in the groin. The scream of pain and surprise filled the air. He opened his guard and it went through the other thigh, in the same place.

– Damn you! – Safeth exploded, no longer able to stand. Jean attacked him again, now at the intersection of his shoulder and chest, piercing it. He dropped his sword, falling to his knees. She advanced, serious, sword raised, pointing at her opponent's throat. He chickened out:

– No, don't kill me... please...

She stopped. With a serious expression on her youthful face, she looked for a moment at the huge but defeated figure. She kissed Planchet's sword and, in a fit of rage, kicked the previously arrogant Safeth in the middle of the face, who fell backwards, covered in blood. Applause broke out. She raised her sword and, with a solemn air, proclaimed for all to hear:

– I am the King of the Beggars! If anyone doubts this, let him enjoy it, while I have my father's sword in my hand.

– Long live Jean, long live the king!

Dr. Girardán wiped away some tears. And he heard Jean continue.

– May this man be expelled from the community. Him and his minions. From now on everything here will change – and he pointed out some –. You, you and you take this disgusting corpse out of here. And never come back, or I will kill you without mercy. Already!

– Already! – Everyone screamed and started throwing stones and everything they found. The men, friends of the criminal, dragged him away.

– Let's burn them – one shouted.

– That's right, let's make a fire.

– No! – Jean reacted. – you shouldn't get their hands dirty with disgusting animals like these. Let them go – and turning to Doctor Girardán – Doctor, my father was here. I know it because I felt it. Doctor, say something, because I have no words.

Everyone turned their gaze to the doctor. This one went a little further and began:

– What to say? Come on, guys, all with me – and he recited the Lord's Prayer.

THIRD PART

Chapter I
War, Always

Justice be done to King Francis I. Although he loved orgies, monumental festivals and hunts, he was a lover of letters and even a good statesman. He founded the College of France, and brought the Italian Renaissance to his country, attracting to his Court great artists of the time, such as the renowned Leonardo Da Vinci, Renevenuto Cellini and many others. He built the palaces of Chambord, Villers– Cotterets, Fontaineblau, Saint– Germain en Laye and many others. Knowing that his predecessors provoked the wrath of the French, particularly those of the nobility under his boots, he reasoned with them, making them experience a luxury they did not have before. Certainly, this caused a waste of finances but, under his aegis, it was a means for the government to attract to itself those that its predecessors had reserved. In this way he kept the nobility always around him. Royal absolutism progressed, although Francis was too frivolous to govern himself. There was always a dispute between the favorites and the successive favorites. Until her death, the queen mother played a leading role in the reign. Francis unified the territory, confiscating the assets of the Constable of Bourbon, gave new vitality to the administrative centralization and replaced Latin with French, making it the official language.

Margaret of Angouleme, his sister, helped a lot. And thanks to him, his brother did not persecute the Protestants, and it was much later, when these religious people put up posters in several cities, including Paris, with the words: "True articles on the horrible abuses of the Royal Mass", which started the repression of supporters of Martin Luther. Abroad, the king, nicknamed 'The Knight King', launched the Italian adventure, emerging victorious against the Swiss, the Holy Alliance in Marignau, a victory that made him famous and lord of the Milanese. Now France was in a critical situation. Surrounded by the Habsburgs, owners of Flanders, Germany, Naples, Sardinia, Sicily, Spain and the Spanish Colonial Empire. Francis attempted to obtain an alliance with Henry VIII of England, but failed. The betrayal of the Constable of Bourbon, who thus took revenge for the intrigues of Louise of Savoy, provided Charles V with a great and unexpected reinforcement. Francisco had gone with the army, since he had nothing else to do but war. France suffered.

✶ ✶ ✶

After the resounding victory over Safeth, the Turk, Jean was hailed King of the Beggars. At first, everything went well. He managed to get community members to collaborate, help those really in need, such as the sick, the elderly and children, stipulating a minimum rate. He arranged for everything stolen and non-perishable to be stored, predicting bad days. However, a king had to have a wife. And "he" was harassed, almost daily, by the girls of the community. Her frequent rejections were starting to draw attention. When she was not on 'duty' in the streets, supervising her subjects, she stayed at home, read, or went to Dr. Girardán's residence. Thought; However, in Alençon... Jeanpaul. Could he still be there? One day, the doctor made her sit before him and reported:

– Jean, it's time to tell you everything your father trusted in me.

– And what is it, doctor?

– To start the conversation, I must tell you that you are a rich girl, very rich.

– How rich, if I have nothing? – She stirred, surprised.

– And how rich, dear!

He confirmed, standing up and going to the shelf. He soon returned with a small chest in his hands. He placed it on the table, opened it, took a thick leather envelope and passed it to the girl.

– Come closer and read what is in the documents.

Jean obeyed, removing a bundle of parchment that was 1st, interested. Although it was like that, her face was changing.

These were documents provided by the most famous banking house in Paris, based in Switzerland. There, in her hands, were titles of incalculable financial value, deeds to luxury houses, including a small palace in Avranches. And the amount of current currency exceeded thousands of louis

– *Mon Dieu* ! – She exclaimed, putting her hand to his forehead –. How, how do I own all this?

– These are your father's savings and smart investments, daughter.

– *Mon Dieu*! But my father was almost illiterate...

– However, he had exceptional financial acumen. He knew how to invest his savings, entrusting their management to bankers, who by the way were very honest.

– Oh, father! He deprived himself of the comfort he could have enjoyed...

– He reserved everything for you, my daughter.

– Ah, my dear Planchet!

– He loved you so much. He knew that his madness of "making you a man" would be harmful to you. Everything is in your name. You only need to go to the bank with me to complete the legal details, with a view to taking possession of the assets. I was already there with a document signed by Planchet and everything is fine. We should go there tomorrow.

— A palace in Avranches. Where is it?

— It's far.

— And who takes care of it?

— There are employees. The bank takes care of everything.

— And residences here in Paris...

— Exactly. Rented, generating good money.

— Farms and estates.

— Also.

— And gold coins...

— Thousands, daughter.

— What do I do, doctor?

— First, go to the banking establishment. Then you decide what to do.

— So, I'm rich.

— I'm going to set up a hospital for you, my dear doctor. I will buy a beautiful house so you can move out of this dirty street. Go...

— You're not doing anything – the doctor interrupted – . I do not need anything. Age does not allow me to run a hospital. And as for transferring from here, I don't want to. I have roots in this place. My patients need me.

— But doctor...

— However, there is something you can do.

— Whatever, doctor.

— I want you to support Lenoir.

— Soon you will be alone in the world.

– Why do you say that?

– I'm old now, daughter. And he, despite his corpulence, is not yet forty years old.

– You still have a lot of life to live, doctor. Don't worry about Lenoir. You won't be alone. I promise.

– I know, daughter.

Jean started rummaging through the trunk. He took out his hands full of precious gems between gold coins.

– Rich! – He exclaimed –. "And poor at the same time" – she mused thoughtfully.

– How, daughter?

– Will Jeanpaul accept me?

– Wow, even Francisco would do it.

✳ ✳ ✳

Six months had passed since Jean left the Luzard house. The duke had postponed his return, due to the latest events involving France and which culminated in the war it was waging against Charles V. However, the day of return finally arrived. Jeanpaul was elated.

– Do you miss your friend Jean?

– It's true, mother. I miss him.

– Us too, son. What's up with Michelle?

– Oh! It wouldn't even work. Yesterday I updated it. I do not love her.

– I know.

– Françoise is the one who is crazy about Jean... besides, after that kiss...

– Mischievous! This one will never have Jean!

– Why so sure?

– Well, son, it was clear that he had no major interest in her.

– Maybe.

– Do you want to take the horse?

– No, no. I would like to take Diana.

– Oh! This one, your father won't give up. And what time do you plan to leave?

– I think early. The grumpy old man is madly in love with Mary. It won't be long in Paris.

Paulette laughed amused.

– How is it, brat! – The duke shouted when he arrived, carrying some packages –. Are you ready?

– Yes, old man.

– Old man, huh? Well, I'm younger than you think.

– I know and I thank you, of course, Mary.

– Child! Respect your grandfather, rag!

"You looked for it, my father," Lord de Luzard said smiling.

– You still defend him...

– Aren't you going to take the blunderbusses, grandpa?

– Me – For what? Do we have wild boars in Paris?

– Oh! No, but you can go to war.

– Hold this rascal, I'm going to beat him up.

They parted.

– Give Diana a kiss for me, dad.

– Don't you want to see her?

– No, no, we would both be sad. I will return in spring.

– Go with God – said Paulette, kissing her son.

– Dad, put a flower for me at grandma's mausoleum.

–And remove the weeds... from the tomb of Diana I.

They got into the carriage. There was a single horse tied at the bottom. Mary approached and handed a basket to the duke.

– Sir, they are boar meat dumplings and some pieces of pheasant.

– Mmm, food for kings! See you soon, Mary.

– That's all? – Jeanpaul asked.

– Except that?

– Aren't you going to kiss her?

– Jean! – The duke shouted –. Jean de Luzard, I cannot guarantee that this brat will arrive safely in Paris.

– Be careful with the gout, old man – Paulette joked.

– I have never been treated so badly in my entire life. Come on, coachman.

The carriage left. In the distance the Duke's laughter could still be heard.

– This father of mine...

– You never get old, darling. Are you crying, Mary?

– No, no ma'am, it was a speck.

– I know – and she looked meaningfully at her husband.

✻ ✻ ✻

Let's leave our friends traveling, unhurriedly, along dusty and bumpy roads, towards Paris and we will return with our Jean, "The King of the Beggars."

The news circulating in Paris was that King Francis had been defeated and was in prison. The atmosphere among the nobility was boiling. People were in need, the increase in prices had reached levels never seen before. The rich, owners of estates or farms, moved in the hope that better days would come. But what about the poor of Paris? To do? Those who managed to grow vegetables and fruits on their properties, on the outskirts, and had some livestock, took them to the market square to sell them or exchange them for other items. What happens to those who had nothing? For them there was only one way out: steal. Even the beggars in the Courtyard of Miracles had a hard time.

– What did I earn today? – One complained – This doesn't even pay for the horse meat I put on my leg! This is misery! – Jean listened to the complaints, giving them her full attention.

– That's right King, today I asked and I was surprised when the man asked me if I had anything for him, he didn't respect my status as a beggar! Are those times? at this pace, very soon our profession will end due to the existence of too many beggars. And we'll ask each other? This has to stop!

Jean smiled.

– Take it easy. Here you will not miss anything. We have food stock for everyone. However, you will have to pay for them.

– Pay? But how, if we are talking precisely about lack of money?

– It doesn't matter if you pay with coins. You can contribute by working.

– In what?

– Well, sweep, clean the environment, disinfect the houses, wash clothes.

– How horrible. Planchet didn't force us to do any of this.

– *Mon ami* – he considered, seriously –. My father is no longer here. I am the King and I try to be fair. If we have food stored it is because I forced them to set aside some to face days like these. We have never had a tank so full. But can it remain empty if we cannot renew the stock and how can we replenish it? Contributing the minimum. Those who cannot pay effectively with money will do so with service. Everyone will have to work.

She knew better. In reality, the stock would not last long. That's why she paid for carts and carts of food for the warehouse, claiming to be part of her contribution. She resolved disputes, provided medical care, found a teacher for the children, had drinking water transported to the community, pretended to be austere, and was feared in the wake of her duel with Safeth. But, on the other hand, she was constantly harassed by the girls of the community, who longed for "him." And the situation became complicated when a father, in order to draw attention to his daughter, advised him:

– King, you have to get married. Where have you ever seen a king without a queen? Another, with the same objective:

– You are Planchet's son, Jean, and at your age he no longer knew how many wives he had.

And one more:

– My daughter pines for you every day. She's a talented girl – and he lowers her voice – and she's a virgin... it's hard to find a virgin around here, much less in all of Paris.

Jean listened to everything and then just reflected, like a bovine ruminating, on all those offers.

– It is difficult to find a virgin in Paris! – And what am I? Idiots! – And the thought flew to Jeanpaul. And when she got bored she would go to Dr. Girardán's house, look for the room, get rid of all her clothes, leaving only the nightgown. And then she listened to stories that the good doctor told, she learned about the progress of his affairs but, as always, questions rained down on her. On this occasion, in order not to deviate from the rule, she asked, while refreshing herself with a fruit juice:

– Doctor, why did I have the impression that I already knew Jeanpaul?

– Surely you met him in a previous incarnation.

– Does he believe it too?

– It's possible.

– Tell me. When we die, what happens immediately?

– Oh! There is no general standard. Sometimes the spirit, when deeply rooted in the body, does not leave it immediately. He is even buried with it, or even, leaving it, accompanies his burial and remains next to the grave for a long time. In this case, you are in a state of confusion, you do not understand anything.

– And can you spend a lot of time in this situation?

– Yes you can. When he understands that he no longer has a physical body, he decides to look for the people he knew, his family, his friends. Then, his disturbance deepens even more, since no one sees him, no one hears him.

– How awful!

– That's how it is; However, as soon as he realizes his new condition and asks for help, he is sent to his rightful place. There he receives instructions and then begins to understand the entire process he went through.

– And then finds other loved ones?

– Always. But, when he disincarnates, he can immediately become aware of his situation and not waste time staying close to the body.

He then heads to the spiritual places, where he will meet those who came before him.

– Does this happen to everyone?

– No, daughter, no. There are those who took their own lives, barbarian murderers, who will atone for their sins in regions commensurate with their mortal stage.

– Hell?

– Not the one imagined by the priests, but in a way yes.

– And do they suffer?

– And how!

– But do they get out of there?

– Yes, Yes. God is a father and a father always wants the best for his children. Always gives them a chance.

– What does it mean to return to the physical body?

– Naturally. In this way you will have all the means to study in the school of life and progress gradually.

– And when they arrive their memory is erased, they do not remember what they were. Wouldn't it be better if they remembered it? In this way they could better correct previous errors.

Girardán, benevolent, smiled and clarified:

– No, it wouldn't be. Think about it. A certain spirit, when incarnated, lived at its peak, in the condition of an all – powerful king. Disembodied. When he returns to physical life, he does so in the body of a beggar, devoid of everything. Remembering that he was accustomed to the existence of a nabob, would he settle?

– No, but if it were the other way around, the beggar from before would love to be king.

– Evidently. To avoid further compromises in existence, perhaps even suicide, the memory of past time is erased. If the beggar has to be king one day, he will be, and vice versa. However, there are cases in which memory is allowed, in fact, then the spirit will already be in possession of a very high degree of moral advancement. However, he suffers from the memory, because he knows that if he does not behave satisfactorily, it will take longer to free himself from the earth's crust, where he lives, and move towards a better place. In this case, in a way, you have to help others in some way, alerting everyone about what is happening. As an example, we have writers, who spread notions of a healthier life through books; researchers who currently expose doctrinal points that time has almost erased.

– In my case, what would it have been?

– Do you really want to know?

– Of course, doctor – and crossed her legs. The doctor cleared his throat and continued:

– As far as I know, you revealed yourself with your ability to animate a female body. You wanted to be born a man, forgetting that the spirit is always the same, whether it is expressed in one gender or another. You feared the impositions that weigh on women's shoulders.

– But I was born a woman.

– Without a doubt, and what happened? Your father, full of daughters, could no longer bear the mockery they made of him for "being a maker of daughters." At the same time, unconsciously, doing the same thing. With old Planchet's decision to hide your gender from you, you were glad and followed exactly what your father wanted.

– Does that mean I was to blame too?

– Evident. It was not only for obeying your father's will but also yours.

– It would be much easier if you had been reasonable and now you want to be a woman, but due to the responsibilities assumed you suffer from longing to be next to the one you love, without powers, because you also cheated on him.

– *Mon Dieu* ! And what will I do? – She asked distressed.

– Oh! Come here, sit here on your knees, I'll tell you – she obeyed. Affectionately, the doctor kissed her forehead and, placing the index finger of her right hand on it, advised her:

– You will do exactly what this pretty little head tells you. The whole solution is within. Think now. You have free will and a beautiful woman's body, whose organs are being abused. Think. The solution is within you.

– Oh, doctor! – She whined –. Help me!

– This is one thing I can't do. The decision has to be yours.

– The water is ready, Jean – announced Lenoir, who had arrived, with a huge smile. She looked surprised at the doctor and then at the servant.

– Now! – He roared. – Do I just have to come to this house and then get into the bathtub? I almost feel like I smell like a skunk. Am I offending your nostrils?

Dr. Girardán laughed mockingly. He looked at the young woman seriously and explained.

– It's not that, daughter. You don't smell bad, on the contrary, you smell good. Lenoir's concern is that he, like me, knows that in the begging community you are not in a position to bathe daily, since they do it almost collectively. There is no danger here. And we have that ointment that did you so much good. Now, get rid of that offended face and go to the bathtub. Now – and he patted the girl.

– I'm glad this is true – she murmured, heading towards the room, where right in the middle, the water was steaming.

She smiled satisfied, undressed and entered the bathtub. It took almost an hour. When she came out, she put on her men's clothes and went to meet the doctor.

– Ready! Are you satisfied?

– Undoubtedly. The woman turned into a handsome young man! Take that pot off the shelf – and pointed – When you can't come here to take a bath, use it all over your body – referring to the ointment in the pot.

– Thank you Doctor. You are an angel and – to your assistant – , Lenoir, I will need your services tomorrow.

– New purchases? – The doctor asked.

– Yeah.

– The usual, miss?

– Don't call me miss, Lenoir. Not while dressed as a man.

– Oh! Sorry sir.

– That's better. Yes, the usual. The people is in need.

– I understand. I'll go to the market very early.

She kissed the doctor and left. At that very moment, a beautiful carriage stopped at the door. Curious, she crossed the street and looked. He saw an elegant gentleman get out, shake hands with an older, but still beautiful and elegant woman, and, after leaving her, walk towards someone who was inside the vehicle. He spent a while talking, since it seemed that the person did not want to get off. However, after a few minutes he gave in and abandoned the vehicle. He was a handsome young man, tall and blonde, who seemed to be the same age as her. His face showed his dissatisfaction when responding to the old man's call. He knocked on the door several times, using the large ring. The hatch opened and, soon after, the door. Everyone entered.

– Who will it be? – She thought, dying of curiosity. The children surrounded the carriage. She approached and asked the coachman:

– Excuse me...

– Yes, gentleman?

– I am the grandson of Dr. Girardán. I was leaving when these people arrived. Can you tell me who they are?

– Oh! Yes sir. The Duke of Morriet, his wife Mrs. Constanza and their son, Felipe de Morriet. They are visiting the doctor, who is a great friend of theirs.

– Oh! Aren't they from here?

– No, gentleman. They are from the Nantes district.

– *Merci* – and she left. He wanted to go back to the house, under the pretext of forgetting something, but she gave up. He returned to the Court.

He spent the rest of the day in audience with the population. There were complaints, the most diverse demands. Thus, she knew that Turk Safeth, although lame, had recovered and was active.

– Where he is?

– He wanders around the Market Square with his three accomplices and at night he takes refuge in the Nesle Tower, or stays in the cabarets[35] on the Rue des Marmousets and Glatigny.

– Well, in the Valley of Love.

– That's how it is. Between prostitutes and homeless people.

– I hope I never encounter him, otherwise I would kill him. But what does he do?

– From what I've heard, he robs houses.

– Houses?

– Yes, King, he and his associates take advantage of the houses whose families have left the city, temporarily moving to the countryside and invade them, stealing cutlery, etc.

---

[35] Cabaret, at the time it was a large inn, where meals were served.

– Miserable! – she exclaimed indignantly –. This could cause us a lot of damage. We will be pointed out as the cause of these abuses.

Chapter II
On a single Horse

Francis I, despite being defeated, lived in luxury, including all comforts, in the Charterhouse of Parma. Negotiations intensified and the sister, with her companions, did everything possible to free him, while also taking care of local affairs. Since history already tells us what happened and in our first book *Love is Eternal* we focused on everything, let's forget this part, to just deal with our characters in that suffering Paris.

Jean went, as soon as she could, to look for Dr. Girardán. As she always did, she soon undressed and put on a nightgown. She was tired and worried. She sat in the room, waiting for the doctor who was attending to a patient. She opened the curtain that separated the room from the hallway, rested her legs on a stool, caressed her youthful breasts, sore from the pressure of the vest, and stopped thinking about the problems the Turk could cause to her community. She knew of the musketeers who had remained to guard the city. They were rude and unscrupulous men. The cream of the army accompanied the king and at any moment these fearsome creatures could attack the Court of Miracles, attracted by the wave of robberies that the members of the community did not commit. But how to clarify these invasions carried out by isolated groups?

– Your water is ready.

–Lenoir! – she screamed – . That's all you can say? Just see me and offer me water to bathe? By any chance, when I enter here, the atmosphere becomes fetid?

– Child, forgive Lenoir – he said, apologizing, respectfully – . I didn't even think about it. I just figured, seeing the girl so apprehensive, that a nice cold bath would be nice. No, you don't smell anymore. On the contrary, the smell is similar to that of lilies. Sorry. It's up to you. The doctor will be there.

He left, he was leaving when she, repentant, called him:

– Wait... Wait, Lenoir. I'm sorry.

– You're welcome, miss.

The big man's eyes showed no resentment. She stood up and hugged him, reaching right up to his waist.

– Sorry, friend, sorry. I didn't mean to offend you.

– The girl is tense.

– Yes, *mon ami*, yes, I am – and she made him lean down to kiss his forehead – . Do not be mad at me.

– Lenoir never will, girl. I'm leaving now. The doctor will be back soon. Take a bath.

– I will do that.

– It is good and cold, with essence to calm. I already cleaned your boots and leather pants. Your sword is shiny and draws easily. Do not you worry about anything.

– Thank you, dear – and she went to the bedroom.

***

– Grandfather – said Jeanpaul, sitting at a table full of delicacies that only Jacob, the innkeeper, knew how to prepare for the duke.

– Speak, brat, and quickly, I'm going to attack this boar.

– Can't you wait? Jacob went to get the sauce.

– Oh! With sauce or without sauce, how hungry!

– And when you are not?

– Speak, brat. I will do my best to listen to you.

– We are close to Paris.

– Okay, we are. Why? Don't you know that?

– How to find Jean?

– Ragbag! It was you who found him, not your grandfather. What can I tell you? – And putting his hand to his forehead –. Ah! Dr. Girardán. He is the best person to inform you about it. But what is this love for this boy?

– I want to help him, grandfather.

– That's why you have your grandfather. What does he do? Is he literate like you, or does he just know how to fence and kiss... kiss, you said it?

– I don't know. I feel like something is missing that I can't explain.

– Oh! Grandson, if he fell in love with Françoise, he already has everything. Her father is rich and she adores him. Leave it alone.

– Grandfather! You do not like him?

–How not? Yes, I like him and I will do what I can for him. After all, he is my grandson's dear friend. But that's all.

– I have the impression, as I said, of having already met him.

– Grandson, the sauce arrives. And also, enough talking. You talk about Jean like he's your favorite! Jean is a man, *petit* . Let's go to the boar.

Jeanpaul reflected before turning his attention to the food. In the end, it would not be the duke who would eliminate that schism. After the meal, the duke, satisfied, patted his grandson on the shoulder:

– Let's go to the "siesta", as the Spanish say.

– You go, grandfather, I prefer to ride for a while.

– Horseback riding after lunch?

– Sleep after lunch? – the young man joked.

– Now...

– Grandpa, walk a little first, drink water instead of wine, then, yes, sleep a little. At your age...

– What's wrong with my age? I'm strong!

– I know, but, extravagant at the table, look at your belly. Mary won't like this.

– What?

– It's true, grandfather.

– But isn't the belly a sign of fullness?

– Yes, for those who want to take something from you. Every potbellied person is rich. Now let's go! A woman wants a slim man.

– Go ride – and shouted – Jacob – the butler arrived, all helpful.

– Do you have something to start with?

– Yes sir. A tea.

– I want one.

– Check it, eating and not sleeping. You are fat. Does your wife complain to you?

– I didn't understand.

– Women don't like fat men?! – Oh! Mr. Duke, for these people it doesn't matter if the man is fat or thin. You just need to have money.

– Come out, Jacob, come out. I will walk. Prepare the tea.

Jeanpaul walked away down the road. He walked at a slow trot, thinking about what he would do when he got to Paris. He had received several teachers at his parents' house, many of them coming from Paris to teach him his first letters. When he grew up, his father sent him, under the care of his grandfather, to the Fontein Academy, where he graduated in science and literature. He spoke fluent Latin, which until recently had been the official language in France, until Francis suppressed it, imposing his mother tongue, English and Italian. He was also thinking about Michelle. Now, why had he rejected her? Didn't he love her? The union of both would only be beneficial for the families. They would unite their properties; they would be richer. Why didn't his father and mother urge him to marry her? Did they accept his refusal so naturally?

He had already traveled a good number of kilometers, without realizing it, when, in a natural curve, he came across three men, mounted on two horses. The one in front, who came alone, a little chubby, dirty and with a huge black beard. He stopped, signaling with his hand to the two who followed him, mounted on a single horse. Jeanpaul automatically grabbed the handle of the pistol at his waist.

– Calm down, gentleman. We are passing through.

– Well, leave it – said Jeanpaul, without removing his hand from the butt of the gun –. Just get out of my way – The one who looked like a leader shouted to his companions:

– Rascasse, let the nobleman pass – and he made to take off his hat.

– Where are you going? – Jeanpaul asked.

– Far. Nantes, perhaps.

– Nantes? But Nantes is in the north.

– And what do we care about the cardinal points?

– There is an inn nearby.

– Gentleman, continue on your way. We, ours. You can come in.

– No, you go first – and he took his mount to the side of the road.

– You are cautious, young man.

– I really am, sir... sir...

– Brisquet... that's how they know me. Come on, come on – he shouted to the others and they resumed their march.

The young man rode for a while longer and then returned to the inn. He found his grandfather awake and walking.

– Didn't you sleep, grandpa?

– No, I wasn't sleepy.

– Oh! What news! Did you happen to see some men passing by?

– One who rode alone and two on a single horse?

– Yes, grandfather, yes.

– I saw them. They dismounted here.

– Well... and they go to Nantes.

– Son, that fat, bearded man was my friend.

– He was?

– Well, years ago. Is younger than me.

– And who is he?

– The Count de la Tour.

– Count?

– Yes, why do you ask?

– He told me his name was Brisquet.

– Brisquet?[36]

– That's what it was called.

– Oh! The unfortunate man wanders throughout France. It is a long story. I'll tell you later. Now, now I'm going to sleep.

His grandfather left. He wasn't sleepy, like every young person. The nap is for those who have reached a certain age and have the now and the future before them. In his case, he had to act in the now, pointing to the future. Why sleep? I slept at night, because yes, I was made to sleep, to replenish the energy expended during the day. But how many, in old age, continued to work to support themselves and their homes? This is the great difference between the creatures. Because some are born with a silver spoon, others have to suffer to achieve a better situation, right? Do you know what I'm going to do? – Thought – . I'm going after those three. I have a horse at my side, as two ride one.

No sooner said than done. He hit the road in a hurry. As the three could not get very far, as the weight of two men on a single horse slowed their progress, he soon caught up with them. Pairing the animal next to the bearded individual, he smiled at it.

– You again, young man?

– Yes, sir, Comte de la Tour.

– How, young man? Do you know me?

– No, no.

– If I remember correctly, I said, call me Brisquet.

– I know.

– So?

– My grandfather is your friend. He was the one who informed me about your real name.

---

[36] See *Love is Eternal*.

– Your grandfather?

– Yes, the Duke de Luzard.

– Oh! – And he stopped the animal, raising his hand so that his companions could stop.

– Is Luzard your grandfather?

– Yes he is.

– Oh! Young man, it's been so long... yes, I passed by his son's manor.

– My father.

– Shall we dismount for a while?

– Certainly. And look, I brought you an animal, so your friends don't have to ride just one.

– Scratch! – shouted the man, dismounting –. This nobleman gives us a horse. Assemble it yourself later. And thank you.– He went to his saddlebag and took out some pieces of, perhaps, smoked birds. He offered the young man a piece of bread, put his enormous hat on his back and invited:

– Come, let's sit on the side and talk – Jeanpaul obeyed, nibbling on the meat.

– Salty, he observed.

– Oh! Canned salt, boy. And at the same time, it makes us thirsty, to compensate for the sweat we lost.

– The water, you mean.

– Yes, it balances the metabolism. So, we replaced the lost water and traveled.

– You're smart.

– And you, not so much.

– Because?

– What is your name?

– Jeanpaul.

– Oh! Jean...

– Why am I not so smart? – Brisquet laughed out loud.

– Because? – The young man repeated.

Still laughing, the big, obese, bearded man took out the dirty sword and pointed it at the chest of the seated young man – Because, Jeanpaul, we are bandits, we are criminals, *mon petit* – and placed the tip of the sword against the young man's shirt, looking at him to the eyes – . Get up, young man – and he holstered the gun. Don't trust everyone. I thank you for the animal and for your courtesy towards me. Now go in peace.

Jeanpaul was livid as he stood up.

– Tell your grandfather that the Comte de La Tour has been dead for many years. I'm Brisquet.

"Sir," the boy stammered, but the man had remounted.

– Go, Jeanpaul. The late count gives the duke a big hug. And, boy, don't believe all the people in this ungrateful world. *Au revoir*[37] de la Tour? I prefer Brisquet.

He mounted and returned to the inn. He changed his clothes, went to the waterfall, enjoyed the last rays of the sun, swam, snorkeled, thinking about the friend he would see again. in Paris.

– Tomorrow or later we will be there.

When he returned, the innkeeper was already lighting the candles and oil lamps. He changed and went downstairs. Night had arrived. Grandpa arrived, all in good spirits.

– So, rag, are you awake yet?

– Oh! How hungry!

---

[37] Bye bye.

– The only thing you think about is eating, grandpa?

– Now look... why do I have this belly? To fill it, right? – He consulted the innkeeper.

– Yes sir.

– Grandpa, you slept with a full belly. Do you wake up and fill it again? *Par example* !³⁸

– Not for now, grandson. Let's play chess, after all, we slept all afternoon, sleep will take a while to come.

– I reject the invitation.

– What?

– Today I have already eaten salted meat and I am sleepy. Tomorrow morning yes, I will eat. I'm going to bed.

– Sleep? – The duke roared.

– Yes, grandfather, I can't stand up anymore.

– Now...

– Leave him alone, Mr. Duke – the butler intervened.

– Leave it? – Jeanpaul had already left –. How to leave it? Will he be sick? We slept all afternoon!

– No, sir – reported the innkeeper –. Only you slept, not him.

– How not?

–He left on horseback and only returned a few moments ago. He went to the waterfall, took a bath, came back, changed and returned to the living room to wait for him. Meanwhile, he nibbled on something.

– But, then he didn't sleep?

– No. And he took one of our horses, returning without it.

---

³⁸ For example.

– These young people, I don't know! They can't stand upright. Come the boar. And as for the horse, I will pay you.

– I know, sir.

* * *

In this narrative, we don't care much about what happened in France. That King Francis had been imprisoned in Italy and sent to Spain. We only say what is necessary, since the story of our book takes place in that period. Therefore, from now on, historical facts will only be mentioned when they are essential. If you want to know more, of course, there are encyclopedias. We stick, as has already been said, to the characters' own history.

* * *

Saying goodbye to his client, Dr. Girardán left the office. He crossed the curtain and found Jean sitting, her legs stretched out on a stool. His eyes were closed and he seemed to be sleeping. In order not to disturb her, the good man left slowly, very carefully.

– I'm not sleeping, doctor – she said without moving. The doctor stopped, smiled and greeted her:

– Hi girl. You seem tired.

– And I am – she confirmed, sitting upright, removing her legs from the furniture – I already took a bath, if you're interested. After all, it's the first thing you tell me to do as soon as I get here.

Girardán sat down.

– I'm tired too and now I'm going to take a bath. It's a healthy habit, you know?

– Doctor...

The doctor got up, approached her, kissed her forehead, smiled and sat down again.

– Have you been waiting for me for a long time?

– I don't know.

– Let me calculate. Lenoir prepared the water, you talked for a while, you went to the bedroom, you took off your clothes, you got into the tub, then you dried off, you put on your nightgown... about two hours.

– Much less, old man, she replied, smiling and, moving away from the chair, she approached the old man's lap, who hugged her.

– Except that the water was cold, Lenoir did not heat it – and kissed the scientist's gray hair.

– You are heavy, girl.

– Who were those people who visited you yesterday?

– Visits?

– Yes. When I left here, a beautiful carriage stopped at your door and a man got out of it with a lady and followed by a young man.

– Oh! They were friends: the Duke of Morriet, his wife, Lady Constanza, and their son, Felipe de Morriet.

– It seemed to me that the child did not want to go.

– Oh! Felipe is like that...

– I think I've already heard about the duke. Wasn't it Marquis?

– Yeah.

– Who is worth more, a duke or a marquis?

– Well daughter, of course he is a duke, in heraldry we have...

– I know – he interrupted – are count, viscount, baron, duke and marquis coming?

– More or less... with intersections.

– Beautiful, the boy. What a bearing! How elegant!

– Yes, he is all this and more, he is a born fencer. It seems that he was born with a sword in his hand.

– Was his father a winegrower?

– Yes. He made the best wine in France. It still does, but on a smaller scale. Now he breeds Arabian horses.

– Oh! I know... – and jumped into the doctor's lap, making him moan.

– Oh... slower, miss.

– I know. The horse that Jeanpaul received for his birthday came from Nantes. Son of Tigger, from the stables of the Duke of Morriet. I remembered. At the moment, they also talked about their son. He had beaten the son of another duke.

– He was. Colby. Every court knows it. The king punished him.

– Punished?

– In a certain way. He forced him to go to his father's property for a few months.

– Is that a punishment?

– Well, in a way. To keep him away from possible revenge and – he laughed – so that his subject could sit without feeling pain.

– I didn't understand.

– Oh! Colby, yes, because he was strapped to the seat. The king knew he was right.

– Excellent young man! And where are they now?

– The parents returned to the Nantes district.

– And he?

– Probably in some residences of the father's friends. He is a very good friend of Leonardo.

– Leonardo?

– Little girl! Leonardo, yes.

– The Italian?

– But of course, who else?

– I would like to meet him.

– Leonardo?

– No, Felipe.

– Get down, get off my knees, I can't stand it – he stood up. – No, you don't want to meet him... not as a woman.

– Is it so dangerous?

– No daughter, it is not... he is predestined. Proud, but docile and friendly with his friends. Fierce against villainy. Willing to help those who need it, and abandon those who do not deserve it. He is fearless. He does not measure sacrifices to sustain himself, but woe to those who do not satisfy him, disturbing his interests.

– What about women?

– They say that Diana of Poitiers drags her wings towards him.

– Diana? The Lady of the Court? But she is much older than him.

– They are malicious statements. Felipe loves Angelica.

– Angelica?

– Yes. They are from the same region.

– Oh! Then he's committed.

– What do you want? Did you forget Jeanpaul?

– Never, doctor – and she stuck out her chest –. No Felipe has yet been born to make me forget Jeanpaul.

– Good. But tell me, are you tense. What's happening? – She sat down again and put her feet on the stool.

– Safeth, she said.

– Safeth. But hasn't he already abandoned your community?

– Yes, but he continues to act on his own. I'm afraid he'll hurt us.

– Come on, girl, tell me – the interested doctor responded.

– Now he robs houses. Precisely those whose owners are absent. He beats the servants, steals, and heads to the Valley of Love, or the Tower of Nesle. The Musketeers will soon focus their attention on our community as the promoter of these raids. So, I don't know what will happen.

– That's true, and what do you plan to do?

– I don't know, doctor. I never killed anyone. However, I am able to get rid of this individual if necessary. Now I regret only having injured him.

– My daughter, come, sit on my lap again. Lenoir, bring us some juice.

– Yes, doctor.

– Honey – the doctor continued –, forget it. Go to the Gendarmerie and report that the man no longer belongs to your community.

– Come on, doctor! And is the Court of Miracles a legal institution? Everything illegal that happens in Paris is immediately associated with it.

– It's true. It's time to get out of there, daughter.

– And abandon all those people in need of protection and help? Never. Eliminates tumors, right? So that? Save the patients.

– That's how it is.

–Then I will have to remove this tumor called Safeth so that my people can live in peace.

– Jean...

– There's another way?

– You told me there would never be anyone. I believe. Who knows, you might even have killed him on the day of the duel. After all, you defended your life. But now, deliberately searching for him to kill him is a crime.

– Crime? – She screamed – . Crime only when I want to defend innocent people?

– Calm. You can't go to Gendarmerie, I understand that, but don't take the law into your own hands.

– And who will do it?

– I already told you. Get out. You have possessions, take some to your properties. End the community. You can do it.

– Can I, can I do it with some and with others?

– Daughter, the Court of Miracles is a cancer within society. It will have to be removed, like the tumor you mentioned before. Those who want to stay, let them stay. Save the majority.

She remained silent for a while, thinking.

– So? – The doctor urged her.

– How many properties do I have in rural areas?

– Oh! Daughter! A lot.

–And can I, alone, take care of everything?

– No, no. You will elect and hire administrators. They will survive thanks to work and their fortune will increase. And they will have a more dignified life than the one they lead, removing and replacing bloody noses, sealing eyes and exposing fictitious wounds, seeking simple alms. No, Jean, with what you have you are doing them an injustice.

– And I will have to reveal the truth.

– What truth?

– I am a woman.

– Seriously, daughter, such an act must be put to an end. Do you love Jeanpaul or not?

– Of course I love him. However, I fear his reaction. Will he accept me, after I've deceived him all this time?

– Honey, you are no longer the Jean of Planchet's time. Let them say what they want about him, but he knew how to love you. Remember that he tried to reverse the situation with you. He rewarded you, daughter, giving you the means to benefit whoever you want. Obviously, Jeanpaul will understand your motives and will welcome you into his heart. You are beautiful, just the way you are, in this women's nightgown. Go, daughter, attend to this friend of yours.

– I can think?

– As long as you want. Now get off my lap. I'm the one who's going to take a bath.

– Can I stay here today?

– Daughter, the house is yours. And by the way, it's a great day to stay.

– Because? Something special?

– Today, Jean – said Lenoir, who remained silent the entire time – is the day the doctor talks to the dead.

– Oh my! – And she put her hands on her chest.

– Are you afraid, Jean? – The doctor asked.

– No, doctor, no. I'm gonna change my clothes.

– It is not necessary. Stay like that.

– But doctor...

– There is no lack of respect, girl, in the way you dress. You won't be questioned about this. After all, we are all born naked. The evil is in the head. Wait for me.

Chapter III
The Apparition

Safeth and his henchmen had not forgiven Jean for what she had done to them. The lame Turk blushed furiously when something reminded him of Planchet's son. And he went, in his own way, attracting other bandits, with the intention of invading the Court of Miracles, and putting an end to the "brat" who had mutilated him. He hid in the tower of Nesle Castle, whose guardian, bribed, let him enter. The walls had already fallen around them. The staircase was steep and inhabited by bats. In that tiny space, just after the stairs, there was only a patio and a kind of room with a window. There he remained, followed by his henchmen. In his proverbial foolishness, he did not even know that, in that room, now inhabited by rats, Princess Margaret received her courtiers and then killed them, throwing their bodies into the Seine. Until she killed her own children without knowing it. It was there that Buridan, her first lover, slapped her and there she was executed with her own hair. The criminal was unaware of all these details. For him, the Tower only served as a hiding place and a suitable place to devise his plan of revenge, helped, unknowingly, by spirits who were in tune with him. There he learned, through one of his companions, that the Duke of Luzard had traveled with Jean and Jeanpaul. That they were friends. He then plotted to invade the duke's house, stealing everything since he was away. A little revenge, he thought. End with what the duke had at home, since his grandson was a friend of the man who had defeated and crippled him.

– Oh! Let's get rid of that house. Then I catch him myself, him, the King of the Beggars. I kill him, without mercy.

✳ ✳ ✳

In the evening, Lenoir arranged the table, placing a crystal vase of water and some glasses in its center.

– Sit down, Jean – invited Dr. Girardán's assistant.

She did so. Soon the doctor appeared and, without saying anything, took a seat at the head. Lenoir did the same at the other end. The doctor looked at the girl who remained expectant. He smiled and took one of her hands.

– Don't be afraid, dear. You're tense – She managed to crack a half smile.

– Following instructions from our friends who no longer carry the carnal envelope, every week, on the same day, I sit down with Lenoir to talk to them. They bless the water you see, making it fluid, and it does us a lot of good, it even cures some diseases. Leave your little hands, palms down, on the table. Try not to think about anything.

– Are any dead going to appear? – The doctor laughed.

– If it appears, they will not kill you, as you think. But I do not know. They decide... – and he closed his eyes, with his hands on the table and his head held high. Then he said a prayer and fell silent again.

There was complete silence in the room, dimly lit by a single candle on the shelf some distance away. Suddenly, Jean shuddered. She closed her eyes, afraid. He felt two hands rest on his shoulders and the smell of wildflowers. He didn't have the courage to open his eyes immediately, despite his intense curiosity. He endured the gentle pressure on his shoulders and realized that one of the hands had moved to his head. There he gained greater understanding. He risked opening his eyes, very slowly. In front of her she saw several people sitting, adopting the same position as her. Who would they be? The doctor had not warned her, but naturally Lenoir had opened the door for them, while she remained with her eyes closed. He slowly turned towards the head of the table, where Lenoir was. And she got scared. He even tried to get up, thinking about helping the man. But the grip on her shoulder kept her still. The man had his head resting on the high back of the chair and a substance identical to thick wisps of grayish – white smoke emanated from his mouth, nostrils and ears.

– My God! What is this? Who's holding me? – Thought. She looked away to the other side. Dr. Girardán, calm, remained in the same position. The type of thick fog coming out of Lenoir floated in connection with the unknown creatures that were there. The pressure on his head and shoulders ceased. And he heard: "In the name of the Eternal Father, I greet you, Jean de Foiers.

– Huh? – She said scared. – The voice came from behind. She tried to turn around.

– Don't turn around, the voice continued. I'm going towards you, close and open your eyes – She obeyed and saw, among those who were sitting, a beautiful woman. Surprised, she asked:

– Who are you, madam? – The vision moved from one side to the other. He stopped and smiled.

– My name was Suzanne.

– Lady Suzanne, Jeanpaul's grandmother?

– You can consider me like that.

– But I helped clean your mausoleum. We gave her flowers... she's dead, lady!

– So, you think? Are you afraid?

– No, I can't be afraid, you are beautiful lady! I am dreaming?

– No, you are not. Come, get up and touch me. Do not be late. Our brother, who makes my visit possible, is bothered.

Jean got up excited and went to meet the vision. She extended her arm, whose hand Jean held.

– You see? I am a ghost? Do you feel my hand?

– Yes ma'am. It's hot.

– What do you want from me, madam?

– Tell me, dear, since we will be together in the very near future.

– Together? – And Jean put her hand on her chest –. I will die? – Suzanne smiled and shook the young woman's hand.

– No, honey, no. You're already dead.

– I? – Jean shouted. – Did I die?

– No – the vision responded smiling –, not as you think. You are alive to give life to those who need you.

– I don't understand.

– Do you love Jeanpaul?

– Yes, ma'am, yes. And a lot. But what do I do? He sees me as a man.

– I can't advise you. Follow your heart.

– Give life to those who need me? Can't you be more explicit, madam?

– You're a woman.

– Yes I am.

– And Jeanpaul, man.

– That's right.

– Together they will not give life?

– But madam...

– My blessing for Paulette and Jean... kiss the duke. Hug Diana. And receive a hug from someone who loves you very much, but who can't be here right now. I'm leaving, Brother Lenoir suffers.

– *Mon Dieu*, lady, who sends me the hug?

– You will have to overcome the barriers of death, you will suffer, my dear, for that stubbornness in wanting to be the King of Miracles at all costs, succeeding your father. He's fine.

The vision, now clear, let go of her hand, approached Dr. Girardán and kissed his head. The entire room seemed to smoke, those at the table began to turn transparent. Already almost diluted, but still visible, Suzanne reported:

– Pierre.

– Pierre? Died? – Then everything disappeared. And he found himself on the other side of the table. The doctor at the head, Lenoir lying back on the other end of the table, without those strange "things" coming out of the orifices of his body. He noticed his intense paleness.

– *Mon Dieu*! – She said, out loud, amazed.

– Calm down, girl – she heard the voice of Doctor Girardán, who was getting up.

– Doctor, Lenoir feels bad.

– Fill a glass with this water – he replied –. Give it to him.

Jean did as the doctor ordered and approached his prostrate friend, held his head and raised the glass to his lips.

– Drink, man, drink.

Lenoir sipped the liquid, stirred it, and rested his head on his arms on the table.

– Doctor, are you not doing anything? – Asked.

– You also drink this water. I'm going to do the same.

– And Lenoir?

– He will be fine soon. Come, we'll talk before dinner.

– But, the uncle?

– Calm down, come on, give me your hand.

Jean was still under intense tension and wringing her hands.

– Cover your breasts, girl. Does this set have buttons? She looked at him for a long time and then, obeying, answered:

– It was you who didn't let me change my clothes! Now, are you telling me to hide my breasts?

– Did you notice anything? Did they reproach you?

– No, no, but you...

– I only advise you, so that you do not forget that you are a man.

– Oh! Doctor, what was that?

– What?

– Lady Suzanne, Jeanpaul's grandmother.

– Oh! – The doctor pretended to be surprised.

– Oh? Well, doctor... she talked to me!

– She talked with you? – The doctor simulated.

– Doctor... don't play with me.

– Come here, sit on my lap – she didn't hesitate, she jumped up and was already sitting on the doctor's lap, with her arm around his shoulders and her head resting on his chest. Typically, feminine attitude.

– There you have it, grandfather. Now answer.

– Answer to what?

– Lady Suzanne...

– What did you think of her?

– Oh! Doctor...

– I prefer grandpa.

– Oh, grandfather! How beautiful! Was she an angel? – Girardán smiled.

– Did you notice wings on it?

– No, no, but how beautiful she is! How much goodness she radiates! My God, I've never seen a dead person!

– Don't talk like that, daughter. Actually, we were the ones who died here.

– Grandpa... and those strange people sitting at the table? Where do they come from?

– You saw them?

– Yes I saw them.

– They are my friends. They are always present at our meetings.

– They are dead?

– Jean...

– I mean, are they spirits?

– Yes.

– So, what need do they have to participate? Don't they know everything?

The doctor put his arms around the girl, kissed her hair and smiled.

– No, they don't know everything. They join our group to learn.

– But...

– I understand your doubts. They're like students, honey. They are sent here, to become familiar with the world they left. They attend our meetings and participate in them. This process is adopted all over the world. Even among the savages, who have their gods, they, likewise, gather in ceremonies. One day in the future, there will be many houses that will handle this exchange naturally, allowing the spirits to act more satisfactorily. For now, my dear, those who dare to receive them may end up at the stake.

– How barbaric! But what harm do they do?

– None. Clergymen fear that the hegemony of the Church will be shaken. However, they know everything.

– The priests?

– Not all. I am referring in particular to the Holy Inquisition.

– I have heard something about it.

– Do you know about Martin Luther? For presenting theses contrary to certain dogmas and practices within his religious community, he and his Protestant followers are considered heretics.

– Grandfather...

– Tell me, my rose or my carnation?

– Rosacravo – and pulled his ear –. You are in danger?

– I?

– Yes, you know who I mean.

– I am immortal, *ma cheri*, they cannot harm me. –But, from what I understand, it would have taken away the right to help the poor, in this organization. Certainly. I would help them in another way.

– Oh! grandfather! – And he hugged the old man again –. I will defend you by killing everyone. The entire population of Court of Miracles will come to your aid. And me with Jeanpaul at the head!

Girardán laughed, amused.

– You laugh? I speak the pure truth.

– I know, I know – and he caressed the girl's hair. And, to open up to her, he sniffed her, asking – . Have you showered yet?

– Well, old man – she shouted, making to get up –, so do I smell bad? – And she grabbed both ears of the doctor, who was sobbing with laughter. – Oh! You're kidding, right? You clever old man!

– Of course. You smell like a wild flower.

– What was that coming out of Lenoir's mouth, nose and ears? That pasty smoke?

– Well, it's difficult to make you understand. It is a substance that spirits need to materialize.

– Is it always like this?

– No, not always. They just wanted you to see them.

– And Lenoir? Does he suffer?

– No, no. Naturally he feels weak for a few minutes. After all, all the energy comes from him.

– Poor. Is it the same every week?

– No, no. Hardly ever.

– So...

– Because of Suzanne, she wanted to talk to you, in addition to showing herself as she was.

– I didn't understand the meaning of the words she said to me...

– ... since you will be together in the near future? – The doctor asked.

– Oh! You listened?

– ...and you will be alive to give life to those who need you?

– Grandfather! Did you hear everything? You seemed to be sleeping.

– I heard and I saw.

– So, what did she mean? In the near future will we be together and live to give life? Answer, grandfather, what was trying to make me understand?

– Why didn't you ask her?

– Wow, grandpa, she seemed so rushed!

– Of course, Lenoir wouldn't last long.

– Are you going to clarify everything for me or not?

– She said it, dear.

– What did she say?

– Have you forgotten? Put your head to work.

She made an effort, recapitulating the entire encounter. Little by little, she said, separating the words:

– "you are a woman... and Jean Paul, a man." That's what she said.

– And then?

– Oh! – she pouted –. It's no use. I know that I am a woman and Jeanpaul is a man. And? Already knew.

Girardán smiled. He stroked her hair again and in a jealous tone recommended:

– Don't torment yourself. You will soon know. Forget it.

– Forget it? How? I will remember it.

– Then do it. I can't help you now.

She suddenly looked melancholy and covered her face with her hands.

– And now what happened?

– Pierre... Pierre died... Oh! – and sobbed.

– He just left the body, darling.

– Oh! Jeanpaul must be sad, Lady Paulette, Monsieur de Luzard, the Duke, Mary, everyone.

– And he is simply happy.

– Grandpa, how can you say this? He Died!

– And then? What did Suzanne tell you?

– That he had sent me a hug.

– So then?

– He remembered me! I only saw him once! He called me girl! Oh! Pierre...

– He already knew everything.

– Oh, what a mystery!

– Someone like her?

– We went to his tombstone.

– Are you afraid of me, Jean? – Lenoir said.

– Oh! Silly, how can you think that? – And she jumped off the doctor's lap to hug him.

– But you stayed silent, girl.

– Today I'm going to be afraid to go to sleep.

– I'll stay with you until you fall asleep.

– Thank you.

Lenoir, Jean was afraid, not of what he saw, but of Suzanne's words that he could not interpret.

– A smell of man – he exclaimed.

Lenoir's specialty, whenever we read our king, is to have the camera in the kitchen,

– Not after the meetings?

And the doctor scratched his head.

– Lenoir will need to replenish his energy. Besides, I'll let him tie up what he untied.

– He did something useful and pleasant.

– Could you say what it is?

– He's preparing it. The aroma is going to make my mouth water.

– Can't you guess?

– Some wild boar, partridges, over a lit fire, like the first time I went with Jeanpaul, but I don't know the smell.

– Roasted beef, with mushroom sauce, grilled garlic, mixed with egg and pressed rice.

– Pressed rice?

– Yes, it is his specialty. Blend the rice with the celery fat, when the particles are burning, take it out, strain it and it will remain alone, but with a dark color,

– Oh!

– A lot of fat for you, daughter. You should eat little.

– And you?

– Me, well, I'm already quite old...

– For now I shouldn't oppress him – she completed

– I'm back– Lenoir said, carrying two large bowls in his hands – Here is the appetizer, which Jean likes – and he left it on the table, returning to the kitchen, returning later with two more bowls –. There's my specialty – he exclaimed, nodding – Help yourself.

– But like Lenoir?

– What's wrong, doctor? Don't you like it too?

– Yes of course. However, today I don't want to eat with my hands... we have guests!

– Oh! I'm sorry, doctor... and he got up quickly, went to the closet and returned with some iron cutlery that he placed on the table.

– Sorry, Jean, I forgot.

– I will point out the omission to you, but not to grandfather.

– And because?

– "We have a visitor" am I a visitor then?

– You're right, girl, you're right. It's the tradition.

– But with me?

– Jean... do you remember those people you saw sitting at the table?

– Yes, those who disappeared, yes.

– Good. Well, they still remain here.

– How come I don't see them?

– Because I only see them now.

– How come nothing comes out of Lenoir?

– It is not necessary... that is only for materialization, I already said it.

– And the cutlery for them?

– It is something simple, but you will have to learn it, through observation.

– Grandpa... do you mean they are watching us eat?

– Yes that's how it is.

– *Mon Dieu* !

– The act of eating, dear, as a family, no matter how frugal the food may be, should involve all possible education.

– But not everyone can do that.

– It's true; However, if there is someone who does it, it is already a beginning. But let's forget this. Let's go to the beef.

– So I'm not so hungry anymore!

– Let's go to pray.

– And does this matter to God?

– Maybe he doesn't. We are the ones who should care about what He gives us.

– I'll tell the duke.

– Duke?

– I don't matter, grandfather, doesn't matter.

✱ ✱ ✱

– You returned, dear, to the physical plane.

– Yes, I went. I wanted our future mother to meet me.

– I don't understand why, but since you did it, it was probably for something serious.

– My dear. You are still attending school. While you are there, with the acquiescence of our mentors, I took the opportunity to visit our friend Girardán, who protects the one who, as I told you, will be our mother.

– And you were successful?

– Like always. She will understand everything.

✱ ✱ ✱

– Grandfather...

– Yeah? Did you finish your food?

– Of course.

– Then let's leave the table with Lenoir.

– Why?

– He has a bigger appetite than us – and the man who was stuffing himself –. Will you excuse us, Lenoir?

– Sure, doctor.

They sat in chairs, facing each other.

– What is the question now, daughter?

– Lady Suzanne, told me that I would have to overcome the barriers of death and that I would suffer for my stubbornness in wanting to take my father's place. What does it mean?

– Calm down, honey, you will soon know.

They talked until late into the night. She later left. Lenoir took some blankets and spread them on the floor.

– What are you going to do?

– Sleep here. And there's no point in saying no, dear – the doctor added. He won't leave here.

– Very good. Leave a candle burning.

– He doesn't even listen to you anymore. Already fell asleep!

– Poor! – She said regretfully, looking at her friend lying covered up to his head.

– He is tired.

– I'm sure of it. Good night grandpa.

– Good night, *chérie*

Chapter IV
The Ambush

Philip Augustus, king of France, in the 12th century, ordered the construction of a defensive wall for the city of Paris, made up of several small towers, not far apart and with several gates that opened onto the countryside. The fortified wall began on the right side of the Seine River. There stood a large round tower, which the locals called the "corner tower." In front of this tower he had another built, about fifty meters high. Of considerable diameter, a second one was attached to it, narrower but higher, which contains a staircase that leads to the "corner tower." From there to *Saint– André– des– Arts* Street , there was a wall in which a door opened, which they called " *Porte de Brie* ." From this gate to the Seine, the wall continued. Inside this here is where the Nesle Palace was built, which gave its name to the tower, there the most horrendous crimes were perpetrated, with Princess Margaret of Burgundy as the protagonist, and there, in that room impregnated with evil vibrations, they were housed. Safeth and his companions. The surrounding residents said that, from time to time, they heard heart– rending screams coming from that sinister tower and attributed those screams of terror to the victims, who, after a night of love, were murdered and their bodies thrown into the Seine. They also heard the muffled screams of the beautiful princess who was strangled by the executioners, using her own hair. Some swore that, on moonless nights, they saw the crazy woman appear through the tower window.

– Well – said Safeth – it will be dark tomorrow night. We will be able to enter the residence of the Duke de Luzard. They say he has a huge collection of weapons.

– And cutlery.

– But...

– But ?

– For everything to go well, we have to attract the King of the Beggars to that house.

– The King of the Beggars? Jean, Planchet's son?

– That same one. Then my revenge will be complete.

–How do we do this, Safeth? And for what?

– You really are a fool.

– What will we do?

– He, knowing that we intend to rob that house, will surely try to prevent it. We'll make sure he knows the time.

– The time?

– Of course, we will get there sooner. And we will remain hidden. When he comes, we will fall on him. Then we'll steal what we can take. When the gendarmes arrive, they will find it and deduce that it is the work of thieves from the Court of Miracles. My revenge will be complete, as they will invade that den of traitors, leaving no stone unturned.

– How will we act to let her know our plans?

– Easy. We still have some friends there. One of them will report seeing us making plans. Of course he will run.

– And will there be time for this?

– Tomorrow morning we'll see.

✷ ✷ ✷

– Wake up girl... wake up...

– Huh?

– Wake up, Jean – Lenoir called.

– What? – And she got up halfway out of bed –. You wake me up? Why?

– It's already six, girl.

– But I was dreaming.

– Don't you have to go back to the Court?

– *Mon Dieu* !

– I'm going out so you can change.

A while later, around the table, they had breakfast.

– You woke up late, Jean – commented the doctor.

– Yes, but also, grandfather, I have never had such an interesting experience. And, indeed, I was in the middle of a beautiful dream and this brute – she pointed to Lenoir – woke me up – the man smiled, continuing his meal –. Grandfather – she continued –, why do we dream? What value do dreams have for us?

– A lot and nothing.

– In what way?

– When we sleep, dear and, naturally, without using herbs, sleeping pills or alcoholic beverages, it is as if we were dead in the flesh. The spirit leaves the body, only connected by a silver "cord." Then we can go to regions where our spiritual friends are, even learn something from them. It is a normal dream.

– And those who drink, those who take sleeping pills? It is not the same thing?

– In a way, yes. If such medications are prescribed, observing the need for their administration, the less harm.

However, when they are used without diagnosis, just to escape reality, they lead creatures to become easy prey for the "enemies" that seduce them. They look for each other.

– What happens to those who drink alcohol?

– Too much, you mean.

– Yes, a persistent drunk.

– Well, they tune in to those who need it.

– About what?

– For drink. Generally, the meeting is with others like him, who induce him to do what they want.

– And that cord?

– Remains attached to the body.

– And the enemies don't see it?

– Clearly. That is why they use their machinations, so that the unwary always return. They no longer have the cord. They take advantage of those who come there to send the message.

– *Mon Dieu* ! And they can't escape this?

– But of course they can. Just listen to common sense.

– Common sense?

– Yes. Everyone has the sense of discernment. It is enough to add it to the requests and supplications of family and friends, so that, by stopping feeding the addiction, you can free yourself from those who encourage it. It's difficult, I know, since now we only talk about the spirit, as if it can do everything. Because you are "dead" do you have to know everything?

– But, grandfather, don't they know?

– Yes, daughter, they already know.

– They know it, girl – Lenoir joined the conversation – however, they cannot and do not have the power to tell you what you have to do, how to act, etc.

– Why not? It would be much easier...

– Because if they did so they would be nullifying the possibilities of the right of action of those incarnated, acquiring experience in their successes and failures. The spirit is the same, girl. Only the body changes. If those there helped them with their minimum needs, what merit would they have?

– Did you understand what Lenoir explained? – The doctor asked.

– Oh! I have a lot to learn! I mean, in short, that they, the disembodied, are like us, in other places?

– Yes.

– But they can help us.

– In the end yes. There is no difference, you understand? Naturally, the most evolved come up with something to instruct us and they do it. They can heal, they can do everything. However, we go through the school of life to learn. The spirit does not work miracles. Only God makes them. Having passed on to the other side of life does not mean that a friend becomes a very intelligent being to turn to in case of any difficulty. We are what we are. We were what we are and we will always be what we are. There is no other rule.

– And what do I do?

– Now? Get out of here, run to your community, if that's what you want, crazy, and defend it, protect it and feed it.

– You don't like this, do you, grandfather?

– You know I don't. Actually, I respect your feelings towards those people. Come on, you're a man now. – Jean hugged the doctor, kissed him affectionately and did the same with Lenoir.

– I don't know when will I return. There must be a lot to do...

– Your storages are full, *ma chérie*.

– I know, Lenoir, I know. But they just want more and more.

– Who to blame? To you or to Planchet?

– To me, grandfather, to me.

– Why's that...?

– Because Planchet gave me the means to help them, even forgetting about his other women. Do you remember? He only made daughters. How many sisters do I have? And they think I'm a man. Grandfather, I want all my sisters and their mothers to be protected. I'm going to finish off the Court of Miracles. Don't I have lands and even palaces?

– Yes, daughter, you have them.

– Tomorrow or the next day I will send a messenger, where I will express all my intentions in this regard.

– God protects you.

– And everyone here.

– Go, little man – said Lenoir.

She held the hilt of the sword, and with a serious voice, she said, looking at his friend.

– Do you want to go out and fight a duel with me? Your size doesn't scare me.

– Yes, I will – roared Lenoir.

– Ok let's go...

– My flag will be a nightgown and underwear.

– Coward! – and hugged him, kissing him.

– Take care, Jean. If you need help, call me. I would give my life for you.

– I know. And you, take care of grandpa. See you around! I love you.

– *Au revoir*, miss!

* * *

Jean returned to her reign. Naturally, when she walked away, she left behind someone who answered for her. He had chosen one of her sisters for this, despite not knowing who her mother was. She liked the girl, much older than her, but the only one among the others who had a propensity for honesty. Her name was Cecille.

– Everything alright, Cecille?

– Yes, king, everything.

– Don't call me king. You know my name.

– So be it, Jean.

– Sit down. And the nursery? Did all the children take the medications I recommended?

– Not all. You know, some are distrustful...

– Yes – and she stroked her hair –. I know how difficult it is now to force the population to take precautions. They have always lived with rats, to eradicate this you have to give them time.

– That's how it is.

– Cecille, my sister – he began to say cautiously.

– did you call me sister?

– And you are not, dear? Aren't you Planchet's daughter?

– Yes, I am, but...

– I know, you are a woman, like the others.

– It's true. We were relegated to the background when you were born a man.

– Poor! He was already very old. But, Cecille, I haven't forgotten and I have a job for you.

– Job? Which?

– Calm down, Cecille – he said smiling –. You have done very well in my absence. What I ask of you, sister, is that you find out how many sisters we have whose father was Planchet. And their respective mothers, of course.

– For what?

– Maybe an inheritance?

– Oh!

– Soon I'm going to get everyone out of here, this is not life, little sister.

– Oh! Jean, why do you say this?

– Because I suffered here, little sister, we all suffer. And it's time for us to have a better life.

– I know, brother Jean. Just with what you did to the Turk, you were a great help to us. Don't get involved in anything anymore. We are what we are, brother.

– And the inheritance?

– Well – and the young blonde, dressed in rags, a scarf holding her hair on top of her head, put her hands on her waist and continued – what will the inheritance be for us, whatever the amount? We know nothing more than to beg, to steal, to rob. Where would we go?

– Did you not like your father?

– Oh yeah! And how! At first, when I was a little girl, he put me face down, straddling him. Then another came, another and so many more that I grew up and he didn't even remember my name and we barely saw each other. Not just mine, but everyone's. Then, when you were born a man, he completely forgot about us – and lowered her head, crying – . I loved him, yes. After all, being the king's daughter had some advantages. "She is the king's daughter" – they said and left me alone – . I loved him, yes, I loved my father. I even think the others loved him too.

– You were the one who stayed next to his grave, after everyone left.

– Yes. And I understand that you were not even there after that duel.

– It's true. I've arrived late. But I heard about your devotion.

– I brought him honeysuckles. He loved them. I miss him, with that grotesque way of looking like a brute, but what a heart he had!

– Come here, Cecille – and Jean got up, entering the room where she slept. The young woman followed her.

– Do you remember who lived here?

– My father.

– No, Cecille... before.

– Oh! Paulette... but she disappeared!

– Good. Paulette is alive and she is the mother of a young man – he said, unbuttoning her belt, which she let fall to the floor, then her blouse, before the perplexed look of Cecille, who already had other thoughts in her head, fearful. Understanding, Jean continued – and I love this young man... no, I will not commit incest with you. Look, she opened her blouse, her vest, letting her breasts stick out.

Cecille staggered, stunned.

– Jean! – She shouted, covering her mouth with her hand –. What is this?

– I am a woman, sister, I always have been – She took off her pants and showed herself naked before her sister – You see?

– Jean...

– It's our secret sister, you can't tell anyone anything.

The girl knelt in front of her sister, holding her by the waist, crying. Jean also stroked her hair, crying.

–How, sister, how did you defeat Safeth?

– Our father raised me as a man, remember?

– What a man, sister – she stood up and hugged his sister –. Dress up quickly. Your secret will die with me.

– No, it will not die.

– How, Jean?

– Our father left us an incalculable fortune. I have place for all my sisters and whoever wants to follow us.

– Do you intend to destroy the Court of Miracles? – While dressing, she responded:

– I cannot do it. I intend to take with me only those who wish to change their lives. There will always be beggars no matter where in the world. But we who live and suffer here have a duty to help them.

Cecille looked at her in surprise.

– I ask you to keep my secret for a few more days.

– Don't worry, Jean. For me no one will know anything.

– I know it. Do what I asked you. I want to know how many sisters we have.

– That's how it will be, sister, agreed the blonde, who couldn't contain her joy.

– Then go, I'll stay here tonight. Stay with me?

– Stay, yes.

– Aren't they going to talk?

– Talk?

– Now, Cecille... I am a "man", you are a woman...

– And does that matters? Aren't you the "son" of Planchet? – Jean smiled.

– Yes, I am.

– Then let them talk. The worst are those who love you as a man.

– I choose you.

– Okay, my 'dear young man' – said the blonde, bowing.

✳ ✳ ✳

The news in Paris was mixed. They said that Francis was imprisoned in the Charterhouse of Paima, others in Pavia. One, in Italy, the other, in Spain. The truth is that he was imprisoned in Italy and sent to Spain. As I have already explained, only what interests us in this context is the object of information. But the situation in Paris was one of fear, of anguish, yes. After all, how many sons were there in the army and how many fathers? No matter how bellicose people are, they go to war to defend something. However, no one likes war. Peace would be ideal. But what to do if those at the top of royal hegemony want to annex land and more land? Francis lost Burgundy... he regained it later, without war. Read and you will see that wars are only encouraged without listening to the people. Poor France, which soon, just a few centuries, would completely turn in on itself and the people would cry out loud. What happened is an example for the world – *Egalité, Fraternité et Liberté*.[39] – But that is in the future. Let us stick to our story, taking little interest, as has been said several times, in what was happening at that time. The truth is that Jeanpaul and his grandfather, the Duke de Luzard, were ahead of schedule, arriving in Paris a day earlier than expected. And it was morning. There was

---

[39] Equality, Fraternity and Freedom.

an iron gate at the entrance and a high wall surrounding the property. To access, after the door, there is a grass garden up to the door of the residence, on whose walls the vines climbed almost to the ceiling, clinging deeply to the interstices of the stones of the building. A very large balcony extended outside, on the upper floor.

The coachman took out the luggage, while the duke searched in his pockets for the keys to the padlocks and the door.

– Grandpa… where are Sigfrid and Helga?

– Well, we arrived a day early. And today is Friday, their day off. That's why they closed everything. They went to their parents' house.

– These Germans.

– It's natural. You will see that everything inside is clean and tidy – he finally found the key to the padlocks and opened them.

– Leave your suitcases – he said to the coachman –. Take the carriage, clean it, feed the horses and you'll be free for the rest of the week. Take. With this money you can have fun… but the rest I will only give to Mrs. Aubry. This is just an advance.

– I know, I know, sir, and what an advance! – said the coachman, examining the coins –. I'm going to buy her a gift.

– Go away, ragbag. Monday, here, very early.

– Sir, you will be alone. The Germans aren't here. If you want, I will bring my Aubry to serve you.

– *Merci, merci* – the duke thanked, placing his hand on the servant's shoulder –. But my grandson and I know how to cook, right, Jean?

– Jean? – The young man responded.

– Jeanpaul, can't you get your friend out of your mind? Didn't we call you Jean before?

– I don't know what you were talking about… it's not what?

– We'll cook together, right, brat?

– Oh! Right, cook what?

– I have everything prepared and smoked. Thomas and I fixed everything.

– Boar?

– And how not? Also, pheasant, partridges. We have food for about three days.

– Everything salted.

– And long live the salt, grandson, long live the salt.

– And your gout...

– Boy... go, take the bags.

– Go ahead, see if you don't take long to open the door. I want a bath now.

– You only think about your friend, or about taking a bath; Are there no women in this head?

– Go, grandpa, I'll carry the bags.

✻ ✻ ✻

– Suzanne, does this need to happen? Will our sister, who will receive us as a mother, have to go through such vicissitudes?

– Yes, dear, yes. There is an outstanding debt to pay. Deep down she knows it.

– Is that Jeanpaul?

– God is lavish in benign surprises. This way she will know everything and then they will be together.

– Didn't you tell her when you were at Dr. Girardán's house?

– Yes, but it cannot be explicit, as you expected. I used a metaphor.

– She understood?

– No, but Brother Girardán does.

– Well, who am I to comment on something I don't know?

– At least you show good feelings, worrying about what happens to our future mother. Come on, let's pray.

✳ ✳ ✳

– But how come you didn't find it, rag? – Safeth shouted, red with anger –. Did you go to the Court? To the sewers?

– Yes, I went and looked for your friend there. He informed me of his absence.

– Damn it! – The Turk shouted –. Go back, go back and wait there. Contact the man I sent for you. We can't waste time and he has to know it.

– What if he arrived and your friend gave the message?

– That's what I need to know, stupid. It is necessary to follow the plan that I have already made. Come on, it's still morning and don't come back again without news.

✳ ✳ ✳

Once her sister left, Jean began to think. She mentally reviewed the properties she owned, calculating how many people could live in them. And she was scribbling on a piece of paper when someone called her.

– King!

She stood up and left, her hand on the hilt of her sword and the cameo that Paulette had given her shining next to the wide leather that crossed the center of her body, holding the sword.

– What do you want, Villiard?

– King – the man began, holding the dirty hat with both hands, close to his chest – I have news...

– News? Whose?

– Safeth, king.

– Well, what do I care about Turk?

– Oh, king! I heard he's going to break into a house tonight.

–And isn't that what a naughty dog always does? What I can do? I'm busy, if you want, tell the Gendarmerie and leave – returning inside the house, when the man added:

– Yes, I will... and when they know that the house belongs to the Duke of Luzard, they will surely take action. Thank you, Rey, and turned to leave – Jean reacted quickly.

– Wait, Villiard.

– Yes, *m'sieur*.

– Did you mention the Duke of Luzard?

– That's what I heard.

– And how did you know?

– Well, at work I heard them plotting everything, next to the Nesle Tower.

– And are you sure?

– But if I am here, King, in the middle of the night, around two in the morning, he and two of his henchmen will invade the duke's residence. Do you still want me to go to the Gendarmerie?

– No, don't go.

– And why not?

Jean was furious. She looked for a quick answer:

– Well, Villiard... what do we have to do with this?

– It's true sir, I just wanted to tell you.

– You did it well. Thank you – and she entered.

She leaned over the table, her head between her hands. – How should I act? – Thought – . I can't let that animal steal from the duke. I have to do something. It's not yet ten in the morning. God! I have to go back to Dr. Girardán's house. I need to think. I will send someone to look for Cecille – However, she soon arrived smiling:

– I already have some... – but upon seeing the apprehension on hwe sister's face she stopped, asking:

– What's going on? – Jean informed her of everything.

– *Mon Dieu* !

– Take it easy. I won't stay with you tonight. I'm going to Dr. Girardán's house.

– What do you plan to do?

– Prevent that disgusting Turk from desecrating the duke's house with his presence. And there is no one there!

– Will you let me go with you?

– For what? You're a woman.

–And what are you?

– There is nothing to discuss about the fact. Continue what I asked you. I'll be here tomorrow.

– Be careful, Jean – The girl left.

✳ ✳ ✳

– But my daughter – commented Dr. Girardán – this is crazy. The duke must have servants in his house. Don't go, Jean.

– I'll go with her, Lenoir shouted.

– No, nobody. I'm going alone. If I came here it was to sleep.

– Sleep during the day?

– Yes. I have to be wide awake at night. Can you help me, grandpa?

– Daughter, the Turk...

– I already beat him once. I will beat him again. And I will be defending the home of the man I love.

– Jean...

– Grandpa, if you don't want to, I'll leave. I came to seek peace here. I thought about your messages and your essences that make us relax. If you deny me, I will return to the Court and there I will wait for the moment to act to prevent the Turk from carrying out his intentions. You have no obligation to me.

– I don't, Jean?

– No, do not interfere with my purposes, except what you and I already know, I hope, that you will do. If something happens to me, my sister Cecille, who I told you about, has a list of people who will benefit. Do whatever you want, including providing help to others as you see fit.

– And Jeanpaul?

– She lowered her head.

– It is for him that I do this. If I don't come back, tell him the truth. And tell him I love him!

– Girl... – and hugged her.

–Lenoir...– she said.

– Yes, Jean.

– I want hot water and my nightgown. Grandpa will give me a massage.

– That's all, Jean.

– And that all– black outfit, remember?

– Yeah.

– I want it.

Lenoir left to prepare everything. She began to undress, leaving only her shorts. The doctor looked at her.

– To think that when I told you to take off your clothes, when you got here, you almost attacked me with the sword – She sat on the doctor's lap.

– *Je t'aime* , grandpa.

– Me too. Let's go to your room.

There the attendant came with water, filled the tub and then left. The doctor had his back turned while the young woman was bathing. Then, with the large towel around her body, she got out of the tub, lay down, submitting to the massages of the kind and concerned old man.

– Now go to sleep and when you wake up you will be in shape. I'll wake you up in the afternoon – and he left the room –. *Mon Dieu* – he thought –, help this girl. Mrs. Suzanne, is it really necessary for her to go through this?

– Apprehensive, doctor? –Lenoir asked.

– Yes, and a lot. Dismayed by my helplessness. I don't know what will happen to her. She could suffer a lot.

– If you want, I'll go with her.

– No, our friends know what they are doing.

There was a knock at the door. It was a client and he proceeded to give medical attention, completely supressing his feelings. He let the girl sleep until after five, when he woke her up. He sat by the bed, stroked her hair and, before waking up, she murmured Jeanpaul's name.

– Wake up, calm down, daughter. It's me, Girardán – She opened her eyes. She looked at the doctor for a moment, then stretched and threw herself into his arms, in a long daze.

– What happened? What did your dreams tell you?

– Not much. I only saw Jeanpaul.

– How did you saw him?

– He ran on a black horse, Tigger's son and I, on the white one I used there. However, no matter how hard I tried to reach it, I couldn't. It was agony.

– And finished?

– No; Then I saw myself as a woman, holding his hand, in the crenellated tower of a small castle. It was only a dream?

– I cannot tell you. There are dreams and dreams. You can have nightmares when you eat too much and sleep on your stomach. There are those who, too tired, have other dreams and there are those who really leave the body. They visit friends and family.

– But can these dreams also take us to the future?

– Of course. These are called premonitory dreams. And this is inherent to being human, girl. It has nothing to do with religion... – and he touched her nose with his index finger.

– And how do you know the difference?

– Oh! This is just the moment! Come, get dressed. It is advisable, in addition to black clothing, to wear a scarf of the same color that covers from the nose to the chin.

– Ma I going masked?

– Yes, you will.

– Why? Safeth knows me.

– I know. But if someone shows up, they won't recognize you.

– It's true.

– Come, come, eat something light. And, as soon as you return home, we will be waiting for you. We won't sleep. For now, just wear the shirt. Black suits only when going out. I leave to prepare everything.

– Should I take another bath?

The doctor smiled and patted him.

– No, you smell good. Do not be late.

Chapter V
The Black Figure

Near the second hour of the morning, a black figure walks between the sleeping walls of the deserted streets of Paris, blending into the blackness of the night. Except for the rustling of the wind in the leaves of the trees, a wind that heralded the storm, all was silent. The figure moved close to the walls, holding close to her body, with her right hand, the cloak that covered her. The other hand seemed attached to the hilt of the sword, as if it were an extension of it. From time to time, at the slight flicker of a firefly, her eyes would illuminate with the dim light. But only her eyes reflected the fleeting light. She was wearing a scarf the color of night that covered her face. She walked cautiously, yet quickly. She walked through alleys, crossed squares, dodged trees and finally stopped in front of an immense walled residence. She approached the iron door. She looked from side to side and quickly climbed it, jumping over the wall, quickly sitting up and letting herself slide to the other side. She ran towards the wall covered in ivy and vines and stuck to it. She looked at the balcony that projected from the upper floor. She felt the solidity of the thick vines and, like a feline, she began to climb cautiously. About five or six meters separated her from the balcony sill. With gloved hands clinging to the aerial roots of the plant, feet resting on the walls carpeted with branches and flowers, she finally managed to swing one leg over the balcony balustrade, standing up and entering the small balcony. Automatically her hand grabbed the hilt of the sword and pulled it out of the sheath, putting herself on guard. With attentive eyes and ears, she approached the large glass door. Inside there was a curtain that prevented her from seeing what was inside. She leaned against the door and then stepped back, surprised. I was just leaning! Why? Did they forget it open or were the thieves already there? She redoubled her care, sharpening her ears and eyes.

It was Jean, dressed like the darkest night, who had arrived with the intention of defending the residence of her beloved's grandfather. The storm was approaching. Lightning, from time to time, dimly illuminated the sleeping city. What to do? If the criminals had anticipated her, she would have had to be very careful: she stood to the side, near the wall, and pushed the door just enough to allow her passage. She risked a look. Only darkness. She , sword ready, and entered, pulling the door behind her and pressing against it. There was no way to orient herself. She didn't know the inside of that house. She stopped when she felt his body touch something. A piece of furniture or a colonnade. She fumbled, shifting the sword to her left hand. It looked like a small column, she surrounded it. She stopped, trying to listen to something. Nothing. She closed and opened her eyes several times, hoping to accustom them to the darkness. She returned the weapon to her right hand. She sighed deeply. Her left hand held the cameo that she carried next to her chest. She was sweating. She remained motionless, leaning against the wall, waiting. With a brighter flash of lightning, she had an idea of where she was. A room full of furniture covered with white covers. A large crystal chandelier and some more furniture. But it was too soon to get a better idea of the place. She wished for another lightning bolt. However, the thick curtains on the door prevented more light from entering. There was also a glass door on the other side. She waited for another lightning bolt. She heard a click. She got goosebumps all over. At the same time, the room lit up. She screamed in fear and surprise. He saw two men holding large torches, one in each corner of the room, next to him. The light from the flames made the crystal pendants of the enormous chandelier shine. There was another lit torch, almost next to him. The three men, who, in the light of the flames, looked more like demons from hell, all carrying swords, advanced.

– Stop! – a resonant voice was heard – and behind a spacious armchair the figure of his greatest enemy appeared.

– He's mine – Safeth roared – and took the center of the room, laughing mockingly, illuminated by the flickering light of the resin torches.

– Screw you! – Jean roared, leaving the corner where he was.

– I'm going to kill you, brat – he responded fiercely – the time for my revenge has come and he threw himself at him limping.

– Let's get rid of him, Safeth – shouted one.

– Calm. Me first. Then it's your turn... – and he attacked. Jean defended herself, parried the blow and then lunged at the Turk who dodged it.

– Are you wearing a mask, fighting chicken? – Another attack, another defense. Her arms trembled. The man's strength was enormous, even more because of the hatred that made his half–closed eyes shine. Jean retreated, sometimes advanced. One of the men tried to push her. Quickly, Jean cut him off, making him scream in pain and recoil.

– One less! – She shouted, stopping the Turk's successive blows – And, at the first carelessness of the antagonist, who seemed driven solely by hatred, she pierced his arm at the wrist.

– Damn! – He roared, holding his wrist. – Kill him!

The men advanced. The first attack was repelled. Safeth pulled a gun from his belt, but because his arm was injured, he had difficulty aiming. It was then that the inner door opened and two armed men entered, with lamps in their hands. The Turk shot Jean, who fell heavily to the floor with his hands on her head. One of the men fired a shot, hitting Safeth in the face. The other imitated him, knocking down another. Jean managed to get up, covered in blood. She caught a glimpse of Jeanpaul advancing. Gathering all her strength, she ran, burst through the door leading to the counter and jumped, landing in a crouch on the street. It was already raining. Stumbling, clinging to the walls, she slipped away, covered by her cloak.

She felt weak. Blood flowed profusely from her head. Her vision was blurry. With a supreme effort she managed to keep moving. She crossed the square and, at the beginning of Saint Germain Street, everything went dark. She fell.

* * *

We return one day before the events we have just narrated.

– Who prepares the food? – The duke asked his grandson.

– Grandpa, you ate so much on the way and are you hungry?

– Why do I have a belly?

– Well, you do it. I settle for fruit.

– But everything is already prepared, naughty. Just remove the salt.

– Okay grandpa, okay, I'll do it. But, on another occasion, bring Mary on your back.

– Brat! – Grandfather roared –. How dare you desecrate the name of a beautiful and pure young woman?

– How I miss her, eh, old man!

– Old? – And he advanced towards his grandson who ran.

–I'm going to take a bath. Then I'll take care of your boar parts. Immediately afterwards I go to Dr. Girardán's house.

– Do you only think about Jean? Why don't you invite him to live here?

– I'll think about it.

After the bath, in the kitchen, Jeanpaul prepared the appetizers that his grandfather brought, who, at his side, gave him instructions.

– Why don't you come and do it yourself?

– Because I have allergies.

– Allergy? To what?

– To the food I make.

– You know pretty well that you are becoming obsolete.

– Do you call your grandfather obsolete? Well, you know, I'm only seventy– five years old, you bastard. And I don't know if you will reach this age.

– I hope not. Getting older must be a horrible thing. I don't know what Mary saw in you.

– Again, Mary? Look, you are burning the pheasant, reckless boy.

– Oh! Did you change the conversation? Don't you want to talk about Mary?

– Boy...

– Come on, tell me grandpa... how is she? Here among us.

– Make sure you respect your grandfather, child. Did I ever ask you what you were doing with your Michelle?

– Well, what did you think? Nothing really.

– I know, your friend Jean did better with the viscount's daughter.

–Françoise? Oh! Yes, the boy knows how to kiss. It left her steaming from her ears, but your food is ready.

– Excellent. You are not going to eat?

– No, not now.

– Look...

– Don't worry. I already saved what I want.

– I knew it and what are you going to do? Are you really going to go to the doctor's house?

– I will go. And among other things I'm going to ask you for some medicine so you won't be so hungry.

– Spoiled brat!

– Go, grandfather, go eat.

– Are you going to change your clothes?

– It's almost noon, I'm tired. I have to unpack my bags, start unpacking everything. I think I'm going to get some sleep.

– Sleep? Oh! I'm going to take a walk around the area. I'm going to the banks of the Seine!

– See the washerwomen? Or eat the junk food they make there?

– Maybe... the fried fish there is excellent.

– Well look... a duke!

– I'll see if I can get some men to take care of the house for us.

– Are you afraid?

–Afraid, the Duke de Luzard? Come on!

– Well, I'm leaving. Let the door open. When you come back, wake me up.

– Go, brat, go.

– Tomorrow I will look for Jean.

– Alright.

Jeanpaul left and began to open the suitcases, hanging his clothes in a large closet. He took off his clothes and held, for a moment, the cameo that his mother had given him. He smiled and put it in a jewelry box. He took off his boots, thought about taking another bath, but lassitude and fatigue took over him. He threw himself on the bed and soon fell asleep. At night the grandfather returned. He opened the bedroom door and looked at his grandson, deeply asleep. He smiled, lit a candelabra with two huge candles, covered the child with the blankets and murmured in a low voice:

– A storm is coming. It's going to be cold – And he closed the bedroom door. He walked through the house, closed the doors and curtains of the living room, crossed it, closing the large gate that separated it from the other rooms, and retired, lighting a candle, placing his pistols on a nightstand. He yawned and slept. It seemed to him that he had barely fallen asleep when he felt himself being shaken. It took him a while to wake up. The candle was still lit.

– What – he shouted.

– Silence, grandfather.

– Jeanpaul… what's going on? – he sat down – I barely fell asleep.

– We have visitors, grandfather.

– Visits? At the moment?

– Thieves.

– What? My pistols – and he got up quickly –. My clothes.

– Forget your clothes, don't make noise.

– How you know…

– Listen.

– Hell! They seem to be dueling. *Mon Dieu* ! My sword.

– Without swords. I have my guns, you have yours.

– Ah, Paris! The king is to blame. Where are they?

– In the hall. And they have torches.

– Torches? They are going to burn the house down.

– They seem to fight among themselves. Come on. Turn on the lamps.

– Let's go now – the duke hastened, lighting two resin torches

– Be careful, grandpa.

– Come on, they can only be bandits and they fight among themselves because of some disagreement. Who knows, because of the robbery division.

– Shoot only when you are sure who it is.

– Oh, I'm going to shoot.

– Each gun has one bullet each.

– So, there are four.

– Come on.

Anxiously, they ran to the door, which they opened suddenly. They saw when a bald man, of enormous stature, shot another, dressed all in black. The duke fired the pistol, causing the bald man's face to almost disappear at the impact of the bullet. Jeanpaul shot the another, who fell. Quickly, he pulled the trigger of the gun to shoot the masked man who ran towards the counter.

– Shoot, Jeanpaul – the duke shouted –. Kill the scoundrel – But the man in black managed to jump onto the street. He ran towards the counter.

It was raining. He didn't see anything else. They came back.

– We have two dead – the duke announced.

– Yes, one more injured and this one unharmed, for now.

– Don't kill me, sir – the criminal shouted.

– And why not?

People were already screaming in the street, desperate to be shot.

–What is happening there? – shouted one. Jeanpaul came to the counter and shouted:

– They robbed us. Please, someone call the gendarmes, and he came back.

– *Mon Dieu* ! They have everything covered in blood! – The duke complained.

Jeanpaul tore a rope from the curtain and tied the criminal firmly.

–Keep an eye on him. I'm going to get dressed. Then you will leave – and he was leaving when he saw, on the floor, something shiny. He crouched down and, surprised, asked:

– My cameo?

– You lost it?

– How? I left it when I left to y bedroom, in the jewelry box.

– Well, you should have grabbed it.

– No, no… I'll check it – and he ran towards the bedroom – he opened the room impatiently. The cameo was there!

– *Mon Dieu* ! What's happening? It's the same as mine! – He dressed hurriedly, girded himself and returned to the hall. His grandfather had another surprise.

– Look – he said, extending a sword, with the blade stained with blood – it is the same as yours.

– *Mon Dieu* !

– There is no other like it, grandson. Just yours and the one you gave to Jean.

– And the cameo? Mine is in the jewelry box.

– I fear the worst.

– What do you think, grandfather? – He asked worried and nervous.

– These individuals stole these items from your friend.

– They did it?

– This one will have to be revealed.

A carriage stopped at the door. Jeanpaul went to the counter and came back.

– Grandpa, the gendarmes.

– Come down, son, make them come in.

✶ ✶ ✶

– Doctor, a storm is coming.

– Yeah?

– And Jean did not shelter from the rain.

– What are you up to?

– He should have returned by now. I'm going to look for her, doctor.

– If you want, go, Lenoir. I can't stop you. Take a cloak.

– I'm going – and the man left, dressed in a thick cloak. The rain fell heavily on the dark streets of Paris, sometimes dimly illuminated by the bluish light of lightning. Lenoir was almost running. He was reaching the square when he saw, in the intermittent light of lightning, a figure staggering towards him. He stopped and watched, holding the hilt of the dagger. Suddenly, he saw the figure fall heavily to the ground. He ran with his heart in his hand, because he recognized, in that figure, the black clothes that Jean was wearing. He approached quickly. He knelt down and checked: it was her.

– *Mon Dieu* ! – He exclaimed – and seeing the blood that flowed – Oh! Oh my God, no! – And he picked up the girl, livid, and started to run, bathing in the girl's blood that gushed out. It seemed like there was no weight to carry. Upon reaching the house, he kicked the door several times, shouting for the doctor, who soon ran there.

– Hurry up, doctor, Jean is dying – and he entered the office with the precious bundle, placing it on the table.

– Light candles, quickly, Lenoir – The white of the tablecloth that covered the table was quickly dyed with the bright red of the young woman's blood. Lenoir appeared with the candles lit. Girardán opened the girl's clothes and, in the light of the candles, discovered the enormous wound on her head.

– Give me bandages. Get that pot quick. Scissors, Lenoir, and began to apply the potion to the wound, while pressing the girl's temples.

– She will die? –Lenoir asked.

– Take off her boots. Massage her feet. Poor thing... so much blood! – And he applied the bandages smeared with the potion. He managed to stop the bleeding.

– Was it cut?

– No, they shot her. The scalp around the wound was burned. Light closer. I have to put the ends of the wound together.

– She doesn't react, doctor.

– Give me thread and needle. Bring that pot – he dipped the thread in the substance of the pot, threaded the rustic needle and began to suture the wound.

– It will leave an ugly scar.

– The hair will cover it when it grows.

– Will she be alright?

– Only God knows. Give me sugar water, she has to drink it. Then go to the garden and bring poppy leaves.

– She's soaked, doctor.

– Bring the shirt.

With great care, the two men removed the wet, blood-stained clothes from the girl, who did not move.

– Doctor, her lips are purple.

– I saw it already. Go, fetch the water and gather the poppies. Quick, Lenoir: he carefully cleaned her body, removing all the dirt, and then put her nightgown on. He received the water and carefully made the girl swallow it. Then he placed his right hand on her forehead, closed his eyes and began to pray. He heard a deep sigh from the young woman. He opened his eyes hurriedly. The girl remained in a coma. Lenoir returned with the poppies.

– Macerate them well, Lenoir – and continued pouring the sugar water directly down the girl's throat. Once the poppy infusion was ready, he spread the paste on the wound and applied a bandage.

– Now we just have to wait.

– Her breathing is very weak.

– She lost a lot of blood.

– The day dawns.

※ ※ ※

At the duke's residence, after the bodies and the prisoner were taken away, the two were talking.

– When the day is completely clear, we will go to the doctor's house. He will be able to tell us about this strange appearance of Jean's cameo and sword in this house.

– The criminal could not say anything about the incident. It really seemed like he didn't know anything.

– Remember, grandfather, that one of them, the one dressed in black, escaped. Maybe he knew something.

– I didn't understand why you didn't shoot.

– He was fast and with those clothes, in the dark, I had no chance.

– I don't understand how Jean, who fights so well, allowed them to take away his sword and his cameo!

– This also worries me. Any betrayal?

– I just hope he's okay.

– What a night! I have to find some men to clean up all this mess... so much blood! Even on the balcony...

– The one who escaped must be injured.

– It was that brute, the one I shot, who shot him. I don't know how he didn't kill him!

– What reason would have led them to fight each other?

– Maybe share problems.

– But, Jeanpaul, if they wanted enter the house... they wouldn't leave the hall.

– It's true. Perhaps they were fighting for leadership.

– I don't know... It's daytime. You go to the doctor's house. I'll meet you there. I'll take care of getting someone to fix all this. And I still have to go through the Gendarmerie.

– Okay, I'm going. And I'm going on foot.

– It's true, we don't have anyone to hitch the carriage.

– Well, it's not that far away. And I need to walk, grandpa.

– Go away, brat.

– Good aim, grandfather, you miss when you shoot a wild boar and hit a man.

– I prefer to think that I killed an animal. I feel better this way.

– Do not doubt it. Well, grandpa, I'm leaving. I'll wait for you there, at the doctor's house.

– Go away. But I'm going to get someone to harness my horses. It is not in good taste for a duke to walk the streets.

– Do what you want. I wait for you.

The sun, although still fearful, hidden behind black clouds, managed to illuminate the city, whose streets boasted immense puddles of water. Sometimes Jeanpaul had to jump small streams that, noisy, entered the sewers. He looked for some trace of the man in black's passage, but the rain had washed away everything. He didn't pay any more attention and continued. At that moment, already in the square in front of the entrance to the street where Dr. Girardán lived, he stopped at one of the countless vendors that populated that square every morning. He bought a basket of peaches and raspberries, drank a hot broth with two small smoked herrings, chatted with the seller, and continued on his way. The streets were already full of people, large carts loaded with the most varied items, carriages passing each other, men on horseback, a group of musketeers returning to the barracks. The city was already awake. Finally, he arrived at the doctor's house. He held the big iron hoop and hit it several times. It was not answered. He waited and touched the knocker again. Nothing.

– There's no one at home? – Thought. He waited a few more minutes and called again. The door opened and Lenoir's great face appeared.

– What do you want? – Asked.

– Sir, don't you recognize me?

The man behind the door took a closer look, then smiled and said in a pleasant tone:

– Oh! You are the Duke's grandson! Wait, sir... With the door closed, Lenoir ran into the room.

– Doctor, Doctor...

– What's wrong with you now, Lenoir?

– The grandson of the Duke de Luzard is here. What I do? Do I dismiss him?

– Jeanpaul? – Asked the doctor, whose dark circles stood out on his tired face.

– Yes, that same. What do I do?

– Praise God! – Girardán exclaimed.

– What do I do then, doctor?

– Let him in.

– But what about the girl?

– Take him to the living room. I will talk with him.

– Are you going to tell him everything?

–This might be useful to her, Lenoir. Their hearts are spiritually united. It is excellent therapy for her.

– But she is so weak...

– Make him come in.

Lenoir went to the door, removed the heavy bolts, and opened it.

– Please come in, Mr. Duke.

– I am not a duke, sir... The duke is my grandfather. I'm just friends with Jean. Is he in here?

– Come in, the doctor is waiting. I will guide you – and he led the boy to the living room –. Sit down. The doctor is coming. Do you want a drink?

– No, thanks. I'll wait.

The doctor didn't take long to appear. He stood up, respectfully removed his hat, and placed it on the table.

– Hello, Jeanpaul – Girardán greeted him.

– My respects, sir – and he handed the fruit basket to the doctor.

– Oh! Peaches and raspberries, so good! Thank you for your courtesy, young man. But sit down.

– Doctor, you are tired. I notice these huge dark circles under your eyes. You have not slept?

– Young...

– Forgive me – said Jeanpaul – I ask you, knowing that you are a tireless protector of poverty. Jean told me.

– The truth is, I'm tired, I barely slept. But this doesn't matter. It is always a great pleasure to welcome you. How is your grandpa?

– Good, he will come to pick me up soon.

– When you arrived?

– Before yesterday. We arrived a day ahead. We arrived in the morning. I wanted to come right now to visit my friend Jean, but you know what happens when we come back from such a long trip. Suitcases to open, clothes to unpack, employees left. And so many other things, besides exhaustion. Why? Something happened?

– No, calm down.

– Isn't Jean here?

– No, not Jean.

– Doctor, I am very worried. I hope you can clarify some doubts for me.

– Everything that is in my power, I am at your disposal – and for Lenoir –. Stay by our patient's side. Give him the water.

– Yes doctor.

– Sorry, sorry, I don't want to bother you, since you have a patient – and he tried to get up. The doctor stopped him.

– No, do not worry. Truly, you are the best medicine for him. Jeanpaul looked at him surprised.

– I? I don't understand.

– You will understand soon. I'm ready for your questions. You can start.

– Doctor – and the boy put his hands together, crossing his fingers, seeming a little nervous – they robbed us last night, around dawn. Five criminals broke into my grandfather's house. I don't know why, they fought among themselves. I don't think they expected us to be home – and the boy talked about what had happened.

The doctor listened attentively.

– What I don't understand, doctor, is how the cameo that my mother gave to Jean, on our anniversary, and which is the same as this one, appeared in the living room of the house – and he showed the beautiful jewel hanging on his chest – in my grandfather's house. Likewise, Jean's sword, just like mine. Tell me, doctor, was Jean robbed?

Girardán scratched his hair, sighed and began:

– Listen, Jeanpaul. Listen very carefully.

– Speak, doctor.

–Yesterday morning, very early, Jean was here. He was angry.

– What are you talking about? – The boy was visibly nervous, almost distressed.

– Let me talk, son. Take it easy.

– Sorry, continue.

– He learned that some criminals, enemies of his father, among them a bald brute, whom he had defeated in a duel when he returned from Alençon, were planning to invade your grandfather's house to rob him.

– A huge, bald man?

– Yes, he was the boss.

– My grandfather shot him with a pistol.

– Well, he asked me to stay until night, revealing that he would wait for the criminals at his house, to defend the duke's belongings, who were absent at the time. I tried to change his mind without success.

– Why didn't you tell the gendarmes?

– He ruled out that suggestion. He insisted on going alone, to avoid the stealing of the property of those who had been so kind to him. He slept all afternoon and we talked until the early hours of the morning. Lenoir tried to follow him. He rejected it. The night was dark and predicted a storm. He dressed all in black, a scarf covered his face and left, first asking me that if something went wrong and he didn't return, I would tell you everything and support his sister Cecille and he disappeared into the night. He wore the cameo on his chest.

– *Mon Dieu* ! – The boy, restless, got up and walked nervously from one side to the other –. Dressed in black? With a huge cape?

– Yes, Yes.

– So, it was him who the bandit shot, when my grandfather and I entered the living room! – The doctor shook his head.

– Then he got up and looked at us. I saw it by torchlight. My grandfather killed the man, I shot the other. I saw the one in black running towards the counter. My grandfather told me to chase him, yelling at me to shoot. He jumped into the street. I still tried to catch a glimpse of it to shoot, leaning over the counter, but I couldn't; the darkness was total. There was blood, a lot of blood on the porch. It's hurt? Dead? – And his eyes opened like saucers –. No, doctor... say no, please.

– Sit down, young man. I'll bring water, wait – and he went to a shelf, took water from a container and came back. Jeanpaul had his head in his hands.

– Here, son. Drink.

With trembling hands, the young man took the glass and drank greedily.

– *Mon Dieu* ! What recklessness! Alone, against four criminals... he left one out of the fight; and he had a sword wound. How brave! Come on doctor, where is he?

– I told you, when you arrived, that you would be the best medicine for him.

– Yes, yes, what did you mean?

– He loves you very much, Jeanpaul.

– I know, he and I… we are like brothers.

–Like brothers...– the doctor murmured.

– You better believe it, sir.

– That's what worries me, son.

– Why?

– You'll see it soon.

– Doctor, why so much mystery? Where is Jean? I know you're with a patient. I saw you giving orders to your assistant. Why don't you save us time? You will be able to return to your patient's side.

– Listen... – there was a knock on the door.

– It must be my grandfather who picked me up.

– We'll see.

It was the duke. The doctor opened the door.

– Good morning, doctor! – He added.

– Good morning, Lord Duke. You can come in.

– It is not necessary, doctor. I just came to pick up my grandson.

– I'm sorry sir, but your presence is necessary. The duke, suspicious, took off his hat and entered.

– What's happening? – Asked – . Something with Jean?

– Oh, grandfather! So much...

– I'll take you to Jean.

– Excellent. Grandpa, that man in black who ran away, do you remember?

– Why? – The duke asked surprised.

– It was Jean, grandfather.

– Jean? What story is this? And what was Jean doing in our house, in the middle of the night?

– To defend it, grandfather.

– Boy, what is this story? – and the duke stopped, looking at his grandson.

– He knew that they were going to rob the house and ran to try to avoid the action of the bandits.

– But...

– This is how we found the cameo and the sword.

– Heavens! So he's hurt. The animal shot him.

– Excuse me, Lord Duke – the doctor interrupted – you will soon find out the details from your grandson. Now the two of you will go to see Jean.

– Is he badly injured?

– He is. But prepare for an even bigger surprise.

– *Voyons* !⁴⁰

They entered the office. Lenoir was sitting next to the table where Jean lay.

– Here he is.

The two approached. A young woman, pale as wax, had her eyes closed. Her face was serene. Bandages covered part of her head. Lenoir stood up.

– God, how pale is he.

– He lost a lot of blood.

– How did he get here?

– It was raining. Lenoir decided to go look for him. And he found him fallen.

– Poor. Has he come to his senses yet?

– No.

– His life is in danger? – Asked the duke.

– It's serious, sir.

– We can transfer him to the Court doctor.

– He cannot be moved yet.

Jeanpaul approached the young woman and put his hand on the sheets. With teary eyes, he instinctively murmured:

– Fight, Jean, fight. You are strong, you have already defeated many. Don't give up friend, fight – his grandfather hugged him while he talked to the doctor – what do you think he will need, doctor? Just say it. We will do everything possible for this brave man. I have no words to thank you for this gift of friendship

---

[40] Come on.

– and, in turn, he took Jean's other hand, which until then had been covered, since the doctor had removed the sheet.

– It's cold...

– It's natural, calm down.

– Such a little hand, who would have thought that he could hold a sword in a duel! How delicate... – Girardán looked at Lenoir significantly. He later stated:

– It's not just the hand that is delicate. The whole thing is – Jeanpaul looked at his grandfather, the latter at the doctor, without observing anything. The doctor pulled the sheet further, exposing half of the young woman's body. A white nightgown and underneath the outline of her free breasts. Stunned, both of them, with eyes wide open, contemplated the evidence, until then inconceivable.

– What?

– Jean is a woman, gentlemen.

– Huh? – The duke almost shouted.

– Women? – Jeanpaul staggered, straightening himself, leaning over the young woman – *Mon Dieu* ! Always was? The doctor smiled.

– Of course, since she was born.

– But how can this be? How were we deceived? My parents, my grandfather, me, everyone...

– Not your parents. They were aware of the situation.

The boy ran his hands through his hair, annoyed. The duke remained silent, contemplating the girl's serene face. He leaned over, put the back of his hand on her forehead, and said sincerely:

– Poor girl, she is so beautiful!

Jeanpaul left. Doctor Girardán was going to follow him, but the duke stopped him.

– Leave it, doctor, leave it. It needs time and a lot of reflection, and taking the young woman's hand, he kissed it and then adjusted the sheets, covering her – . You have to get well, my daughter. God will be kind to you and allow you to get out of this dream.

– Give her more liquid, Lenoir – the doctor recommended – . and change the bandages.

– Is she still bleeding?

– No, just serum. The infusion I am administering is healing and anesthetic at the same time. She doesn't feel pain.

– And the liquid?

– Recovers the water she lost and compensates for the serum you have also been depriving yourself of.

– Blood transfusions are already performed in England.

– I know. I could do it... arm in arm... and maybe I will. I'm just waiting for orders.

–Orders? Whose?

– Your grandson is the best medicine you have, dear Duke.

– I don't understand and who do you expect orders from?

– From certain friends.

– Oh! Have you consulted other doctors?

– In a way.

–And how does my grandson get the medicine he needs?

– You'll see it soon. Come on, let's go with him. Lenoir will take care of her – They left. They found Jeanpaul leaning over the table, sobbing.

– My grandson... – said the duke, stroking his hair. He raised his head. The face was covered with tears.

– Why did he deceive me, grandfather? Why?

– I don't know, boy, I don't know.

– We spend a lot of time together. We rode, hunted, and even dueled.

– And dated girls.

– He kissed Françoise. I was proud, but jealous.

– Gentlemen, listen to me. You deserve an explanation and I have it. Listen to me please. So, Jeanpaul, you tell me if you want to save her.

– Save her? And it depends on me?

– You will know.

Now he listened and the doctor began to discuss the events that culminated in the situation Jean experienced. In silence, they both listened with respect and admiration.

– Amazing! – The duke exclaimed. – How can a father inflict such suffering on a son? This man must had been crazy.

– No, he was not. He should not have adopted such an attitude; However, in return, he showered his daughter with an extraordinary dowry. He lived for her. She is now a lady of respectable fortune.

– But exposing herself to so many dangers...

– It's true. And, before leaving to defend your home, she was with one of the sisters to whom she entrusted everything. And I meant to tell you what happened. However, she is afraid of the reaction of Jeanpaul, whom she loves very much.

– Notre Dame of Paris! – The young man exclaimed, sobbing again –. Now I understand certain things.

– Which are?

–Her refusal to accompany us in the bath, in the lake, remember, grandfather?

– Of course.

– Riding, sleeping in the same room as me, always wearing that vest...

– And Françoise's kiss?

– Pure acting. How bad it must have felt!

– She always complained of having a sore throat.

– Yes, and my mother, aware of the truth, always supporting her. Now I understand everything.

– Court of Miracles! God, how horrible! – The nobleman reacted –. How much she must have suffered! Poor dear!

– Doctor, Doctor! – Lenoir's distressed voice, which appeared in the room, caught the group's attention. All stands up.

– What happened?

– Her temperature dropped. She holds her breath.

– *Mon Dieu* ! – And they ran to the office –. The doctor let them in and stayed outside. He put his hand on his forehead and walked a little.

– Doctor, run, it's wrong, the duke shouted, appearing at the door. What are you doing, man? Come on...

The doctor regained his composure. Jeanpaul arrived, holding Jean's hand close to his chest. He cryed. The girl sighed from time to time. However, she did not move or open her eyes.

– She is cold. My God! Do something, doctor.

– Well, I will send for the Court doctor – roared the duke.

– Calm down, sir – Girardán said.

– Didn't you say wait for an order? Whose?

– I already received it. Calm down – and for the assistant – Lenoir, bring that table and add it to the one Jean is on.

– But it's too tall, doctor.

– For that very reason.

– I will help – the nobleman offered.

Putting the tables together, the doctor approached a piece of furniture, took out a long tube from a container, dried it on his apron, put two needles made from what looked like bamboo stalks on it, and, looking at Jeanpaul, said smiling:

– Didn't I tell you, son, that you would be his main remedy? – The young man seemed surprised.

– Come, lie down on this table – and Lenoir – Throw it aside so I can stand between the wings. Come on, young man, lie down.

Jeanpaul looked at his grandfather and then climbed onto the table and lay down. The doctor, without any type of asepsis, rolled up his shirt sleeves, with two fingers he tapped the vein at the junction of the arm and forearm, held the tip of the needle with his fingers at the end that faced Jean, and stuck it in. Calmly, he did the same with the girl's arm. Everyone seemed expectant. They saw the blood running through the tube, controlled by Girardán, now raising it and now lowering it. Jean stopped sighing. After a few minutes, he pulled the needle out of the boy's vein, pressed the tip, and then quickly released it. A thin stream of blood gushed out. He pressed again and took the other one out of the young woman's arm.

– Bend your arm, Jeanpaul – he did the same with Jean's –. Give her water, Lenoir. And for our friend, make some juice with the raspberries he brought me – The Duke looked at him perplexed –. And, Lenoir, wrap her in a very thick quilt. When she starts sweating she will be out of danger – and he left.

Lenoir followed the recommendations to the letter. Jeanpaul got off the table, examined the needle prick, fixed the sleeve of his shirt and walked over to Jean, took her hand and kissed it.

– I'm leaving, son. I will provide some fruit. Then I'll see how the house is cleaned. I will be back soon.

– Go, grandfather – and remained vigil.

Lenoir wrapped the patient and offered the juice to the boy, who drank it. Then he brought him a chair. Sitting down, he continued to hold the young girl's hand. Lenoir left. He found the doctor sitting with his elbows on the table.

–What about him?

– He is carnivorous. If I know him well, he will bring meat.

– Lenoir will put some armchairs in the office, so we will be better accommodated.

As Jeanpaul had predicted, his grandfather returned with a large suitcase.

– Here there is fresh fruit, fish and beef. And how is she?

– Ah, grandfather, getting better and better.

– Thank God, grandson – and he patted him on the shoulder –. You saved his life, grandson.

– I?

– Tell him, doctor.

– It's true, son. You were the instrument for his recovery! The duke handed the suitcase to Lenoir and asked the doctor:

– Doctor, why didn't you give him the transfusion before?

– I had thought about this. But like I told you, I was waiting for orders.

– But whose orders? There was no one here. The doctor ignored the remark and continued:

– I needed to know if your grandson's blood was compatible with Jean's,

– And it was?

– Of course.

– And who said it?

– Oh! My dear duke, that is why they consider me a witcher.

– I don't understand.

– Grandpa, the doctor communicates with the dead. I heard mom talk about this. Let's forget what happened. What interests us is that Jean is reacting.

– Yes, my stomach too.

– My grandfather, how you eat!

– I need to maintain the body. Sigfrid found out what happened and returned to his wife. Everything is in order. The survivor confessed that the entire incident was the result of a plot hatched with the aim of killing Jean. They didn't know we were back.

– Misérables!

– They got what they deserved.

– Well, while you talk, I will stay next to Jean – Jeanpaul warned, and so he did – she seemed to be sleeping peacefully.

–How is she, Lenoir?

– It seemed like a miracle to me, doctor. The feet feel warm again.

– Miracles exist, friend.

– We haven't slept since yesterday, doctor. Why don't you go get some rest?

– No, I'm not tired. I want to be there when she wakes up.

– I will light the fire. When he comes to, who knows, maybe he won't be hungry?

– Leave some vegetable broth ready. You'll warm it up if she wants.

Leaving the room, Jeanpaul hurried toward them. The doctor raised his head.

– What happened, young man?

– Are there women here, doctor?

– Not because?

– A nurse?

– No, there isn't, but what happened?

– She got all wet, doctor, he declared, a little embarrassed.

– Oh! How good, thank God! – exclaimed the doctor, raising his arms.

– Doctor – the boy continued – I tell you that she got all wet.

– You mean she urinated.

– Yes, yes, that's all.

– This means, young man, that the body has begun to react. It's a great forecast.

– And there isn't a manager to change her clothes?

– Take it easy. I do this.

– You?

– I am a doctor. Bring some shorts and a sweater, Lenoir. And warm water with a towel. Dr. Girardán did not spend much time in the office. As he left, smiling, he said:

– Ready. Everything clear. She started to sweat. Breathing is normal.

– I can stay?

– Of course, boy. And you should. But you need to feed yourself.

– Don't worry. Grandfather went to look for fruit. He will be here soon – He took her hand, kissed it and was fascinated looking at her. Then he bowed before her and declared:

– I love you, crazy – and he kissed her lips, which were already hot.

Dr. Girardán had removed the thick quilt, leaving only a sheet on top. Her forehead was covered in sweat.

– Did you need to do what you did, my love? I don't know if I suspected it... it was something that was going through my head. I'm sorry, my love, for not being able to interpret the feelings that animated me. I felt jealous. That strange feeling when you kissed Françoise... Ah, Jean! I loved you and I didn't know it. I came to doubt my masculinity, my love, because I loved you and a man cannot love another, except parents, brothers... but you were a man.

As he spoke, he shook her hand, stroking her hair.

– Fight, my dear, fight, so that you live and I can kneel at your feet and ask for your forgiveness.

He felt two hands rest on his shoulders. He was afraid, he wanted to turn around, but the pressure increased. A jealous voice spoke to him:

– Take it easy. Focus your gaze on her.

– Who is it?

– A friend.

– Why are you holding me?

– I don't, you can turn around.

Jeanpaul turned around. And rising, he found himself face to face with a young man with long hair, dressed in a shirt with a lace front, whose loose sleeves reached up to his wrists, girding them; The shorts were loose from the waist to the thighs, thereafter the legs were sheathed in fine mesh stockings and the feet were placed in low shoes, with a large buckle at the top.

–Then why didn't you call me? The doctor left me alone with her. What do you want?

– There is no need to apologize. When you wake up, you will gradually remember everything. Keep talking to her. You know, she's listening.

– But who are you? Of course, a friend, since the doctor let you in.

– You have a lot to give us.

– Give? As?

– Take it easy. Go back and talk to her like you were doing – He went forward, placed his hands about two centimeters from the young woman's head and, after a while, continued:

– Stay with her. Keep talking. I'm leaving.

Jeanpaul watched the stranger leave the room. He turned to the patient and took her hand. However, he wondered: how did the doctor allow this man to come in here? Without a doubt another doctor. Keep talking? But wasn't that what he was doing?

– I love you, girl. Wake up for me. Talk to me. There's nothing left to think about. I love you Jean.

✳ ✳ ✳

– Do you see, brother, how love redeems everything? Through suffering, the spirit is purified.

– You knew everything, didn't you, Suzanne?

– Yes dear. The kind brother doctor contacted Dr. Girardán and told him how to proceed. And he followed everything to the letter.

– Was it necessary for her to go through all this? Suffer so much to reveal herself as the woman she is?

– I think so, or it wouldn't have been the way it was. She, of course, as I said, must or should have some trace of old guilt, I don't know what. Or something that we will only find clarification through our mentors.

– What about us?

– As?

– After we incarnate as her and Jeanpaul's children, will her way of the cross end there, as well as ours? – Suzanne hugged him smiling.

– I don't know, honey. If the carnal life is a school, let us try not to repeat ourselves, striving to obtain a diploma that gives us the right to enter a higher school. But, and you, you went to see her...

– Yes. He was there, like a guardian. He questioned my presence. It almost got worse. But I gave you the pass you asked for.

– Great, honey. Everything will be fine.

✳ ✳ ✳

Night had fallen. The lamps were lit in Dr. Girardán's house. Lenoir had arranged some chairs in the office. Jeanpaul continued holding the patient's hand.

– So, grandson? It moved?

– No, grandfather, no. But it's hot, it seems like she's sleeping soundly.

– That's right – the doctor intervened –. And as for you, young man, you must eat.

– I'm not hungry.

– Well, we have roast beef.

– Eat it yourself, grandfather.

– Eat? But I already did it, grandson. Only you are missing.

– I knew it, you really don't stop eating, except when you feel bad. Doctor, give me some medicine to prevent this. He's already old. Girardán smiled, while the duke reacted vehemently:

– Old? It's only old people who want it, son. Those who stop to peacefully contemplate the ruin of their cells. But those who do not have time to age and keep their minds agile, even recover cells in a phase of decrepitude. Therefore, they are mentally young until their bodies can no longer handle it.

– Doctor – and Jeanpaul turned towards him, carefully leaving Jean's hand on the bed – this young man who was here, why didn't you tell me?

– But what young man, my grandson? Nobody came in here.

– Now, grandfather, let me talk to the doctor. And I only do it because I'm afraid I've treated him badly. After all, you yourself said that no one would enter the room. Who was he, doctor?

– Damn! Didn't you say that me, the doctor and Lenoir were together? Who would enter without us realizing it? Are you delusional? Or is it lack of food?

– Grandfather – and Jeanpaul was about to get up. The doctor put his hand on his shoulder, calming him:

– Calm down, son, calm down.

– But the man was here. I felt the pressure of his hands on my shoulders. Then he asked me to continue talking to Jean, that she heard everything and that she would remember. He then placed his palms some distance from his head. And he told me "you know brother, you have a lot to give us" – And he went out through that door, no one saw him? He was wearing old shorts, no weapons.

– *Voila* ! – The doctor exclaimed. – Calm down. I know who it was. Sure enough, I let him into the room and he winked at the duke, who was about to speak.

– I didn't have time to warn you.

– Ah! – He calmed down, taking the girl's hand in his again – Grandfather, the sword and the cameo?

– They are in the carriage.

– Please bring them. I want them here.

– But...

Jeanpaul's look disarmed the old duke. He left the room without saying a word and then returned with the pieces.

– Give me the cameo.

Carefully, he attached it to the young woman's nightgown.

– And the sword?

– Leave it there – and pointed to a corner next to the shelf.

– He still has clotted blood.

– I'll clean it up, said Lenoir.

– Bring, Lenoir, please, a basket of fruit. Leave it next to Jeanpaul. And the broth?

– I'm keeping the fire burning.

– It seems we will all stay here – said the doctor.

– If you allow me – said the duke – I will sleep in the carriage. I'm very fat.

– No, Mr. Duke, you will stay here. When Jean wakes up he will be happy to see us all – Jeanpaul roared.

– But, grandson, the space...

– Bring your pillows from the carriage, put them on the floor and lie down.

– And you?

– I stay here.

– You do not eat?

– I'm not hungry.

– Well, I'm going to look for the pillows. I dispatch the carriage.

– No, grandfather. The coachman can sleep here.

– And the horses?

– I'll take care of them, sir, said Lenoir. Don't worry. And you stay here. I'll bring the pillows... and he walked away.

– See? As always, everything is at hand – Jeanpaul observed – and added – please, doctor, tell my grandfather to calm down. And a single lit candle.

– Alright, son. We will stay outside the office. Lenoir will bring some cushions. Stay with her – and left.

The young man focused on Jean. He kissed her hands, while expressing affection: I love you, Jean. Come back to me. Let's walk through the forest, ride, play with Diana. Wake up, love, or I will die with you too.

The boy was tired. He unbuckled his belt, letting it fall to the ground, along with his sword. He did the same with the blouse and, bending down, let his head fall next to Jean's, he inhaled her hair that smelled of medicine and, taking the young woman's hand, he soon fell asleep. In dreams he saw himself in the most diverse situations: sometimes with his grandmother Suzanne, then with his parents, the dog. At one point, he was holding hands with Jean. However, he was a woman, she was a man! He knew it was him in that female body and she, his Jean, the young man at his side. He heard someone declare... "It doesn't matter what body houses a spirit. "We are all equal!"

It was early in the morning. He felt a caress on her hair. He opened his tired eyes, thinking he saw his grandfather next to him, but he found himself leaning over Jean's bed. And the hand continued to pass over his head. He turned around, slowly. Only one candle illuminated the room. Raising his head, he found Jean's face smiling at him, eyes open and stroking his hair. He didn't hold back. Tears automatically flowed from his eyes. He got up:

– Jean! – He murmured.

– Dear...

– *Mon Dieu* ! – And he began to cry convulsively.

– I love you, Jeanpaul. Forgive me.

– Jean, Jean – and he began to kiss her face, her lips, until she moaned, waking him up to the true situation.

– Oh my God! Sorry, love.

– Where am I, Jeanpaul? Your house, the bandits... Safeth...

– It's all over, dear.

– Dear? I'm a man.

– I know, I know, you are more than a brave man.

– Jeanpaul...

– I'm here.

– The Duke?

– It's okay, my love, it's okay.

– Cecille?

– Cecille? Who is dear?

– My sister, Jeanpaul.

– Really?

– Your grandmother, Lady Suzanne... I was with her. You called me, I came back.

– I love you Jean.

– This candle.

– It's night, darling.

– Doctor Girardán? Lenoir?

– Everyone is fine, love.

– I wounded one, I injured Safeth, the door opened. Safeth shot me. I saw you, I ran, I jumped... Jeanpaul, are we in heaven?

– No, love, no. You came back from there.

– Where is everybody?

– Sleep my love.

– I'm sleepy.

– I know, love, I know, rest.

– Jeanpaul... I'm hungry.

– Ah! – The young man exclaimed, smiling, while a candelabra with three candles was lit. He turned quickly and found the duke, Doctor Girardán and Lenoir at his side.

– Doctor! – he shouted – she's hungry!

– Light more candles, Lenoir – resounded the Duke's animated voice. – I want to see my patient – and he leaned on the bed –. Hi Jean!

– Lord Duke, she murmured, smiling, with tears streaming down her face, "are you okay?"

– But of course, dear. Do you want a wild boar? I'll hunt it down now, just for you – She smiled.

– Your house...

– I know, calm down, girl. There will never be a way for me to repay your selfless gesture – he kissed her forehead.

– Doctor Girardán – he called –. I'm hurt?

– But of course, daughter, how could you not?

– My sword?

– Saved.

– Cecille?

– I'll call her here tomorrow.

– I don't see Lenoir.

– He went to get you something, aren't you hungry?

– Yes.

– You feel pain?

– My head hurts a little.

– It is a good sign. I will give you medicine immediately after eating and the pain will disappear.

– Did you tell Jeanpaul everything? Have you forgiven me?

– Girl, the boy didn't move from the headboard. While Lenoir arrives with your food. Stay with him. I will prepare some medicine for the pain.

– Jean, I love you.

– Jeanpaul, and Françoise?

– Oh! So, you remember? We'll talk later. Now come on. We have this delicious broth.

–Did the Duke go hunting wild boars? – He looked at the doctor.

– Don't worry, she's putting her ideas in order. Give her the soup – he continued to Jeanpaul, while helping the duke lift the cushions. Solicitously, the young man put the spoon in the patient's mouth. She drank with satisfaction. After a few spoonfuls, the doctor said:

– Enough, boy.

– But sir, she is hungry. He wants more.

– It is not advisable to overeat, for now. Tomorrow you will receive a larger dose.

– I'm hungry, doctor – she complained.

– I know, daughter. But you have to be content with that portion. Have some juice.

– I'm sleepy, Jeanpaul.

– I'm here, darling – and he took her hand.

– And Mrs. Paulette?

– she is alright.

– Stay with me. Give me the sword, I want to hold it.

– Good. You sleep and I will put it in your hands.

– And Lenoir?

– It's here, don't you see anything?

She smiled.

– Yes, I do, including many other people among you.

– Sleep. I will not leave you – The doctor gave her water. She slept.

– Doctor – Jeanpaul asked – she wants to know things you already talked about before, she repeats phrases, what's wrong?

– Don't worry. She was absent for a long time. She's coming back. It is natural to mix previous visions and memories. Now, when you wake up, you will have your thoughts in order. So calm down. It's really good to be with her.

– And my grandfather?

– Oh! Already fell asleep. Do the same.

– Doctor, what if she gets all wet again?

– Oh! Young man, she already has control over her body. She will ask for it.

– And how will I do it?

Girardán smiled.

– Call me, I'll take care of everything.

– I can't sleep anymore.

– Whatever you want.

✳ ✳ ✳

To cut a long story short, Jean recovered and began to walk supported by friends. She stayed at Dr. Girardán's house for five days. The love of other incarnations was now showing. The difference was that she wasn't wearing men's clothes. The duke had returned to his residence, but Jeanpaul would remain. He spent hours in the backyard, sunbathing with the girl, as the doctor ordered. Lenoir revealed himself. He took her to bed, prepared the water for bathing, washing her clothes, combing her hair, and bandaging her. One day, Jean called the doctor and joined him at the table in the living room, just down the hallway. Present, were Jeanpaul and Lenoir.

– Doctor – he began –, I feel fine now.

– I know, honey, I know, but not completely.

– Listen, doctor. I have to go back to the Court.

– What Court? – Jeanpaul asked.

– Of Miracles, dear.

– Jean – he shouted – are you crazy?

– Listen, darling, just listen; You'll agree with me later.

– But, Jean, that filthy den...

– I was born there, remember?

– And what do you want to do there?

– Say goodbye. My presence there is no longer necessary. But I have to catch up on something I owe you. Doctor, will you go with me?

– But of course, honey.

– I'll go too – Jeanpaul offered. She smiled, taking his hand.

– No, dear, you won't.

– But how could I not?

– I don't want you to see that place and, besides, I'm going to wear men's clothes.

– But, Jean, again?

– I have sisters in that place, dear, who I need to help. Don't worry, I won't be long.

They argued for some time, but the boy's efforts to dissuade her from her attempt were unsuccessful. Jean dressed in men's clothing. As before, he girded his sword, put on his hat, and kissed Jeanpaul.

– I will not be late.

– I'll be waiting.

Upon arriving at the Court of Miracles she received a loud ovation, since the news of what had happened had reached the community. As always, these types of events arise, without knowing how. She met with her sister, who provided her with the information she had collected at her request. It was later discovered that she had eighteen sisters, many of them married or living together. She interviewed them all, providing them with assets, providing them with a certain amount to support themselves at the beginning. Cecille preferred to go to the country. She was engaged. Jean was happy and gave her a rural property. After legalizing all the donations with the bankers, she returned to Dr. Girardán's house. On the way, he, who had accompanied her, commented:

– It was a magnanimous gesture, daughter.

– I simply did my duty. I kept the small palace of Avranches.

– Even so – the doctor interrupted –, you are still very rich and you are going to marry a rich man. After so many setbacks, after having eaten the bread that the devil kneaded, you were finally rewarded.

– We still have to compensate someone, dear doctor. The best man in the world. The nicest, the most charitable, gentle and kind.

– Um… is there such a man?

– If it'd exist? Come here and I'll show you – He took the doctor's hand, brought him close to a large puddle of water on the street and said: – Look inside this puddle.

Do you see?

– Well girl, I only see my image.

– Well, there is the man I told you about.

– Little girl! – The doctor was excited –. Then – and his voice rang.

– No one is missing, because my reward was having met you. You already paid me.

– No sir, I am going to renovate your entire house, expand it, equip it with everything for your well- being. I will transform the front part into a clinic, where there will be beds for your patients, with greater comfort.

– No, dear, it is not necessary. But I would like you to support Lenoir. I reiterate what I asked you before. He has no one in the world. You won't be alone.

– Come on! You talk as if you're going to die.

– Who knows?

– In any case, Uncle Lenoir will stay with me.

– Thank you dear.

– Let's change the conversation. We are arriving.

As soon as they entered the doctor's residence, Jean hurried to the room, where she got ready, dressed in clothes appropriate to her sex, and went to talk to Jeanpaul.

– My grandfather, in your absence, was here. Insist that you come to our house.

– Oh! Jeanpaul, I am sorry to reject such an honorable invitation, but I cannot leave Dr. Girardán.

– How not? – The doctor intervened. – Go already.

– Doctor, what do you mean?

–It's the right thing to do. You should get used to it. Are you going to marry the duke's grandson or not?

– But, of course – he was quick to assure the boy –. However, with one condition.

– Condition, Jeanpaul? And what is? – She asked, hugging the young man.

– That you lay down your weapons – The doctor smiled and so did she.

– I already have them in that state. However, I will keep my father's sword and the one you gave me. From time to time we will train.

– Yes – and they kissed.

– You have few women's clothes, Jean.

– Few?

– In fact, you only have a nightgown.

– There! And now? I never thought about this!

Jeanpaul smiled.

– I'll buy all your dresses in Paris.

– I don't want to.

– How not?

– Call some seamstresses. They will make my dresses. I won't go to any atelier.

– Look at that!

– I have to get used to. After all, I was a "man" for a long time.

– Well, dear – added the doctor – you should go. We will always see each other.

– As soon as everything is settled, we will go to Alençon, there we will get married.

– And from there to our small palace in Avranches.

– As you wish, queen. If you were the King of the Beggars, now you are my queen.

– Doctor, will you be okay?

– Of course dear, don't worry about this old man. Remember; however, Lenoir.

– Regarding that, you already have my word. I won't take him with me now, because he himself wouldn't go and you need him.

– Wait – and he went to the office, it took a while, returning smiling, with a small wooden safe in his hands –. This is yours. It's a gift from me. It's simple, but it has been with me for many years. I never left him.

Curious, Jean opened the small safe, lined with red velvet. There rested a small wooden cross, with the effigy of Christ, attached to a silver chain.

– Doctor – he observed, taking out the crucifix – is this the same one you used that night, here?

– That's it, daughter. It is the most precious possession I have.

– No, doctor, I can't accept it.

– Jeanpaul – said the doctor –. Do you remember the young man who was here with you in the room when Jean was still in bed?

– Yes, Yes. How to forget?

– This crucifix is for him.

– But how? – Jean asked surprised.

– Accept it, one day you will give it to him.

– It looks more like one of those that priests use.

– That's how it is. You did it well. Take Jean for example. At the appointed time you will deliver it to him.

– But...

– Not buts. Take it.

– Are you saying goodbye to us, doctor? Come on, we won't leave Paris.

– I know, but I'm leaving.

– What? You are going to travel?

– Yes, I will, dear. But now go. Do you remember Lenoir?

Jean and Jeanpaul left the house. As they walked, they talked.

– It's strange what the doctor told me.

– Well, the poor guy is old, he's tired, but we are so close to him that we can visit him every day.

– Of course.

✳ ✳ ✳

Every afternoon, at dusk, Jean and her fiancé visited the old doctor and brought him fruits and other gifts. One day, when saying goodbye at the door, Dr. Girardán said:

– Be happy. Never let hatred penetrate your hearts. Live forever this love you have for each other. And when you remember me, just a prayer and I will be grateful with you – He hugged and kissed Jean, surprised – . Goodbye, Jeanpaul.

– Goodbye doctor? Because? Tomorrow we will be back.

– I know, son, I know. Come at the same time.

– Of course we will.

– Very good. Whatever happens, do not hate your neighbor.

– But why is all this, doctor?

– Go in peace. Take care.

Hand in hand, the couple continued on their way. And as they passed in front of the Cathedral, they observed some men working, unloading carts with wood.

– What are they doing? – Jeanpaul asked.

– They are going to burn some poor soul – Jean said jokingly, approaching him.

– Oh! Don't joke, Jean. This hasn't been done for a long time.

– Sorry, silly. It must be some church celebration.

When they arrived at the duke's residence, they found him busy packing large suitcases.

– Are you going to travel, grandfather?

– Me, no. Us.

– Us?

– Brat, you have your girlfriend by your side. I'm left alone. Francisco is free and recovers from the defeat in his country house, surely plotting another war. Before this happens, I'm going to Alençon. I have nostalgia...

– From Mary?

– Brat, is this of your concern? I miss everything: the fresh air, the hunting, the wild boars, the pheasants, the horseback riding.

– And Mary's arms.

– Jean – he shouted –, hold this bag so his grandfather can hit him – and ran after his grandson, while the girl laughed. He finished his bravado sitting in an armchair, laughing too.

– We will accompany you – said the young man.

–And I didn't know? Well, I already packed your things and I have good news for both of you.

– Which? – They asked in chorus.

– The two hunting gifts.

– Hunting gifts? Two?

– Yes, your Michelle and your Françoise, Jean, are in Paris.

– Oh! And what did they come for?

– They will remain in Court. The sons of some marquises, I don't know how many, chose them as wives. They will get married at Notre Dame!

– Oh! Excellent! And how did you know?

– I was in the palace today. A friend informed me.

– What beautiful news! – Jean said smiling –. That way I won't have to worry anymore – he looked at the groom.

– Nor I.

– You? Because? – He asked seriously.

– That way you won't have to kiss Françoise anymore.

– You brat! – she shouted, advancing, hugging and kissing the young man.

– Leave this, you will have to get married first, you irresponsible people – shouted the duke. They talked until late. Then they retired to their rooms. Very early, Jean, an early riser par excellence, got up and went to help the butler's wife prepare breakfast. Once the task was completed, he approached the counter and, leaning over the railing, watched the movement of the street. She was surprised by so many people. Some ran, others walked quickly, all towards the Cathedral Square.

– What's happening? – She thought. Heard the bell in the cathedral, perhaps a rich wedding – But how many people run! – She watched for a moment, then returned to the hallway. The groom and the duke were still sleeping. She decided to pack some things in her suitcase, since they were traveling in the afternoon. She noticed, on the bed, the small box that Dr. Girardán had given her. She stopped and thought... But she had already packed it in her suitcase. How was it here? She held it and opened it. The crucifix was there. She took it and let out a groan, withdrawing her hand. It was hot – God, what is this? – She tried to hold it again, she succeeded. Normal temperature. Surprised, she began to reflect: But it was burning! The sun couldn't have shone on it. The window curtains were closed. Without explaining the phenomenon, she held the piece again, kissed it and returned it to the box, putting it in one of the suitcases. She continued packing her belongings, forgetting about what had happened. She remained like that until she was awakened by a knock on the door. It was Jeanpaul.

– You slept more than the bed, love – she said smiling and throwing herself into his arms –. Have you had breakfast yet?

– No, I was waiting for you and your grandfather.

– Then, let's go, or he will it everything.

The Duke was already at the table with a huge napkin on his chest.

– Good morning! – She added.

– Good morning, *ma chérie* – They helped themselves and chatted happily.

– Why do the cathedral bells ring?

– Ah! It was early in the morning and the movement on the street was intense. There must be some party.

* * *

The threat materialized. Dr. Girardán was still sleeping when he was abruptly awakened by loud knocks on the door. He quickly got up and went to open it, just as it was being knocked down with a crash. Armed soldiers entered the room, grabbed him in his nightgown, brutally dragged him to the street and threw him into the car. In a hurry, the vehicle was driven to the Cathedral Square, where a fence wedged between a large pile of wood was already waiting for the detainee. There was no trial. Stumbling, they carried him to the top of the pyre and tied him to the post. No complaint escaped his lips. The population only found out about the execution almost at the moment it was about to take place.

– He is the doctor! – One exclaimed, and the news spread, filling the square with people.

– Why? He is a good man!

A hooded friar began reading a scroll, labeling him a witcher, a heretic, an ally of the devil. He looked at the pale faces of the passers– by and smiled when he saw Lenoir pinned down by several soldiers. He played. The pyre was lit and the fire crackled. Soon, his clothes began to burn.

– He doesn't scream! – One exclaimed.

– Look, his head falls on his chest.

– Certainly, the smoke made him lose consciousness.

They ignored that even before the fire began to burn his flesh, the kind Dr. Girardán, the doctor of the poor of Paris, left his body, in spirit, carried by the disinterested hands of his spiritual friends. Only the body was consumed by fire. A pungent smell of burning flesh spread through the air. The flames devoured all the wood, extinguishing it shortly after. From the body, only charred bones. Lenoir cried like a child. Released, he returned home. He found it sealed. He sat down on the threshold and remained there, his head in his hands. He was no longer interested in life. Everything was over for him.

* * *

– What time will we leave? – Jean asked.

– For me, now – answered the duke.

– In that case, Lord Duke, give me a few minutes to say goodbye to Dr. Girardán.

– You will have all the time you want, daughter. He deserves more than this.

They went to the living room, where they talked, making plans for the trip. At one point, the butler appeared at the door and surreptitiously signaled to Jeanpaul to call him. He got up and went towards him. Soon the two disappeared inside the residence. The servant was nervous.

– What happened? – The young man asked worried.

– Sir... a disgrace.

– Tell me, man, what happened.

– The doctor...

– What doctor?

– Doctor Girardán.

Jeanpaul became furious.

– What happened to him?

– He died.

– He died? No, no! – And the boy put his hands on his head –. As? It just can't be!

– He was burned in a public square, sir.

– *Mon Dieu* ! Burned?

– Yes sir. The Inquisition.

– But it's impossible. Aren't you wrong?

– I wish I was. They gave me the news right now.

– But why? – Jeanpaul was out of his mind –. An old man? He only lived to help people.

– They said he was a heretic, allied with the devil, a witcher.

– Notre Dame de Paris! How evil! And this in the name of the Church.

– Of the Holy Mother Church.

– What Holy Mother Church, what nothing! – he shouted annoyed. – Crazy murderers is what they are. Misérables! – The altercation was heard by the duke and Jean who ran scared.

– What's happening? – Jean asked, running towards her fiancé, distraught and with his eyes full of tears. – Why are you like this, Jeanpaul?

The young man hugged her, kissed her and caressed her hair, hugging her against his body.

– Honey, what happened?

He managed to control himself, sobbed and spoke slowly:

– The bells when they rang...

– Yes, what about that?

– Doctor Girardán was being burned at the stake in the Cathedral Square.

– What? – The duke shouted.

Jean staggered. The young man supported her. But he was surprised by the girl's strength. Intensely pale, with tears streaming profusely down her face, she let go of his arms.

– Bring water, please.

– No, bring brandy – the duke recommended. Jean was a little disoriented.

– The crucifix... the crucifix he gave me was hot. I had kept it, but I don't know how, I found it on the bed, inside the safe. I touched it, it was so hot that it burned my fingers – and she burst into convulsive tears, supported by Jeanpaul and the duke. The butler arrived with drinks. She rejected it.

– How perverse, my love! – Jeanpaul commented hugging her.

– Let's go, Jeanpaul, to the doctor's house.

– But Jean...

– Lenoir is alone now and I promised Dr. Girardán that I would take care of him.

– But Darling...

– Come on, Jeanpaul, let's go – and to the duke –. Send our luggage to the carriage. We'll take Lenoir and leave this cursed city, where I never want to set foot again.

– Darling...

– If you do not consent, I will go with him to my palace in Avranches.

– It's not that, dear, of course I consent to it. The carriage is wide. It's just... how to find Lenoir?

– I know he's there, I'm sure.

– So be it – And for the butler –. You can carry our suitcases to the carriage. Prepare two horses.

– Only one. The one I used is in the doctor's backyard.

– Let us go fast.

Soon they were running through the streets of Paris. As they passed through the square they still saw the smoking remains of the bonfire. Some curious people remained in the place.

– Murderers! – Jean shouted –. I never want to see a priest in front of me.

– Calm down, darling.

They entered Saint Germain Street. They arrived at the house. As Jean had assured, Lenoir was there, sitting on the threshold, his head in his hands. The young woman jumped off and ran hugging him, crying.

– Uncle, uncle!

– Jean… – the man stammered –, they killed the doctor and I couldn't do anything! They destroyed everything I had in life.

– Do not talk like that. You've got me, man. You will stay with me.

– No, Jean, no.

– He asked me and I promised him. It seems like he already knew what was going to happen.

– Yes, I knew it. But I didn't want to believe it.

– Come on man, let's get out of here. Come with me. I will never leave you.

– Your horse…

– I want. You have to go look for it – Lenoir stood up.

– If they knew that they only destroyed the body… The old doctor is alive.

– Yes dear.

– Wait, I'll bring the horse.

Shortly afterward they continued their journey. Lenoir insisted on riding in the passenger seat, next to the coachman.

– Poor! – The duke exclaimed.

– I'll take care of him – Jean declared.

– Us, darling, us.

✳ ✳ ✳

Somewhere, in another dimension, three people were talking.

– So, my dear Suzanne, you have found your soul mate.

– Yes, my brother, yes. We prepare for another pilgrimage in the physical body.

– Soon will be the wedding of those you chose for your parents.

– Oh! Doctor Girardán, I'm glad you're with us. You no longer need to expose yourself to the risks of physical life.

– There is a lot of love in those young people. But the girl, because of what happened to me, began to hate the priests. So much so that to marry he will prefer a Lutheran. Do you know what this means?

– What?

– He – and the doctor pointed to the young man – Fernand chose to be a Catholic priest and the woman who will be his mother hates clerics. Your responsibility will be very great.

– It's true. I will help him.

– I'm sure of it. But knowing Jean, I foresee a lot of discord.

– We will take the risk.

– And your mission will be to change her mind. After all, a sheep does not endanger the flock, as long as it can be satisfactorily trained.

– Thank you brother for everything you did for us.

– Praise God and may his blessings be upon all. One day, the Earth will live as in the beginnings of man, a paradise. The one that men have lost, but that they incessantly search for. God bless them all, and he walked away, with little birds landing on his shoulders and flying over his head.

– Where are the fire marks?

– The inquisitors only freed him from his weakened shell, making him reborn in spirit with all his vitality. Long live God!

END

Zibia Gasparetto's Greatest success stories

With more than 20 million titles sold, the author has contributed to the strengthening of spiritualist literature in the publishing market and to the popularization of spirituality. Learn more of the author's successes.

Romances Dictated by the Spirit Lucius

The Life Force

The Truth of each one

Life knows what it does

She trusted in life

Between Love and War

Esmeralda

Thorns of Time

Eternal Bonds

Nothing is by Chance

Nobody is Nobody's

God's Advocate

Tomorrow Belongs to God

Love Won

Unexpected Encounter

On the Edge of Destiny

The Sly One

The Morro of Illusions

Where is Teresa?

Through the Doors of the Heart

When Life chooses

When the Hour Comes

When it is necessary to return
Opening for Life
Not afraid to live
Only love can do it
We Are All Innocent
Everything has its price
It was all worth it
A real love
Overcoming the past

<u>Other success stories by André Luiz Ruiz and Lucius</u>
The Love Never Forgets You Trilogy
The Strength of Kindness
Under the Hands of Mercy
Saying Goodbye to Earth
At the End of the Last Hour
Sculpting Your Destiny
There are Flowers on the Stones
The Crags are made of Sand

Books of Eliana Machado Coelho and Schellida

Hearts without Destiny

The Shine of Truth

The Right to be Happy

The Return

In the Silence of Passions

Strength to Begin Again

The Certainty of Victory

The Conquest of Peace

Lessons Life Offers

Stronger than Ever

No Rules for Loving

A Diary in Time

A Reason to Live

Eliana Machado Coelho and Schellida, Romances that captivate, teach, move and

can change your life!

Romances of Arandi Gomes Texeira and The Count J.W. Rochester

Lancaster County

The Power of Love

The Trial

Cleopatra's Bracelet

The Reincarnation of a Queen

You Are Gods

Books of Marcelo Cezar and Marco Aurelio

Love is for the Strong

The Last Chance

Nothing is as it Seems

Forever With Me

Only God Knows

You Make Tomorrow

A Breath of Tenderness

Books of Vera Kryzhanovskaia and JW Rochester

The Revenge of the Jew

The Nun of the Marriages

The Sorcerer's Daughter

The Flower of the Swamp

The Divine Wrath

The Legend of the Castle of Montignoso

The Death of the Planet

The Night of Saint Bartholomew

The Revenge of the Jew

Blessed are the poor in spirit

Cobra Capella

Dolores

Trilogy of the Kingdom of Shadows

From Heaven to Earth

Episodes from the Life of Tiberius

Infernal Spell

Herculanum

On the Frontier

Naema, the Witch

In the Castle of Scotland (Trilogy 2)

New Era

The Elixir of Long Life

The Pharaoh Mernephtah

The Lawgivers
The Magicians
The Terrible Phantom
Paradise without Adam
Romance of a Queen
Czech Luminaries
Hidden Narratives
The Nun of the Marriages

Books of Elisa Masselli

There is always a reason
Nothing goes unanswered
Life is made of decisions
The Mission of each one
Something more is needed
The Past does not matter
Destiny in his hands
God was with him
When the past does not pass
Just beginning

**Books of Vera Lúcia Marinzeck de Carvalhoç
and Patricia**

Violets in the Window
Living in the Spirit World
The Writer's House
Flight of the Seagull

**Vera Lúcia Marinzeck de Carvalho
and Antônio Carlos**

Love your Enemies
Slave Bernardino
the Rock of Lovers
Rosa, the third fatality
Captives and Freed

Books of Mónica de Castro y Leonel

In spite of everything

Love is not to be trifled with

Face to Face with the Truth

Of My Whole Being

I wish

The Price of Being Different

Twins

Giselle, The Inquisitor's Mistress

Greta

Till Life Do You Part

Impulses of the Heart

Jurema of the Jungle

The Actress

The Force of Destiny

Memories that the Wind Brings

Secrets of the Soul

Feeling in One's Own Skin

World Spiritist Institute

www.ingramcontent.com/pod-product-compliance
Lightning Source LLC
LaVergne TN
LVHW041743060526
838201LV00046B/891